# MARGINAL AT THE CENTER

# MARGINAL AT THE CENTER

## The Life Story of a Public Sociologist

Baruch Kimmerling

*Translated by*

Diana Kimmerling

***Berghahn Books***
New York • Oxford

First published in 2012 by

**Berghahn Books**

www.berghahnbooks.com

English-language edition
©2012 Diana Kimmerling

Hebrew edition
*Shuli' baMercaz: Sipur Hayim shel Soziolog Ziburi*
©2007 Baruch Kimmerling
Published by Hakibbutz Hameuchad-Sifriyat Poalim Publishing House

**Library of Congress Cataloging-in-Publication Data**

A C.I.P. catalog record for this book is available
from the Library of Congress.

**British Library Cataloguing in Publication Data**

A catalogue record for this book is available from the British Library
Printed in the United States on acid-free paper.

ISBN 978-0-85745-720-2 (paperback)

ISBN 978-0-85745-751-6 (ebook)

This translation of Baruch's book is dedicated
to the Israel he dreamed of and fought for.

D.K.

# CONTENTS

## Part Four: Entering the Public Arena

# ACKNOWLEDGMENT

I would like to thank Jessica Ramer for her devoted, professional work in shaping my translation from Hebrew into a more correct and idiomatic English. Her dedication and enthusiasm made our collaboration productive and fulfilling.

I would also like to acknowledge the invaluable help she provided to Baruch with many of his writings, including *Politicide* and *Clash of Identities*. Her vast knowledge of his subject matter helped him to communicate his ideas to English-speaking readers more precisely.

I would also like to thank Professor Russell Stone for his help and support.

# A Guerilla Fighter for Ideas

I did not pave roads and I did not dry up swamps. I was not a pioneer, a warrior, or even a military officer. I did not establish settlements and I did not build industrial plants. I wasn't exactly a Holocaust survivor or a secret agent. I neither founded nor wrecked political parties. I was never even a member of one or a public figure. I wasn't a pop star, a cultural hero, an actor in the theater, or a player in a stadium. I am not a poet, an author, a sculptor, or a painter. I am certainly not a dancer. So, what actually did I do that would justify the writing of an autobiography and, even more so, its reading?

I was, and still am, primarily a producer, critic, disseminator and examiner of ideas as well as someone who has been trying to shelve several ideas which, according to my values, should be abandoned. At the very least, I tried to argue with their advocates and I like to think of myself as a guerilla fighter for ideas. However, an idea must also pass the reality test; that is, it is necessary to examine, using different methods, how people, groups, and organizations act and react in real life and to ask how their actual practice compares to the norms and ideologies according to which they claim to act. What am I, then? I research societies using a comparative approach, a discipline known in public as "sociology." But sociology also includes the study of history, culture, and economics as well as the examination of ideas, the investigation of social movements, states and the relationships between them, and all patterns of activities of groups of men and women and their identity.

Sociology may be classified in many ways. For the purpose of this book, I will distinguish between academic and public sociology, a concept that is still not widely known in Israel. The academic sociologist whose credentials are well established is secluded in the academic ivory tower and his goal is to advance human knowledge. Whether his findings will ever be used is not a major concern of his and his main audience is primarily his students and colleagues—which is not insignificant. Indeed, he may, from time to time, emerge from the tower to talk to a larger public, mostly when he is challenged by other social agents such as the media, or when he is called on by the public relations department of the university that employs him to support some cause. But these are not his main concerns.

The "public" sociologist (or the intellectual) must be an academic sociologist who is obliged, no less than his academic colleague, to succeed in the area of research and observe the professional ethos. At the same time, in addition to his research, he must also try to influence, with the help of his ideas, the public political, social, economic, and cultural agenda, primarily through the creation and distribution of alternative ideas capable of replacing those that are currently dominant. He also aims to correct what seems to him to be flawed in his own society. The public sociologist sees these activities as part of his duty. The most prominent example, in my opinion, is that of the French sociologist and philosopher Raymond Aron. Aron, after serving in de Gaulle's Forces Françaises Libres, returned to France and became a professor of Social Thought and Political Sociology at the Sorbonne (and a few other universities in France). At the same time, over a period of thirty years, he wrote a column for the newspaper *Le Figaro*. He and Jean-Paul Sartre were of the same vehement opinion about the need to withdraw the French settlers from Algeria. They did, however, differ in their philosophical paradigms and in their ideological approach. Aron opposed Sartre's existentialism and was a rationalist and a humanist and, in contrast to Sartre and most of the French intellectuals of that period, did not sympathize with Communism and did not support the Soviet Union. As a result, he was unjustifiably considered a conservative.

It is unnecessary, I believe, for me to state that I see myself as a "public" sociologist, as will be seen later, primarily in part four of this book.

The creation of an idea is a strange process that I myself do not fully understand, even when it occurs in my own mind. Furthermore, I did not find satisfying explanations for the phenomenon of intellectual creativity. I am not referring here to a single concept, like those written by a copywriter, but rather to the creation of a complex world of content such as a new paradigm. A paradigm contains a system of criteria that permits an examination in the field that either supports or rejects accepted opinions such as, for example, the one claiming that Israel is not a militaristic society. This process includes the precise identification of the types of militarism that do and do not exist in Israel through a quite innovative assumption that militarism does not have a singular and uniform social pattern. Rather, it changes its form in different places and from one period to another and throughout its various forms, it is possible to see a common trait—the over-reliance on the use of force in an attempt to solve social and political problems. Among the public at large and even among many researchers, there is a tendency to relate to only one of the many forms of militarism—the Praetorian type, in which the army comes out of its barracks and the military officers seize power. The fact that this obviously did not occur in Israel is convenient for those denying the existence of Israeli militarism.

However, all those researchers and thinkers who are, presumably, concerned about Israel's "good name" as a democratic state usually highlight, with praise, the involvement of the military and the defense establishment in general in almost all aspects of life in Israel—culture, education, economics and, of course, politics. "The whole nation is an army," is frequently stated with pride. A researcher and close friend of mine once claimed that the fact that most Jewish men in the prime of their active life serve first in the army and then spend at least one month a year in the reserves "civilizes" the army by making it transparent, accessible, and free of myths to most civilians. When I tried to turn the argument upside-down by asking whether it would not be more reasonable to assume that the extended period of time that the Israeli man (and also, to a lesser extent, the Israeli woman) spends in the rigid military framework may burn into his consciousness the values of army and power, or what the professional literature calls the "military mind," I did not receive either a theoretical or an empirical answer to my question. Therefore, I identified two interconnected types of militarism that are found in Israel: cultural militarism, which turns the army and its symbols into a central component of the national culture and identity; and cognitive militarism, which causes people to think in militaristic and aggressive terms without even being aware of it. The problem is not that the army is militaristic, since this is the nature and essence of an army, but rather that the bulk of civilian society is also militaristic.

It is not, however, the intention of this introduction to deal with Israeli militarism but rather to use it as an example of the development and metamorphosis of an idea and a genuine sociological issue that I researched and promoted. This idea gradually developed and matured within me over almost seven years, during which time I criticized and dismantled the dominant thought on the subject through discussions and debates with friends and colleagues and sometimes, while lecturing at the university, through arguments and dialogues with students. I am indebted to my students for several stages in the development of various ideas. In this case, for example, I owe a debt to the female student who said in one of the lessons "We think army" and another student who stated that "Even when we make peace, we do it using power."

The more an idea is accepted, the more ungrateful it becomes. After a while, it enters the public domain and severs itself from you altogether as if you were not its "father-begetter." I often hear many of my ideas flying around the public sphere in the country (and some even in the world at large)—such as, for example, Israel as a frontier society or as a state with multiple socio-political borders, or the confrontation between the two collective identities "The Land of Israel" vs. "The State of Israel"—without any attribution or disguised by another concept. On the one hand, I rejoice when this happens because there can be no greater triumph for a creator of ideas than the acceptance of his idea as self-evident. On the other hand, the terrible little demon inside me squeals and screams, "…but this is my child, mine, mine…" This does not mean that all my ideas were good, and even when I suspect that they weren't too bad, that doesn't mean that they were accepted. The consolidation of ideas is an ongoing process of trial and error: primarily error.

Throughout my public writing, I almost never dealt with social topics such as welfare, but I devoted quite a lot of space to the harm inflicted on the universities and higher education and from this perspective, I consider myself an elitist. I barely dealt with subjects regarding social inequalities (except, marginally, in my Hebrew book *The End of Ashkenazi Hegemony*) not because I didn't consider them important, but rather because I suppose that some "division of labor" must exist in the sphere of public debate and struggle. Apart from that, I also reasoned that those issues are interdependent and that changes in the regime of occupation are a necessary precondition for the radical treatment of problems such as poverty, education (which often functions to reinforce existing social barriers, especially in the geographical periphery of the country), the environment, and more.

I believe that it is proper for all human beings to have an absolute equality of opportunity and self-actualization, and that the state must assist the weak in the society. These core values lead me to believe that the state is obliged to act less as a symbol and a realization of the national identity and more as a welfare state that redistributes the common resources. Nevertheless, I do not classify myself as a member of the left wing. My personal political identity is that of a radical humanist. I do, however, find myself in most matters to be close to the left although I am critical of its ideological stagnation.

This book is a combination of my life story and, briefly, that of family members from previous generations whom I consider part of my story, together with the most important expressions of my works both as an academic and a public sociologist. I was able to mention only a few of the hundreds of articles that I published in Hebrew and English and the arguments I made; otherwise I would never have been able to complete this manuscript and no publisher would have published it. The story does not necessarily unfold in chronological order, and the connection between the autobiographical sections and the other content is primarily associative. This structure may make it more difficult for the reader, but this pattern of thinking is typical of me and is part of me.

Is there any connection between various events in my life and my public stances? I don't know and, in truth, this does not concern me.

Jerusalem, February 21, 2007

# PART ONE

## AND THIS IS THE STORY

# 1

## SO THAT THE CHILD WOULD NOT UNDERSTAND

Passover, 2000. As usual, I woke up well before Diana and even if I could, I would not have moved in bed. I knew that once I woke up, I would not be able to fall asleep again and thus decided to use the time to compose in my mind the lecture awaiting me at the conference in Beer Sheva, whose date was fast approaching and for which I still did not have a clear and definitive topic. On the whole, early mornings and the wee hours of the night when I cannot fall asleep are hours of grace during which most of my best ideas are conceived. These are the hours when even the dogs who fill our home with their presence do not bark. My younger daughter Naama calls them "quality time." She has such excellent expressions. Some say that of my three children, she is the most like me.

This time, however, the thoughts running around in my head are uncontrollable and undirected. They jump back and forth in the time tunnel and I am unable to focus them on the problems inherent to the formation of democracies in the Third World, a topic with which I decided to surprise the conference participants since Charles Tilly (one of the greatest sociologists of our time), who will be appearing with me in the opening session, will talk about the formation of democracies in France and England during the nineteenth century. During the last decade, Tilly seems to prefer studying subjects that are both temporally and geographically distant in the same way that some of my veteran colleagues in Jerusalem tend to do so as not to deal with the here and now. Because of this, I devote myself, almost with delight, to the thoughts racing wildly through my mind, thoughts I didn't deal with for years.

For some reason, I was reminded of the first Passover evening that was ever etched into my memory. It seemed to me to be an enormous event, mostly because after it took place, everything went awry. I think it was the Passover of 1943, and although I sensed the fear that permeated my family, life continued as if everything was normal. My grandmother and the maid cleaned the house in an excessively meticulous way. Each part of the house that was cleaned became a sterile and isolated zone, "Kosher for Passover," and entrance there was forbidden to me while the purified kitchen became the center of activity. All of the kitchenware was replaced with festive utensils and porcelains that were brought up from the cellar and then the cooking for the *Seder* night began. Ten days prior, the red beets used in preparing the *borscht* were placed in special bottles to ferment. The *borscht* was one of two soups, the other being a rich beef soup that was full of *kneidlach*. The tastes of these two soups stayed with me as part of the smells and tastes of childhood.

My role in the *Seder* was frightening to me in its importance. My mother undertook the task of teaching me the four questions. Aside from the Hebrew songs that my mother used to sing to me ("Between the mountains and the boulders a train is flying"), the words of the "Ma Nishtana" ("Why is this night different...?")[1] were the first I learned in Hebrew. At that time and in that place, they avoided taking the child to the synagogue, even though I heard that there had been discussions, and perhaps even a dispute, about this issue. It seems to me that my grandmother ruled in favor of my mother and my grandfather gave up. Apart from reciting the four questions—and of course, I got confused as soon as I began—I was supposed, when the men went out to engage in the ritual hand washing, to find the *afikoman*,[2] a task which turned out to be easy to complete, and then negotiate for its return.

When my grandfather, who was greatly amused, started negotiating the return of the *afikoman* and asked me what I wished for in return, I blurted out "a gun." At the big table that seemed gigantic to me and around which were seated not only my immediate family but many uncles and aunts—some of whom I did not recognize while others were frequent guests in our home—an astonished silence prevailed. "A gun?" asked my grandfather in order to ascertain that, indeed, he had properly heard the child's wish. "Under no circumstances," blurted out my mother while giving me a shove under the table in order to underscore her objection and her repulsion at the unexpected request. "Where did you get this idea?" asked Yantzi Bachi, somewhat amused. Yantzi Bachi was the uncle who was always invited to all of our family events. In fact, he more than anyone knew that outside there was a constant flow of German and Romanian convoys carrying soldiers to the Eastern Front and that these soldiers carried an abundance of weapons.

I had been coached that bargaining with my grandfather about the *afikoman* might be tough and I acted accordingly. "Either a gun or the *afikoman*." All of the guests at the table participated in the bargaining. Finally, my father intervened and said "I will get you a gun," a promise that he actually kept.

I tried to turn my thoughts back to the women of Ghana and Sri Lanka and to the connection between their anti-government organizations and the question of whether these could advance or delay democratization and improvements in their status because I had decided to take a stand against Tilly: if he was going to talk about nineteenth-century Europe, I would talk about Africa here and now, and whoever is able to understand will understand. Indeed, at the conference he understood the hint and during the discussion he called me "an anarchist." A few years later, he came to Toronto where I was on sabbatical and at a formal dinner with several local faculty members (a dinner in which I did not participate) he actually praised me a lot. However, during those sleepless hours, several other *Seders* flashed before my eyes in no logical order.

The next big *Seder* that popped into my head and would not stop bothering me was the one that took place in Giv'atayim after Aunt Yardena was granted her apartment for long-term citizens that she shared with my grandfather and grandmother. This was an attempt, at the end of the austerity period, to reproduce the large *Seders* we had in Romania. My father, my mother, my brother Adam, and I arrived on the eve of the holiday from the Dora neighborhood of Netanya, where we had been fortunate to receive a small apartment after wandering between transit camps. The table was already set in brilliant white with some of the porcelain that we brought from Romania as a precious treasure. My grandfather could hardly see but he knew the entire *haggadah* by heart anyway. Either because my grandfather wished to pass on to my father the status of "head of the family," or because he simply did not have the strength, he included my father in the reading of the *haggadah*. Adam, my younger brother, read the four questions fluently from the prayer book and my grandfather overlooked this innovation of not reciting them by heart. The spiced eggs had the taste of the old days, as did the red soup and the chicken soup with the *kneidlach*. Everything else was smaller and more modest. My grandmother quietly cried the whole evening. "Eva," whispered my mother to her sister. Eva, the daughter born to my grandparents in their old age, had never returned from Auschwitz.

*    *    *

Sixty-seven is a strange age. Outside the circle of my profession and a few other "prestigious" occupations such as politics, business, and journalism, this is considered very old age, when society loses interest in the existence of people. In some areas of the creative arts and in politics, people are at the top of their form at this age and some of my colleagues in their eighties are still almost as active and productive as they were several decades earlier. Even though Israeli universities require people to retire at the age of sixty-eight—in the U.S., they do not, since it is considered age discrimination—it is still possible, afterwards, to teach, research, and supervise students voluntarily. What university policy denies pensioners are the internal research budgets and the participation in meetings and committees that determine both the fate of individuals and the future of the academic community as a whole. A few months before writing these lines, I would not have believed that because of a change in circumstances, I would also be a retiree. For many it is a relief but for many others who are addicted to the internal politics of the university, this is a real demotion in status and self-image. I, apparently, belong to the second group.

I therefore decided to take advantage of the maximum amount of time remaining to me before retirement and work for two more years. However, for reasons that will become clear later on, I was compelled to retire immediately. But what has really preoccupied me, mostly in the last few years and without any connection to that, was when and how it would be appropriate to retire from the world. As a free person and an atheist, death does not frighten me and

I can certainly comprehend, both intellectually and emotionally, the passage from physical and mental existence to non-existence. The real problem is whether I will know when my time has come and whether I will be in a physical state that will allow me to put an end to myself without anyone else's assistance because it is doubtful that I would ever receive such assistance nor would I want to involve someone in this act. In point of fact, this issue has interested me since the surgery I underwent in 1985, and during one of my sabbaticals I even read Derek Humphrey's book *Final Exit* carefully. From this book I learned that it is actually not all that easy to kill yourself without at least some passive assistance.

Autobiographical writing of this kind is, in a way, the beginning of a process—which I hope will still take some time—of departure from the world. I would like this autobiography to be published since I feel a certain obligation to tell those interested, and perhaps also myself, why and how I acted as I did in the professional and public domain. I would like to do this without being didactic and arrogant, even though in all writings of this type there is a certain amount of hidden megalomania. Even if these lines never reach "the public," however, I would still like them to be read by my children, and perhaps even by my grandchildren, as a kind of "connection to one's roots," even though I doubt that most of them will be interested in Grandpa's stories. Perhaps, as is the fashion these days, I will reach a virtual audience via a site on the internet. I assume that it will be a "celebration" for all of my professional, and especially political, opponents, who will be glad to make numerous unflattering connections between my physical difficulties and my "non-conformist" views, but who cares about them?

* * *

It is customary to start an autobiography at the beginning, even though it is difficult to determine what this beginning is. Perhaps my very beginning was my birth, even if it was preceded by many generations before me who also have a role to play in this story. The birth in this case was not "routine," but problematic and it left its mark on the course of my entire life.

I was born on October 16, 1939, in Turda, a Transylvanian town which was not very big. At that time, it was a border town in an area that remained under Romanian control while, a few kilometers away, lay Hungarian Transylvania, a generous gift from Nazi Germany to the Hungarian collaborators. Across the border that had arisen suddenly, there lived another part of our family. At that time, a world war broke out somewhere far away, but this war, with all of its implications, was destined to reach us soon as well. I, too, was in a hurry to emerge from my mother's womb—that is, after only seven months of pregnancy, a premature baby who was hardly ready to breathe in oxygen and pass it on to his brain. My maternal grandmother would often remind me of this when she said that I was always in a hurry and that I hurried too much. And perhaps even now I rush too much. My premature birth had far-reaching consequences that will, directly and indirectly, make frequent appearances in this life story. The result was damage to the brain center that is responsible for the coordination of movement, an injury that was diagnosed years later in Israel as "brain paralysis," a poor translation for an injury known as cerebral palsy, or C.P.

Aside from my premature birth and its consequences, this was, as mentioned, a bad time and place to be born in despite the fact that in comparison to most of my relatives and family members, I was lucky. Unlike the rest of our extended family across the border, our lot was a good one. The mere fact that our small family (that is, my grandmother, my grandfather, my uncle, my mother, father, and I) survived was, under the circumstances, a significant accomplishment and a successful outcome.

My mother married relatively late in life to a man two years her junior. According to the pictures found among the ashes, both my mother and father were good looking. My mother was an impressive and proud woman until her last day at the age of eighty-five. At the time my mother and father agreed to marry, he was a traveling salesman who sold the renowned Hornyphone radios. In his two suitcases, which looked gigantic to me, he carried catalogues and samples of radios and shiny electrical appliances, symbols of the progress and technology of the period. During his sales trips on the Romanian railway, he traveled from the far northeast, the heart and center of the Romanian state, to the border region that was in dispute between the Romanians and the Hungarians. Since there were no more suitable young men left in town for my mother, my grandfather, Adolf, and my grandmother, Esther, had almost no choice and agreed to the betrothal of Ilush, my mother, to Marco, my father. My prosperous grandfather was proud of being Hungarian outside the home and Jewish inside it. He was also proud of the fact that he had acquired his high status there on his own (his grandfather, like my grandmother's grandfather, came to this region from Galicia). Only his sense of humor exceeded his pride. My father was always considered by the family to be a foreigner and somewhat inferior, "a Romanian," a status he accepted with surprising resignation. His revenge manifested itself in his frequent betrayals of my mother although he never abandoned his home in order to pursue another woman and he was a conscientious father and husband.

When my mother and father met, they barely had a common language. My father was really fluent only in Romanian, but he knew Yiddish reasonably well too, and as a result, he "understood" German. My mother was fluent in Hungarian and read and spoke German well. Thus their common language at the beginning was a mixture of Yiddish and broken German. However, my mother had a knack for languages and quickly learned Romanian well. Until he died, my father spoke a broken and funny Hungarian, a mixture of various languages and dialects. This is also how he spoke "Hebrew" when we arrived in Israel, a fact that irritated me to no end and caused me to feel ashamed of him. In his youth, he studied in some sort of trade college but I don't know if he had a diploma of any kind. I never saw him read a book for pleasure except when he read me stories. He was an uneducated man who possessed a social and political consciousness and sensitivity that were surprising given his level of education. He possessed a basic naiveté, a great deal of respect for all people, an almost unreserved trust in everyone, and an exuberant optimism in nearly all circumstances, an optimism that he also radiated to his surroundings. Only twice in my life did I see him in real despair.

My mother was in many respects his opposite. She completed a Hungarian high school education with an emphasis on classical studies. This was undoubtedly the most respectable educational accomplishment that a Jewish girl could achieve in those days, under those conditions, and in such a relatively remote place. But, in addition, my mother was an obsessive reader. She read anything that fell into her hands. Her broad and varied knowledge surprised me each time anew.

I learned Hungarian and Romanian at the same time. With my mother, my grandfather, my grandmother, and my uncle Imre, I spoke Hungarian, but I spoke Romanian with my father. The dominant language and culture in our house, however, was Hungarian. I also started to understand German because even after my mother, Ilush, spoke fluent Romanian, she continued to converse with my father in German so that "the child won't understand."

My mother was a pragmatic woman who had a somewhat suspicious and critical attitude toward other people. At the same time, in her youth, she was blessed with a generous dose of romanticism that, to the displeasure of her parents, found expression also in her Zionism. But my mother did not take her Zionism to the point of open rebellion towards her parents, as did her younger sister Yoli (whose Hebraized name later on was Yardena). In 1936, when she was twenty-three, Yoli got up one day and ran away to Palestine. Joining a kibbutz only exacerbated her relationship with her father, for whom Zionism and Communism combined were too much. I don't know exactly what my grandfather felt when he finally arrived in Israel towards the end of 1952 and was lovingly and warmly received by his rebellious daughter. She treated him and her mother with devotion mixed with some degree of bitterness until my grandfather passed away at the age of ninety-six, full of humor, lucid, and up-to-date about what was happening in the world until his last day.

Because my father's travels became increasingly risky and Jews disappeared on the roads when the fascist Iron Guard hoodlums marauded across the country, his father-in-law, Grandpa Adolf, financed the opening of a store for radios and electrical appliances in the city, whose population had burgeoned as streams of Romanian and Polish refugees filled the city. The store had a Romanian "partner" and was managed under the partner's name since Jews were already prohibited from engaging in commerce. I don't think that my father managed to earn much from his store because the atmosphere was becoming more and more suffocating as German soldiers and their Hungarian and Romanian allies filled the city either on their way to the Russian front or on leave prior to going to battle.

Indeed, our city was a major passageway to the Russian front for the German and Romanian armies. Our home faced the main street and from the large living room, glass double doors opened onto a second-story balcony overlooking it. The street curved into a square with a fountain and a tall, impressive bronze sculpture of one of Romania's kings or heroes. The statue stood in the classic pose of a rider with a drawn sword in his hand while the horse balanced on his hind legs. When a German military convoy would pass, with a noise that shook the entire building, I used to sneak onto the balcony despite being strictly forbidden to do so. Primarily, I was deeply impressed by the motorcyclists. Their motorcycles led and ended the convoys and usually had side cars. They wore steel helmets and dressed in grey or black leather coats and long boots. The escorts wore pistols and sometimes sub-machine guns. A little before that, I was fortunate to receive the promised toy gun which in my eyes was the same as a real one, like those of the Romanian soldiers or the members of the Iron Guard. When the convoys passed, I would wave to the soldiers or stand to attention with my arm raised, as I had seen more than once, and yell "Heil Hitler! Heil Hitler!" Sometimes the German soldiers, or whoever they were, would notice me and return my salute with a smile and a hand wave or a weak "Heil Hitler." I never told anybody about this. Now, as I write these lines, I have chills. I was then a very thin boy with blond hair that darkened within about a year.

My "Hungarian" grandfather, Adolf Laszlo, first lost his mother, who died in some mysterious epidemic, and then his father, who owned a tavern. His original name was Levinger, but when he realized that with a name like that he would not succeed in business, he changed it to one with deep Hungarian roots. At the age of six or seven, his uncle apprenticed him to an artisan-tailor in order for him to learn a trade and become a man. As was common in those days, he did not learn tailoring. Instead, he cleaned and scrubbed his master's house and workshop, carried his wife's bags in the markets, watched their children, and sometimes played with them a bit. He performed every job, big or small, as requested. Most of all, he suffered from the wrathful beatings of his master and mistress, from inadequate nutrition, and almost constant hunger. For ten years, he opened his mouth neither to complain nor to contradict them. During his eleventh year, he rose up and rebelled. "Sir, if you do not teach me the trade, I will get up and go," he said impudently. Young Adolf ended up with a dose of bruises and burns on all parts of his body from a heavy, white-hot coal iron. However, when the master's fury subsided a bit, he did take him to the workshop and started teaching him the secrets of the trade. Within a year, he allowed my grandfather not only to take the measurements of respected clients but also to cut the most expensive fabric. Precise cutting of the fabric was the foundation on which both the elegance and fit of the garment depended and required the highest level of skill and responsibility. A suitable cut could also save material and therefore money.

During my childhood, I used hundreds of fabric samples—small rectangles in soft pastel colors and different prints whose sides were cut like shark's teeth—to build magic palaces and anything else that my imagination desired, like the "Lego bricks" of my own children. Every evening, I used to demand stories from Grandpa and he enjoyed telling me, with a great deal of humor, about the adventures of Fussy the Rabbit. Later on, when I used to tell my children these stories, Fussy the Rabbit became Michel the Rabbit and his little son Michelon, both of whom were made entirely out of carrots. But Grandpa Adolf also used to tell me, while I sat on the chamber pot trying to fulfill my daily duty, about his years as a boy working for the artisan-tailor. These were all totally hilarious and non-educational adventures to which my mother and grandmother greatly objected.

At the age of twenty-something, my grandfather left his artisan master as a master tailor in every way and wandered from the rural town to our city, Turda, where he started to work as a tailor in his own right. Despite the fact that he never attended school, his knowledge covered many areas, from astronomy to poetry to literature. He was a logical man who laughed at the many superstitions that afflicted my grandmother as well as the maids and peasant girls who worked in our house. I do not know where he acquired his basic reading ability in English, which is not at all similar to Hungarian, but he had a good understanding of the glamorous men's fashion catalogues that were sent to him directly from Britain even before the war. Apparently, he had intended to immigrate to America at some point, a plan that was never realized because the gates of the United States were closed to immigrants at the beginning of the Great Depression. Almost as soon as he was able to stand on his own, he was betrothed to Esther, a young woman from the Frankel family.

My grandmother's father—or more precisely, his thick beard—was the first person that terrified me. Fortunately for me, he lived somewhere outside the city and trips to visit him were rare. Aside from his beard, which made him very frightening in my mind's eye, he laughed frequently and loudly and used to invite me to join him in a glass of *palinka*, the Hungarian version of Russian vodka, or Scottish Whisky, or Romanian *tzuika*, "offers" that outraged my grandmother and my mother. I always responded to his suggestions with bitter crying, something that increased his laughter and my mother's embarrassment as she tried, unsuccessfully, to calm me down.

Dad-Nagi-Tata, my paternal grandfather's father, looked to me like some kind of demon or magician from a particularly frightening book that my mother used to read to me at that time and whose main character was a northern troll, actually a quite pleasant one, by the name of Goingu. I never managed to locate this book later on in any other language—unlike other books that I loved very much, such as the adventures of Nils Holgersson and the wild geese, or Pippi Longstocking, the mischievous girl who also used to travel all over the country, and Little Lord Fauntleroy, who had a complex relationship with his grandfather.

I also had night fears due to a rather innocent and beautiful song with a monotonous rhythm (I believe by Sandor Petofi) that my mother used to sing to me in order to send me to sleep. The song, despite the inexplicable anxiety that engulfed me anew every time I heard it, had some enchanting magic and I wanted to hear it again and again. It was a song about a moth that flies around a candle flame until it collides with a wall and becomes still.

My grandfather, Herman Kimerling, was born in 1882 in Piatra-Neamt. According to the name and additional sources, the Kimerlings arrived in northwest Romania from Austria. Family tradition, which I was never able to confirm, claims that my grandfather's grandfather was a railway engineer who was sent on loan to the Ottoman Empire in order to plan and supervise the railway system. If that is true, then he played a part in the construction of the Hejaz railroad that was planned in order to transport Muslim pilgrims to Mecca. This might explain how one branch of the family ended up in Romania. However, my factual knowledge of the Kimerling family is limited and fragmented since I grew up in a family that anthropologists classify as matrilocal; that is, its location as well as its family culture was determined by the mother of the family. There was also more than a bit of contempt, suspicion, and hostility towards the Kimerlings in our house. Herman was born to a baker's family but at the age of seventeen, he was sent to Switzerland to study medicine. One year before completing his studies, his father died and he, the oldest son, was called back to support the family, with its many children, and take over the baking business. Herman never finished his medical training and he became a baker and a bitter person for the rest of his life. He married some woman whose name I do not know. Her name was never mentioned in any family context and the mystery concerning the identity of my paternal grandmother persists to this day. When I was young, I did not ask and now there is no longer anyone to ask. I don't know if my vague feeling that the identity of my anonymous grandmother includes some dark story is justified. Perhaps they simply did not talk about her in order not to hurt my step-grandmother Molly's feelings.

My anonymous grandmother bore five children to Herman. One died in infancy or early childhood and I don't know anything about him either. My father, Marko, was the eldest. Gizella, my aunt, was born after him. My Aunt Etti came after Gizella, and Berko, my uncle, was the youngest son. I do not know where to place the child that died, nor do I know his name. My grandmother seemed to have died at a relatively young age (perhaps with the death of my baby uncle or during his birth) and Herman married Molly. Molly was a simple woman who barely knew how to read and write; she always looked like a Romanian peasant to me and perhaps she actually was one. She never had children of her own, but she cared for Herman's children and Herman himself with dedication and love. After the war, Grandfather Herman came to visit us with his wife once, and only once, in Turda. He was supposed to come and visit us once again in Cluj, the big city we moved to several years after the war, but this visit somehow never took place. I met him on many occasions in Israel but by that time he was already a man defeated by old age and dislocations and whose mind was feeble.

The Hungarian side of my family always suspected the Romanian side of financial and emotional extortion. The latter were usually financially entangled and turned to my father for help. After the first few times—that they always promised would be the last time—my mother forbade my father to give any more "loans." Although he dreaded his wife's wrath, my father found it difficult to live with this restriction and resorted to "anonymous donations." The problem was that these gifts were usually discovered quickly by my mother who then tormented him with her sharp tongue. Those were the only times I heard my mother raise her voice. My father kept silent and accepted his suffering, his eyes downcast with humiliation. For some reason, I always supported my father and despite the fact that, influenced by my grandfather and grandmother, I did not like the "Romanians" in the family, I could not understand why it was wrong to help a brother or sister in trouble. I was also angry at my mother for insulting him and his family. For all that, my mother overlooked my father's infidelities with a hurt silence and tearful eyes but I imagine that in all likelihood she imposed other sanctions on him. In those moments, I hated my father. Don't ask me how a small child knows these things that grown-ups attempt to hide at all costs. I simply knew. I probably put together the whispering and the yelling behind closed doors, the conversations in German that I was not supposed to understand, the silences, and the looks.

## Notes

1. Questions from the Passover Haggadah, which are traditionally asked by the youngest child.
2. A hidden piece of matzo, or unleavened bread.

# 2

## FLEEING

Today we use the term "modern Orthodox" and indeed this describes my grandfather Adolf—a believer, but one who was also involved in both the large and small world. He was an impressive man who hated the rabbinate and loved to work. Fervent about his religion, he never missed a single prayer service in the synagogue. He also kept all the precepts, both minor and major, according to his own interpretation. My grandmother Estie (Esther) was also a very devout person. Nevertheless, my grandfather refused to play any role in the Jewish community and at home he used to mutter, "I am not one of the synagogue managers." He was always impeccably dressed, with a suit and tie, a fashionable hat, and a walking stick or an umbrella on rainy days. He looked like one of the English gentlemen who could be seen in his catalogues or like one of the high-ranking people whose photographs appeared in Hungarian weeklies when Grandpa was in the war. Grandma guarded these weeklies religiously in large, heavy binders which we used to leaf through on special occasions. The cover pages almost always displayed a photograph of His Excellency Emperor Franz Joseph inspecting a unit of soldiers on one front line or another and always announced glorious victories. My grandmother used to utter the name of the Emperor with excessive affection even though this Emperor brought hard times upon her. Immediately following her marriage to Adolf in 1913, she gave birth to four children, one after the other. Illush, my mother, was the eldest, Yoli came two years later, and Imre was born the following year. The last one was Eva-Hava who was the beautiful, spoiled baby girl of the family.

When my grandfather received a conscription order from the Emperor, no effort to obtain favors from those who had connections helped, and Adolf went to war for the Emperor and the Austro-Hungarian homeland. For three and a half years, my grandmother Esther did not receive a letter, a postcard or any other information from him. Her petitions to the military authorities remained unanswered and even though he was not declared dead or missing, Esther was prepared for the worst. Esther, a little but extremely active woman, became the engine of our family almost to her last day. In addition to raising her own four children, she brought her nephew Mishi, who was orphaned at the age of ten, into her home. She raised him until the age of nineteen when he was conscripted into the army and from there escaped to California. Esther coped amazingly well with the shortages and uncertainty of war and she also ran what remained of the store, even though it ceased to provide a living after the Great War started. The family experienced difficult days of hunger and privation but eventually Adolf returned from the battle fields, not completely healthy but in an ebullient mood somewhat inappropriate for a soldier returning from the defeated army of an Empire that had vanished almost overnight.

Years later, his experiences in the military became my grandfather's entertaining raw material for the stories he invented for his grandson, along with Fussy the Rabbit and the tailor's apprentice stories which could have easily competed with the stories of Charles Dickens and Emile Zola, except that they actually contained more humor and a more ironic view of himself. However these stories had an authentic kernel and were apparently based on experiences he had during two different periods. In the first period, my grandfather was stuck in the trenches on the Italian front. "It took us fifteen minutes to load a bullet into the rifle. We shot the bullet in the direction ordered by Mr. Sergeant and then we rested for fifteen minutes. We ate, fifteen minutes. We sneaked out of the trench for our needs. One hour. Many received a bullet in the behind because of this, if you don't mind." When recited rhythmically in archaic Hungarian, his stories sounded really funny. Later on, it reminded me of the adventures of *The Good Soldier Schweik* and, of course, *All Quiet on the Western Front.* During the second period of my grandfather's war, the stories started to sound more and more like those of Baron Munchausen. One officer discovered that my grandfather was a master tailor. He took him out of the trenches, rented him an apartment in some picturesque Italian town, and brought him a sewing machine, other tailoring tools, and plenty of fabric. These were, in all likelihood, looted materials since the brave officers were allowed to do anything during the war, just as they are today. The officer dressed himself and his friends in superb suits and dinner jackets and even brought other officers to my grandfather as clients. My grandfather's officer received full remuneration and who knows what other compensation from those other officers while my grandfather received generous tips and was even promised a medal for heroism at the end of the war although, for some reason, nothing ever came of the medal business. The really comical part of all this occurred when the officer also decided to dress his wife, his mistresses, and his friends' mistresses in the latest Viennese fashion. It didn't matter that my grandfather pleaded with him that he was only a men's tailor and that he had no clue about cutting and sewing women's suits and dresses. He had to follow orders and take the ladies' measurements (with pleasure, I think) and make their clothing because war is war. It never became clear why his letters and postcards from the front never reached their destination. Perhaps the Austrian military post was just lousy, or perhaps the letters were never written in the heat of the various battles.

Despite the ups and downs, the years between the two wars were good years for my family. My grandfather solidified his economic status and became a kind of "elite tailor" of the city, a man respected both by the Jews and the Hungarians as well as the Romanians who "liberated" Transylvania from the Hungarian "occupation" and began the Romanization of the district.

My grandfather's daily schedule was carefully planned and unvarying. After he returned home from one of his businesses, he used to dine, rest a bit, and leave for his club. I was never able to determine what kind of club it was but in my imagination now, it appears to have been some kind of men's club. There was always a strong smell of tobacco emanating from him. Even though he never smoked at home because my grandmother didn't allow it, there was always a package of quality cigars in his pocket. At the age of sixty-five, he suddenly felt weak. The doctor thought it was the beginning of heart disease and forbade him to smoke or drink. He stopped smoking that very day but for the rest of his long life, he refused to give up his evening glass of Palinka.

During high school, my mother was active in "Gordonia," a Zionist youth movement belonging to the historical Labor Unity which later on became Mapai. Years of activity in the movement—first as a member and then as a leader—greatly shaped her cultural and political world for the rest of her life. It seems to me that the best years of her life were those in which she lugged around knapsacks while hiking with her friends, boys and girls, in the Carpathian Mountains. On many occasions, I went through the yellowing photo album where I saw happy and mysterious young men and women. For a while, they had a young leader, good looking and arrogant, by the name of Rudolf (Rezso) Kasztner ("The famous Rudolf Kasztner"). He was the darling of all the Gordonia girls, who seemed to have been his darlings. Many years later, when I used to question my mother about Rezso, she would speak about him with a mixture of repulsion and admiration. She would end every such conversation by saying, "Well, what can I tell you? A politician. It's good that we never needed him." This was incorrect at least on two occasions, but I wouldn't argue with my mother.

The first daughter to marry was actually Eva-Hava, the youngest daughter in the Laszlo house. As mentioned previously, they had difficulties finding a suitable bridegroom for my mother, the eldest daughter, despite her classic beauty. Eva was a young woman with a rare beauty and her bridegroom, Mr. Berkowitz, was considered an excellent match. The young couple moved to Cluj (Klausenburg), the regional capital of Transylvania. Their baby, Andrash, was born in 1941 and I remember only the pictures of my baby cousin in his mother's and father's arms. This is also how I remember my aunt Eva—only from family photos. That same year, Transylvania was divided again, under German influence, between Romania and Hungary. We were left on the Romanian side and the Berkowitz family on the Hungarian one. In the spring of 1944, the Berkowitz family, together with all the Jews of Cluj, was confined to a ghetto. The Nazis deported them, in one transport, to Auschwitz. They never returned. My brother Adam, who was born after the war, received his name in memory of our aunt Eva-Hava.

Even before that, an obscure and unbearable sense of dread hung in the air. As a four-and-a-half-year-old child, I could sense it, although it seems to me that its essence was unclear to the adults themselves. I assume that the restrictions placed one after the other on the Jews, the fear of the approaching war, the anxiety about "resettlement" in Transnistria (a notion that was always uttered in a whisper so that I would not even hear it), the anti-Semitic rhetoric of the regime, and most of all, the marauding of the Iron Guard gangs, were just the bare tip of the iceberg. I do not suppose that anything was known at the time about extermination camps and mass murder. It is ironic that my family placed an almost absolute trust and confidence in Hungarians and Hungarian culture while considering the Romanians to be barbarians and Jew-haters. My grandfather, therefore, made great efforts to reach the other side of the border, the Hungarian side, until things calmed down. Through the services of some dubious mediator, a German officer—a man I still remember—arrived at our home one night (my grandfather described him as a pleasant and fair person) and promised to smuggle us across the border in a truck. Perhaps he knew that there was no place to smuggle us to or perhaps he didn't. There was probably an agreement about a large sum of gold coins and my mother started to prepare me for the trip by explaining that I would have to be very quiet and still during the entire journey. Fortunately, the German never returned but he also didn't hand us over. My grandfather used to mention him every once in a while after the war, always asking, "Interesting. What happened to him? Perhaps he was sent to the front."

There is almost no doubt that had we successfully crossed the border into Hungary, our fate would have been the same as that of my aunt Eva and the rest of the family on the Hungarian side. Together with Eva, there were also three cousins younger than she was—Lilly, Mira, and Yudka—and their parents. The three young cousins survived but their parents were annihilated. It was from these cousins that we heard about Eva's fate. She did not want to be separated from her baby and therefore went with him straight to the gas chamber immediately upon arrival at the camp. After her return to Cluj, Lilly married a young man who also survived the camps and named her daughter Eva, after my aunt.

My grandfather had several apprentices who learned the craft of tailoring from him. One of them was a shrewd and diligent fellow whose name, I believe, was Luminsko. Despite his talent in cutting cloth, he chose a different career and later became the head of the local police in Turda. One summer day in 1944, he entered my grandfather's store, and even though it was completely empty, he dragged him to the back of the shop and whispered to him, "Laszlo, even though you are a Jew and a Hungarian, you are an honest man and you always treated me fairly. I want you to know that tonight all the Jews will be gathered for a transport. Take your family and get out of here. However, if you tell this to even one other person, I will kill you with my own hands." My grandfather hung a "Back Soon" sign on the door and rushed home. The Napoleons (gold coins), the jewelry and the diamonds as well as cash—the classic Jewish survival kit from time immemorial—were taken out of their secret hiding place. There were no cars to be found and there was also a severe shortage of fuel, so my uncle Imre went and acquired some sort of Gypsy wagon and a mare. A family decision was made right on the spot: the young family members with the boy (me) would escape but the older ones (my grandmother and grandfather) would stay and decide what to do as events unfolded. To this day, I don't understand what the developments were expected to be. In retrospect, this decision turned out to be the right one. The Jews were not rounded up on that night or any other night (even though, later on, there were rumors that trains were ready for transport in the coal-mining region near the city).

In the early evening, we left the city and suddenly life became completely different. My father and my uncle took turns urging the horse on and in a short while learned to handle the horse and cart skillfully while I sat bundled up in my mother's lap holding my "tokorbe" very tightly. The tokorbe was a light blanket and its name was a garbled, baby-talk version of "Should I cover you?"

The tokorbe apparently gave me a feeling of confidence and it accompanied me wherever I went, at times while sucking my thumb, until the age of twelve. Before we boarded the ship that sailed to Israel, I decided on my own to throw away the tokorbe, which had long since become shapeless. This was probably my declaration that, from then on, I was leaving my childhood and my lack of confidence behind and I was turning over a new leaf in my life.

Within one day after our escape from the city, we became part of a convoy of refugees who were trying to flee, either by foot or in a variety of strange vehicles, toward some unclear destination. I have no idea who was in the convoy, but I remember that among them were many people wearing Romanian army uniforms—the Romanian army had partly collapsed and the soldiers had run for their lives. It looked like they tried to return to their homes without first getting rid of their uniforms. There were also those who tried to board our wagon—some by force, others by begging—and my father and my uncle would push them away.

We were terrified of the Stukas. These were the German, low-flying dive bombers that were equipped with a pair of machine guns. They would suddenly appear just above our heads and spray the convoy with their machine guns. I still remember that during one of these sudden attacks, my uncle threw me off the moving wagon into a corn field at the side of the road. I landed next to a young Romanian soldier who was lying down flat. He smiled at me. A few seconds later his head was shattered by the aircraft bullets and pieces of his brain splattered on me. My whole body trembled and for many years after that event, I would tremble whenever I heard the noise of an airplane engine, even when I was an adolescent in Israel and the planes were "ours." Today, this would be called a "post-traumatic stress reaction."

My father and my uncle decided that remaining with a convoy was too dangerous and decided to travel on side roads leading up into the mountains. During our wanderings, we used to stop at the outskirts of small villages, spread a blanket near a well, and feed and water the mare first. My uncle had come to see himself as a professional horseman since one of his hobbies, besides hunting for beautiful "shikses," was horseback riding. We often bought fresh dairy products, vegetables, and smoked meats from Romanian farmers and then moved on. Sometimes we stayed a few days at the home of a rich farmer, bathed, ate hot (and very dirty, according to my mother) meals and slept on real beds with sheets. Under different circumstances, this could have been a real pleasure trip. I remember two things well from that period, even though I don't have a clue if it lasted days, weeks, or months: one was the fleas that devoured me and the other was the constant dread in my parents' eyes—a look that I never saw again. After all, the same farmers we encountered could quite easily have robbed or even slaughtered us. They could also have handed us over to the Germans or, if they were not around, to the other authorities. Not only were our lives entirely in their hands, one must also assume that they took a risk when they harbored us, knowing without any doubt that we were Jews. However, most of the time it was the other way round. The farmers treated us with respect as the "masters from the city" and the "lady" and boasted about their wealth and knowledge. If my mother had let me out of her sight, their children would certainly have played with me.

What made it very tough on my parents was not knowing what was happening. Who is winning—the Germans or the Russians? Are the Russians advancing and getting closer? How much closer and if so, where are they? The farmers did not have a radio and even if they had possessed up-to-date information, it was too dangerous to show an interest. In addition, we didn't know the fate of my grandfather and grandmother or that of the rest of the family. Nevertheless, whether as a result of information or out of desperation and because of the cold and the diarrhea that afflicted "the child," we began to head down the mountain. The strongest memory remaining from those nights was the burning horizon all around us. The area contained oil wells and gas; one of the warring sides lit the wells, almost transforming the darkness of night into daylight. It was both an amazing and a frightening scene. After a while, the sounds of muffled artillery became clearly audible, a fact that made my parents very happy—the Russians are close by, they decided, or hoped. We tried to carry on traveling eastward in the expected direction of the Red Army's arrival.

I must add that throughout our wanderings, my mother never ceased telling me stories, singing me songs (also in Hebrew: "Put your hand in mine, I am yours and you are mine" or, "Hey, hey, Galia, you beautiful mountain girl"…) and teaching me all kinds of useful things. I do not recall having books or writing implements but nevertheless, I began to acquire the rudimentary concepts of reading, writing, and arithmetic. It's possible that this was one of my mother's ways of coping with the unbearable situation, and especially with the uncertainty of our life.

# 3

## FANTASIES

My outstanding achievement in eleventh grade was winning the "President's Prize" in a short story competition between high schools for "The Occupier," which I wrote in 1960. The story describes a young Israeli soldier patrolling a miserable Arab refugee camp (I didn't know then about the existence of the Palestinians) in Gaza after its conquest in 1956. The protagonist was deeply affected by the sense of power that his weapon, his uniform, and his status as a victorious soldier gave him. The climax of the story occurs when the hero meets a young Arab girl and feels both sexually attracted to her and sorry for her. I didn't dare describe a rape in the story but I did hint that this is what happened. The end of the story was a little weak because I didn't know how to conclude it so I chose an easy solution. On his return trip home, longing for his girlfriend, the soldier hits a mine and is killed. I don't know how this story won the prize or whether anybody actually read it. Today, in all likelihood, a story bearing this title would be thrown straight into the garbage can.

Perhaps the real reason underlying my fascination with the subject of violent power is the weakness of my body. A female friend once commented, "This is very common. Children who feel helpless always fantasize about power. This is said to have been Nietzsche's situation also. Helplessness can be physical but it can also be spiritual-emotional-social. Temptation in fantasy is very common." From approximately the age of four, I carried a secret that I will reveal here for the first time. Every night before falling asleep, I used to tell myself a story in installments. In this story, I was always the sole hero, something like Superman and James Bond combined, who saves the good and destroys the bad—all this without ever having seen a movie or comic strip. As I got older, the power fantasies turned into sexual ones. I had no one to talk about them with, despite the fact that I could discuss anything else freely with my mother, including my failures and successes in courting girls and later women. But we never talked about sex itself. It seems that the topic embarrassed her and she let me manage on my own, which didn't make things easier and resulted in more than a few disappointments when I arrived at university and began to have sexual experiences.

Eventually, my great curiosity about power developed over time in two separate but intertwined directions. On the one hand, my professional specialization led me to study the sociology of politics and the political world, including the investigation of the relationship between the military and society as well as the study of war as a social phenomenon, particularly in the Israeli context. This entire field can be summarized by three questions:

1. When, how, and by whom are different kinds of violent force used?
2. How do violent organizations (guerilla and terror groups as well as armies, police forces and militias) operate and become activated?
3. How is political power used and manipulated?

At times, my rivals in the academy have argued against me (usually not in my presence), by asking how a person who never served in the military can do research on armies and wars. This argument is generally well accepted in our militaristic society but it is irrelevant. To begin with, most sociologists who investigate a variety of social phenomena never experience themselves the phenomenon under study. ("Is it the case that in order to study prostitution, the sociologists must be prostitutes?" I used to respond.) Second, who can guarantee, for example, that a military officer who participated in wars and other violent acts and must therefore justify them has fewer biases than I do? As an aside, one of the greatest researchers of armies and wars, John Keegan, was also disabled and never served in any army.

One of my colleagues, a native-born Israeli and a colonel in the paratroopers, considers himself an undisputed authority on Israeli society and culture. He tends to characterize Israeli society as an indigenous one while I, viewing it from my own perspective, tend to characterize it as a society of immigrants since even those people whose families have lived in the country for a number of generations still carry the characteristics found in power-oriented, immigrant-settler societies.

At the beginning of the 1982 war, when Israel invaded Lebanon and this colleague was discharged [from his reserve service] after a few days, he burst into my office at the university, very excited. He told me about experiencing the power of the large numbers of tanks and the armored infantry that flooded southern Lebanon, trampling and shattering the "Fatahland," and about the soldiers being received as liberators by the Lebanese Christian population with rice, songs, and dances. It reminded me of the short story "The Occupier" that I wrote in 1960, in which I described exactly this intoxicating sense of power accompanied by this same feeling of moral superiority. I listened impatiently and with some astonishment to his speech praising the military power that trampled Lebanon and then asked him, rather impolitely, to leave my room. At the time, he didn't understand why and after a while, when it was already clear to everybody that the invasion of Lebanon was a terrible quagmire, he claimed that he didn't remember the incident. Amnesia is also a common phenomenon in Israeli academia.

A second direction in my development was, perhaps, the consolidation of a pacific and humanistic system of values for which I could find almost no partners or understanding in Israel. This was a long, drawn-out process, filled with internal conflicts. It is still not finished, and perhaps it will never be, because it is impossible on moral grounds to reject every use of violence and war. True, there are no "good" wars, but a war clearly designed to completely destroy evil is, after all, necessary and moral. In fact, I acknowledge only one such war—the war against German Nazism. Even in this war, however, along with this proper worldwide goal, one could detect phenomena of evil. Such was the terrible revenge bombing of Dresden and the refusal to bomb the Nazi extermination camps. Such was also the racist incarceration of the Japanese in concentration camps in the United States (Americans of German origin were not imprisoned). Especially problematic was the dropping of atomic bombs on Hiroshima and Nagasaki. These bombings may have shortened the bloody war in the Pacific Ocean and saved the lives of many American soldiers—although this is in dispute today—but the after-effects were catastrophic and caused irreversible damage, just as the radiation experiments conducted on the American soldiers themselves did. At the same time, perhaps the horrors of Hiroshima have, as of the writing of this book, prevented the further use of nuclear weapons. The war of 1948 was indeed an existential war for the ethno-national community in this country and as such it was necessary from the Jewish point of view, but its morality was substantially stained by the ethnic cleansing that was carried out in the course of the war on most of the Arab population. Was the expulsion a necessity too? It is very difficult to decide that within a broad historical context.

However, I have a vested interest in the continued legitimate existence and prosperity of Israel, and this is one of my strongest motivations for my strident, uncompromising support for a fair solution to the Palestinian problem. But it is an interest that may distort my moral judgment. The world is full of contradictions and contrasts, and since I have no rabbi or guru other than myself, I must find at least some of the answers on my own. This may be one of the primary motives for writing this book, aside from the actual pleasure of writing about myself and my experiences. I have always revealed myself, though, through the pretext of writing narratives about others.

I received my journalistic training at the "Voice of Israel." A short while after arriving at the Hebrew University I came across an advertisement for the position of editor of youth programs on the radio. I applied for the position and was invited to appear before the interview committee. I "appeared" and the unfamiliar people sitting at the narrow, crowded table treated me with extreme politeness; I emerged with a good feeling. However, as soon as I reached the stairs, I was approached by a woman who was on the committee and who had said almost nothing during the interview. "Look, Baruch," said the woman, who turned out to be Miriam Harman, the legendary director of radio programs for children and youth, "We cannot accept you because of your handicap; however, we are starting a workshop to teach the writing of freelance radio scripts. You are invited to participate in it. Perhaps you could write us some sketches." Today they wouldn't have made such a statement and instead would have concocted some more politically correct excuse. Then, however, I did not see their answer as inappropriate. On the contrary, I was elated at the offer.

One month later, I did indeed receive an invitation to something resembling a course in play writing. There were about twenty of us on the course, mostly female teachers and a few writers of children's stories. The first speaker was the professional manager of the radio, Nakdimon Rogel, who tried to explain to us about the medium of radio, its advantages and its limitations. It must be remembered that in the early 1960s, there was no television in Israel and radio was "the tribal campfire," as my friend and teacher Elihu Katz described it. In my eyes at least, the most important program, and the one that I would never miss, was the weekly series of radio sketches called "The Curtain Rises," edited by Michael Ohad. Some of the best actors in Israel participated in it. One of my dreams has always been to transform plays into radio programs and to write original scripts of my own. Most of the course was presented by another outstanding radio personality, a colorful man with a sense of humor, Amnon Ahi-Naomi. From time to time, he was joined by Miriam Harman herself and a young British director, Reuven Morgan.

At the end of the course, I joined the team writing the educational programs that were broadcast to school children in the mornings. I was primarily "in charge" of history and geography. In fact, I carried out a kind of quiet revolution in the way the material was presented to the pupils. Instead of the dry reading of textbook materials, I began to write dramatic and "suspenseful" stories focused on a number of basic elements of the educational material. The representative of the Ministry of Education was quite opposed to this innovation and argued that the students would not learn the material required of them through my programs. I responded that they certainly couldn't remember anything from the recitation of the material other than boredom, while as a result of my scripts they would at least recall what an educated person should remember about the core topics. Observations carried out on a sample of classes (without my knowledge) confirmed my contention. The students paid more attention in class and the programs even triggered curiosity and additional questions by the students to the teachers. My victory was absolute and the other program writers even began to imitate my approach. What was no less important, however, was that I was able to support myself financially during my studies for a first degree.

There was no lack of failures too. At times, I was swept away on the wings of my imagination and as a result, the script contained baseless items that resulted in complaints and protests from furious listeners. I remember that on at least one occasion following a program on the geography of Uganda, my employment was almost terminated as a result of some nonsense, the nature of which I no longer remember. In contrast, years later while working on my master's thesis on Uganda, I was rigorously accurate to the point of extreme boredom.

However, without any doubt, my most searing failure during the time I worked for the radio was the program that aired shortly before Israeli Memorial Day, which commemorates those fallen in battle. I was chosen to write a special script to be heard by all the students of primary schools in the country that had radios. The program was preceded by words from the Minister of Education, Yigal Alon, to all the children of Israel. I did not like the invitation because I knew that I was expected to write clichés for this sensitive commemoration, but I was not able to give up the "honor" bestowed upon me. For the first time since I started to write scripts, the work did not flow and I struggled with every sentence. In the end, I sent the script to the broadcasters very late but it must have been really terrible. On the designated day and hour, they did broadcast "Baruch Kimmerling's script"; however, any resemblance between what I wrote and what was broadcast was purely accidental.

It was the afternoon programs, however, that gave me the most pleasure, and particularly the series I developed based on classic literature. The radio network broadcast series on *The Adventures of Tom Sawyer*, *The Adventures of Huckleberry Finn*, *A Brave New World* by Aldous Huxley and *The Death Ship* by B. Traven, a book I particularly liked. These series were broadcast as reruns on many occasions, often after a new generation of listeners replaced a previous one, and ceased to be broadcast only when radio programming changed completely.

These scripts were also staged with outstanding skill by Reuven Morgan, and especially Ram Levy.

*   *   *

One evening, in the summer of 1944, we reached a town by the name of Hateg. We entered carefully since it appeared to be too quiet. We knocked on doors and windows. Either nobody opened their doors to us or we saw scared faces through the cracks. "Are there Germans in town?" we asked. "No, they left," was the encouraging answer. "Any Romanians?" "No." "Russians?" "No, they haven't arrived yet."

After a short search, we saw a notice on one of the windows: "Room for Rent." We rented it and collapsed on one large bed. We had barely closed our eyes when a muffled sound began to develop and grow louder until it became deafening. We heard yelling in an unrecognizable language. Every so often, bursts of gunfire could be heard. Despite my mother's entreaties, my father went out; a few seconds later, he returned and hugged and kissed all of us. "The Russians. The Russians are here." The men went outside again and a short while later returned with two soldiers in dusty, dirty uniforms. Strange machine guns were slung over their chests and around them was something like a huge round box that turned out to be the magazine. Both soldiers spoke Yiddish and asked for something to eat. My mother took out all the stuff we still had and they devoured it all. Afterwards, we all huddled in the one room and tried to fall asleep despite the fact that the two soldiers brought a terrible smell with them. But that smell was like a perfume to our souls, the smell of relief and great hopes.

Not long ago, I was pleased to serve as an editor for a book based on the exciting thesis of a brilliant student of ours, Svetlana Robertson, on the topic of

Jewish Red Army veterans living in Israel. In strange and surprising ways, small circles of life close. Altogether, one of the most rewarding and pleasant roles I have filled at the university was that of editor of the Eshkolot Library of the J.L. Magnes (Hebrew University) Press, a role I took on for five years. It seems to me that this is the only trace still left of the Chancellor and founding father of the Hebrew University and his legacy. I believe that I helped in the publication of several important books that otherwise might have not been published.

# 4

## ARIEL AND MICHAEL

Before I left for a sabbatical in Toronto, a well-known British publisher approached me with the proposal to write a book about Ariel Sharon's war crimes. I refused since I am not an expert on the laws of war and international treaties, but we ultimately agreed on a political and military biography of the man. During a period of several months, I read all the material I could obtain about this fascinating person. The actual writing of the book did not take more than one month. After I had consolidated the conception of the book in my mind, I wrote like a man possessed. I decided to almost completely avoid gossip about his personal life with the exception of a short description of his youth and the death of his oldest son. As a sociologist, I was more interested in showing his way of life, his actions, his faults, and his views as a personification of parts of Israeli culture of which he was, in my opinion, a product par excellence. I called the book *Politicide: Ariel Sharon's War against the Palestinians*.

The term *politicide* means a process of preventing one ethno-national entity from achieving an enduring self-determination through the denial of its legitimacy and the systematic annihilation of its leadership and its material, economic, political, and cultural infrastructures. This was and remains the central strategic goal of Ariel Sharon, who was educated to see the Jewish state in a zero-sum conflict with the Palestinian entity over the territory between the Mediterranean Sea and the Jordan River. The strategy remained the same even though the tactics used to achieve it changed according to international and internal Israeli circumstances.

I stressed the fact that although he was the founder of the Likud, Sharon did not belong to the Revisionist stream of the Israeli political-cultural map and certainly not to the national-religious one, which he despised to the depths of his soul. In order to understand this, one needs to read his autobiography, which was published in English and never translated into Hebrew—and for good reasons. Sharon was and remained part of the hawkish school of thought of the Labor Unity/Mapai alignment, as did his mentor, Moshe Dayan. Sharon, however, was endowed with an ability to make and implement decisions that was far superior to Dayan's, while possessing the same indecisive, tormented, and sorrowful persona. This was how I saw him following the "disengagement" and how I would have continued to see him if he had had the time to carry out further withdrawals from the West Bank.

On December 19, 2004, in an article in *Haaretz*, "A State in Formalin,"[1] I wrote that there is no doubt that the ability of Ariel Sharon, a distinguished and experienced politician of international stature, to maneuver and survive is astonishing, just as the wretchedness of his partner in the "Unity" government, Shimon Peres, is barely worthy of pity. To fully understand the process of disengagement, we must analyze a phenomenon that was itself completely unexpected: why and how significant sections of the mainstream, on both the left and the right, could support—or at least not vehemently oppose—Sharon's "disengagement plan." In comparison to the Oslo and "This is our Land" periods, the responses of the extreme right and the settlers were moderate at that stage even though, apparently, Sharon's rhetoric in favor of a Palestinian state and his intention to actually evacuate entire settlement areas appeared then to be even more far-reaching than the declared intentions and rhetoric of the leaders of the Oslo agreement.

Alongside the pragmatic right and the center, there existed two approaches that may have justified Sharon's moves as they were presented—in part openly and in part covertly—with a wink to the broad population that elected the Likud under Sharon's leadership. These populations understood quite some time ago that it is not possible in our generation to implement the idea of a Greater Israel that is free of Arabs. Thus a formula had to be developed whereby there would be Palestinians but they would remain under indirect Israeli rule, greatly reducing the cost of the occupation. Indeed, it is impossible to return to the late 1960s or to the merry 1970s, but perhaps it is possible to pacify and police the Palestinians through the services of sub-contractors along with payments in the form of some minor material assets together with some symbolic incentives. As a matter of fact (which must not be mentioned!), this is an improved and upgraded version of the Oslo agreements and represents an attempt to impose them within the context of The Road Map as "the end of the conflict."

Four and a half years of systematic destruction of the infrastructure of the Palestinian society, the physical and political elimination of its leadership, and the persistent harassment of the entire population up to the point of starving large portions of it were intended to prove the true relative power of the sides on the ground and, in effect, to convert the Palestinians into a pliable mass and to lead them to a kind of "Treaty of Versailles," in the context of which they will agree to any Israeli "peace formula."

The Palestinian use of suicide bombers as a means of warfare, which initially appeared to the Palestinian side as an appropriate and equalizing response in light of Israel's absolute military superiority, boomeranged on them since it turned their desperate struggle for independence into an alleged part of international terrorism and granted Israel both internal and external legitimacy for the use of unrestrained force against them.

Sharon's model for an agreement was revealed in his speech at the Interdisciplinary Center in Herzliya (November 5, 2004): within the framework of the Road Map, Israel would evacuate areas densely populated by Arabs but would retain control (and perhaps the intention was also to retain sovereignty) of both the large settlement blocks and sizeable zones of territory bordering them. Since this state of affairs would have divided the Palestinian areas into three enclaves in addition to the Gaza Strip, Sharon promised that they would retain a kind of territorial continuity and be able to drive from Jenin to Nablus to Hebron without having to encounter Israeli checkpoints or Israelis in general via an integrated system of tunnels and elevated highways. All of this was on the condition (reasonable in itself) that they stop the armed activities against Israel and dismantle the various militias. This map actually turns the existing situation on its head: until now, the Jews made efforts to move separately in tunnels, but from now on, the Israelis would continue to rule over large territorial areas and the Palestinians would be forced to move under or over ground. The issues of the refugees and Jerusalem were not considered at all in Sharon's plan because they were meant to remain outside the agenda. However, since the framework of that agreement was supposed to be based on the Road Map, we are indeed talking about the establishment of a Palestinian state with temporary borders and within those territorial parameters and, at the same time, about the continuation of an Israeli presence in all access routes to it through land, air, and sea.

The other version of Sharon's plan—or maybe a palliative for the right— was presented by the Prime Minister's adviser, Dov Weisglass (*Haaretz*, October 5, 2002). According to this view, the disengagement from Gaza was no longer the first step in the plan but rather the last one, and it was meant to be used as a sop for the Palestinians, the Israelis, and the international community, especially the United States. This move was meant to freeze the political process for a very long time ("It will be put in formalin," as Weisglass so mischievously and colorfully put it). It's possible that the two versions complemented each other. Sharon would try the formalin and if that was not accepted and didn't stabilize the situation at least for the rest of his term in office, he would begin implementing the second part of his vision.

In contrast, beyond the natural personal motives of Labor party members, even those in the left-center camp of the political map, there is a certain logic in the fact that a right-wing leader who is identified with the idea of a Greater Israel and who was a central driving force in the process of colonization of the occupied territories would be able to evacuate settlements more easily than a government that is identified with the Labor party and which is detested by broad sections of the population. Evacuation of the settlements would also create a precedent which would refute the concept of irreversibility. From another perspective, the established left rejoiced deeply in its heart of hearts at the brutal blows that the Sharon-Mofaz–Ya'alon government inflicted on the Palestinians because, from their point of view, it was the government—and not the left—that carried out the dirty job of "softening" them and, presumably, reducing their expectations to almost zero. It is only natural then that the Labor Party supported Sharon's version of the Likud because, with the exception of a few eccentrics in it (the majority of which either left the party or were pushed to its margins), the Labor Party's basic views are not and have never been different from those of Sharon, since the latter, as was mentioned earlier, sprang from the fields of Mapai and Ahdut HaAvoda.[2] During this process, other points of view and any possibility of political opposition disappeared from the country, having been thrown into the wonderful equalizing chemical which is formalin.

*    *    *

My difficulties with leaders and with trust in the political system, however, began many years prior, somewhere around the age of seven.

I think that we remained in Hateg as refugees for at least a month, but I don't have clear memories of anything from that period. The Red Army progressed too slowly towards our town and we still did not know what had happened to my grandfather and grandmother. In the meantime, unbelievable rumors began to arrive in Hateg about something terrible that had happened to the Jews "there" and if so to my family as well. No such news was passed on to me as a child but only after a few years and even then in a very general way. "Mother, why does grandma cry at night?" I would ask. "Her heart is aching," was my mother's accurate but extremely incomplete response.

After a while, we returned, this time by train, to Turda. My grandmother and grandfather were not hurt but our house was totally destroyed and nothing much was left of the store since anything that had not been destroyed had been looted. There was a lot of damage in the city as the Germans had fortified it in an attempt to turn it into their own "Stalingrad" and stop the advance of the Red Army there. The Russians responded indiscriminately with heavy artillery and katyushas. They forced the Germans to retreat but many of the city's residents were either killed or wounded.

Nevertheless, an enormous optimism and motivation to rebuild prevailed in the city—or at least this was the atmosphere in my family. What I remember most from this period is my whole family glued to the radio and listening to the program for people seeking lost relatives. They hoped to hear from those who had been taken to the extermination camps. By that time, my parents already knew something about what happened. Little by little, but mostly after the return of my young relatives from Auschwitz, the scale of the family tragedy—but not yet the size of the general catastrophe—became clear. However, there was no time and perhaps also no will to deal with it. Most efforts were directed toward personal and collective rehabilitation out of the belief that, following the destruction of Nazism, the world could only get better from then on. Only my grandmother's quiet sobbing which penetrated thick walls (and that she brought with her to Israel too) marked the fact that something cosmically terrible and irreversible had happened in the world.

The war continued even after our return to Turda, actually until May 1945, and Romanian soldiers continued to fight under their flag, but this time commanded by the Red Army. Political, economic, and social instability continued after the war ended and the Romanian government remained unstable and rather violent too. Governments were replaced one after the other. The attempt at agrarian reform and the distribution of the land for peasant farming—in particular to families that lost their sons in the war against the Germans and the Hungarians—by expropriating land from those designated as traitors and collaborators (meaning, primarily, Hungarian and German farmers) was accompanied by serious violence motivated by feelings of national and ethnic revenge and hatred. In addition to the fact that 1945 was a year of heavy drought, Romania was justifiably forced to pay heavy reparations to the Soviet Union with wheat and, primarily, oil. A special oil pipeline was laid between the oil region of Ploiesti and the Soviet Union. Inflation increased dramatically and the black market flourished. On August 15, 1947, the currency was changed from the "Lei" to the "New Lei." However, only the exchange of a minimal amount was permitted—a move which washed all the savings in Romanian currency down the drain overnight and brought about the impoverishment of broad sections of the middle classes.

During this time, we rented a large apartment in the center of the city. It was actually half of a large house belonging to a widow who lived in the other half. The owner had an adopted daughter—a foundling, half daughter and half servant—a child of farmers who reminded me of Cinderella. Maria had big eyes, a round face, and two long braids which fell over her well-developed breasts. Her image appears by accident in one of the family photographs in which she is peeking out from among the geraniums, and thus she is engraved even more deeply in my memory. I immediately fell in love with Maria, who I believe was two years older than me, but she didn't share my feelings or pay attention to me and I suffered unrequited love for the first time. As it is said, first love is never forgotten. My grandmother, who corresponded with our former landlady from Israel also, told me years later that Maria became a sprinter who represented Romania in the Olympics but was killed in a car accident almost immediately after reaching her athletic prime.

Aside from my love for Maria, the greatest excitement during this period was attending school and the surprises that this held in store. Oddly, I don't remember the children in the class or that I played or conversed with them. Apparently I was a solitary child and to the best of my memory, I remained in the classroom even during recess. The great surprises and discoveries in school were the charismatic teacher, Magda Frankel—who, coincidentally or not, was my great-aunt—and King Michael, that is, Mihai I. When I first entered the classroom, I immediately noticed two very large and colorful photographs hanging on the wall. The same pictures looked out at us from the first two chromo pages of all the school books we received. I quickly learned that the handsome young man (who at the time was in his twenties) dressed in a uniform decorated with medals and who had a look of authority, was my king—King Mihai I. The beautiful woman with the gentle, caring look was the Queen Mother Helena. At home, I was never told that I had a king. Indeed, I sometimes heard the name Mihai mentioned but I didn't know who or what he was.

Almost every morning our studies began, like a morning prayer, with praises of King Mihai, the father of the nation, an heroic soldier who saved our homeland from our mortal enemies, who were not mentioned by name but who I understood to be Nazi Germany, and brought us to the shores of security, freedom, and prosperity. He was even decorated with medals by both Stalin and President Roosevelt in recognition of his leadership in bringing Romania into the Allied camp.

I did not exactly understand what the teacher meant but in light of what had recently happened to us and the continued uncertainly around me, I drew my own personal conclusions from what she said about the king. I concluded that because of Michael, we had been rescued from the oppressors and it was he who would protect me and my family from all evil forever more. This idea was reinforced by the teacher, who said that the king protects all of us personally, just as a father does. Having experienced such upheavals and fears so recently and having seen my parents so powerless, I found a bulwark in my king. Years later, when I read *War and Peace*, I found a description of the feelings of one of the heroes there—Pierre, I believe—who describes seeing the Czar come to encourage his soldiers before they go off to a decisive battle against Napoleon's army. I felt the same way about Michael. And later on, when I studied sociology, I found out that charisma is not necessarily the trait of a leader but rather reflects the need of his followers to depend on him and again I was reminded of King Michael.

One wintry morning in 1947 when I was already in second grade, I arrived at school and immediately realized that something had happened. At first I didn't understand what, but after entering the classroom, I noticed that the photographs of the king and Queen Mother Helena were missing from the wall. Soon afterwards, the teacher strode vigorously into the classroom and ordered "Children, take out all of your books from your bags and place all of them on your desks." There was a strange silence in the room. The teacher passed from one desk to the other, opened each book methodically, and with careful determination ripped out the pictures of the king and the queen mother. In hindsight, this ceremony appears to me to have been grotesque and absurd. After the teacher finished personally removing the pictures I had considered sacred from all the books, she crushed them into one roll, threw them in the garbage, and returned to her podium. The silence prevailing in the classroom seemed to indicate that my shock was shared by all the children. "Children," the teacher began in a celebratory tone, "yesterday something wonderful happened to our country. We transformed ourselves from a monarchy to a people's republic and we exiled the king. From now on, nobody will rule over the people but rather, the people will rule over itself. The king took advantage of the people and milked it dry. He was lazy and a tyrant and gave us nothing, just sucked our blood like a leech and tried to sell our land to foreigners. The House of Hohenzollern is not a Romanian dynasty at all and the former queen mother barely spoke our language. She was, in fact, Greek—but this is all over now. From now on, we are a free people in our land." Years later, when I studied the Prophet Samuel's speech to the people who asked him to anoint a king over them, I remembered the speech of my first teacher, Magda.

My world fell in ruins about me. They took my king away from me. In addition, I didn't understand how my teacher, who had praised and exalted King Michael, could change her taste and faith overnight. My confidence in her and the world around me shattered and collapsed. But since another school book remained at home with the pictures of King Michael and Queen Helena, I hid it carefully and from time to time took it out from its hiding place and looked longingly at the photograph of the exiled king. And like a desperate monarchist, I would pray in my heart that the wheel would come back around and the king would again return just as he had disappeared. In the classroom, however, other pictures were hung—of the General Secretary of the Party, Gheorghe Gheorghiu-Dej, the Foreign Minister, Anna Pauker, and most importantly, the Light of the People, Joseph Vissarionovich Stalin. Our teacher told us a lot about them and their greatness too, but I no longer believed her and from then on no longer believed in any picture or image.

Another important event occurred in our lives during the same period. On January 10, 1947, my brother Adam (named, as already mentioned, in memory of my Aunt Eva) was born. However, Adam's arrival did not really change anything in my life and I will talk more about this fact later on. Adam was a quiet, unproblematic baby who developed "by the book." In those days, when the reason for my disability was not yet understood, it was an act of courage—and also an unusual one—for parents who already had a child with cerebral palsy to bring another child into the world because of the fear that the first child's impairment might be genetic in nature. Perhaps because of Adam's "normalcy" and the family's agreement that "Roby is so bright," most of my parents' attention continued to be focused on me even after Adam's birth, or at least that was how I felt. However, Adam's excellence and his outstanding talents were revealed to my parents later on.

Because of the age difference, I didn't play much with Adam and actually, until his death, we didn't have the warm and intimate relationship one would expect between brothers despite the love and concern we always had for one another. We grew up and developed together, but on completely separate tracks that almost never met.

Here I must add two clarifications about my name. At my birth, for family reasons unknown to me, I received the somewhat aristocratic name André Robert Baruch Tzvi Kimerling but my family had always called me "Roby" (Robert). When I arrived in Israel, I had two options: "Tzvi" (with all of its modern derivations); and "Baruch." I rejected "Tzvi" because it seemed ridiculous to call a clumsy young man after a light-footed animal.[3] I refused to Hebraize my family name despite the heavy pressure placed on me in high school: I felt that "Diaspora" names were part of the Zionist story. My father and grandfather wrote "Kimerling" according to the Romanian style, with one "m," which was the version my brother Adam retained. When I began publishing in international journals, and in order to preserve the correct pronunciation,

I added another "m," as it must have been originally. This is how it happened that we two brothers carried, at least in foreign languages, two different surnames. This subject was never discussed or clarified and each of us did what he thought correct.

*    *    *

At the beginning of 1948, the Communist regime began to stabilize and my father, as the possessor of "underground privileges," was given a good job as the manager of a nationalized steel factory in Cluj, the capital of Transylvania. I have no idea how my family had the necessary funds, but we bought a large house with many rooms in a quiet neighborhood of the city. There were many fruit trees in the garden—plums, apples, pears, and cherries—whose smell, taste and color remain engraved on my memory, even today, as part of the tastes and smells of childhood. In front of my window grew a young apple tree whose flowers turned into the most succulent and tastiest apples I ever ate, or at least this is how I remember them. A year later, the tree suddenly began to wither and all the experts my grandmother brought in were unable to find the cause of the problem. A short while later, the tree collapsed as if it had been split in two and from its hollow trunk emerged a gigantic, ugly worm that had gnawed at it from within. We mourned this tree as if it were a person we had been close to and for the first time in my life, I experienced loss. In Israel, when I learned the verse "because a man is like a tree in the field," I knew what the poet meant.

Furthermore, I also began to study seriously. Since my parents were afraid to send me, a disabled child, to a big school in a city full of strangers, they registered me as an external student in a school where I went several times a year to take examinations. But in order to make sure I learned the material properly, my parents hired Professor Almashan. Almashan was not a professor, but in Romania every high school teacher held the title "professor." Mr. Almashan was a retired teacher and among the best I ever had in my life. First, he related to me as an adult on all matters, but above all his attitude toward the material we studied was fascinating and he restored the lost honor of the teaching profession that had been taken from me by my first teacher, Magda.

We quickly reached a kind of gentleman's agreement—which I never disclosed, not even to my parents—according to which my studies would be divided into three parts. In the first part, I would learn everything written in the books "and these and only these will you use when you take exams at school, young Mr. Kimerling." The second part was: "… And now, after you know whatever is written in the books thoroughly and by heart, I will tell you what you really need to know and how things really happened, and these you will treasure in your heart because one day these will be more useful to you than what is written in the books." The third part of the agreement was what I would call "enrichment studies." Mr. Almashan told me about Greek mythology, comparing it to Roman mythology, and about Greek and French philosophers and he did not hide his hostility towards Marxism. I don't know how much I really understood of what Professor Almashan said, and I'm not sure even that his "truth" was much more true than the one presented in those books, but the very existence of different truths set well with my prior bitter experience. I also learned how to read texts critically and to understand the subtext. Almashan (I will never know his first name) was a true liberal intellectual and in contradiction to his declaration that he would reveal the truth to me, from time to time he would state "...but don't believe me either. When you grow up, you'll examine this by yourself. Perhaps I'm mistaken ... maybe I am misleading you intentionally or inadvertently...." When I speak of my "Romanian-ness," Professor Almashan constitutes the cultural and intellectual heart of it.

"You must be proud of your heritage"—this is how my first book on Romanian history opened. "You are the son of a great nation which grew from the union of two glorious people. The Dacians were a peaceful people of shepherds and the Romans were a nation of war heroes who ruled over the entire world." At points like this, Almashan would stop my reading and comment thus: "I doubt I can be proud of this glorious heritage the way it's described in this book. The Romans conquered and annihilated the Dacians, who were a primitive but rebellious tribe, and it's questionable whether any remnant of them is still left. But you, Robert, can definitely be proud of the heritage of your people, the Jews. They rebelled against the Romans a number of times and although they were exiled from their land, they survived in every situation. And now you are returning to Palestine and defeating all of the Arabs."

This was the first time that anybody had spoken to me about Arabs in the context of Palestine. I believe this was at the beginning of 1949. My parents were glued to the radio at nights, as they had been during the fascist period, and would listen mainly to the BBC and the Voice of America. Exclamations of "We're winning" (joyfully, but whispering) and "they're winning" (anxiously) were, for some time, part of the conversation at home. I more or less guessed who "we" was, but I had no idea about the mysterious "they." By the way, I very much loved books about the heroism of the crusader knights who fought the Muslims (for example, Sir Walter Scott's *The Talisman*), but at that stage there was no allusion to any connection between the Muslims and Palestine, even though the name Jerusalem was mentioned frequently in books. Sometime earlier, contact had been renewed between my family and my Aunt Yoly from "Palestine," whose banishment by my grandfather was revoked after the war, to the joy of the whole family. My aunt sent me a number of school books in Hebrew in which we could see young boys and girls with sublime happiness radiating from their faces as they plowed, seeded, and harvested. This suddenly reminded me of something. Some kind of association began to form in my mind that led me to ask my mother "What? There are Russian communities in Palestine too?" For some reason, my question stimulated great laughter and admiration and became part of our family folklore. It was then that I heard about the kibbutz for the first time. My aunt also sent a number of records with

Hebrew songs, among which the easiest to remember included "A Wagon with a Horse" and "Bab el-Waad."

My mother introduced me to a practical Zionism and taught me Hebrew words and sentences and a bit of reading and writing. Mr. Almashan bestowed on me Zionist ideology and theory. "You too, young Mr. Kimerling, will reach Palestine and with your head, you'll be famous throughout the world." The man had a great reservoir of knowledge about Jewish history and he was the first to talk to me about immigration to "the land of the Jews." This subject was controversial in our home and therefore not spoken about there, at least not in the presence of "the boy." What's more, we were still in the process of becoming established, and it seems to me that, besides my mother, nobody else thought that we would arrive in Palestine within a short time.

Mr. Almashan's sayings about Jews and Palestine also contained hidden and threatening meanings. It was during this period that one night someone sprayed the outer wall of our house with the three-word inscription "Jews to Palestine." The writing on the wall (in its double meaning) plunged our house into turmoil, for reasons I did not understand. My father called the militia and two men in civilian dress arrived along with the militiamen. One of them even entertained himself by making jokes with me. "They are from Security," my father whispered to my mother, using a term which I frequently heard later on. "This is the act of Hungarian fascists," one of them decided. "We'll take care of them. You have nothing to worry about." But my parents and my grandfather were very worried indeed. Within two days, bars were put on the windows and a tall, blue iron door was installed. "They" also promised that we would receive a telephone ("just to be safe"), a promise which was never kept. I don't think that when Mr. Almashan talked about sending all the Jews to Palestine, he actually meant the same thing as those who had painted the graffiti. The fact is that even when we no longer had the means with which to pay his salary, Mr. Almashan continued to give me private lessons and it seems that the affection between us was mutual.

\*   \*   \*

"The Romanians are thieves and of a lower culture; the Romanians are the Moroccans of the Ashkenazi Jews, etc." All of these expressions accompanied me from the time I arrived in Israel and haunted me even during my days at the university. My colleague and closest friend, Dan Horowitz, who supported me as I advanced professionally and who valued my work perhaps more than most of my colleagues, would console himself and me by saying that I was, as a matter of fact, more Hungarian than Romanian. During my stay in Toronto, one of my publishers composed a short biography of me. A friend who read the piece sent me an email from Israel, perhaps in jest, perhaps in all seriousness: "They wrote that you are Romanian. File a defamation suit immediately."

This situation placed me in a difficult dilemma: I am not only categorized as disabled, but I am also "Romanian." The dilemma was that I could just as accurately have defined myself "Hungarian" or at least "Transylvanian" ("Where is Transylvania? Isn't it in Romania?"). In the Polish-Russian-Lithuanian culture dominant in Israel to this day, being Romanian became a fatal label, similar to "chakh-chakh" or "Morocco-knife," and therefore I can easily understand Mizrachi[4] Jews, particularly those from North Africa. But the Romanians in Israel not only failed to "invent" a counter-culture, as a portion of the Jews of Eastern origin did, but they did not push themselves into politics either—neither as a group nor as individuals; rather, they preferred to fade into the background just as they had essentially done in Romania as Jews. It was in fact the ethnic pluralism of Romania that protected them, to a great extent, from pogroms and persecutions.

Since I had the chance to choose my ethnic identity in Israeli society—which is stratified more by ethnicity than by class—I felt compelled to think about the politics of my personal identity when I started high school. Thus over time, I came to the decision to remain "Romanian" in Israel whenever I was required to claim an ethnic identity. I decided to do so in spite of the fact that I never missed Romania, never considered making a trip there to "find my roots," and even avoided speaking Romanian every time that such a rare opportunity arose.

I have no "roots" there and if there were any, I chopped them off. The only roots I have, for better or for worse, are the Hebrew culture and language. At the same time, I cannot completely forget the land where I was born and spent the first twelve years of my life. In any case I was, after all, an immigrant and remained an immigrant throughout my life. Therefore, if the choice was between being "Hungarian" and being "Romanian," I chose—not without hesitation—the second identity, because the Romanians and the Bulgarians were the only people of Eastern Europe who did not, relatively speaking, enthusiastically support the mass annihilation of the Jews. Without a doubt, part of Romania's leadership, even the fascist one, stood out in their favorable attitude toward the Jews, in contrast to the complete cooperation given to the Nazis by both the elite and the ordinary people of Hungary.

This is not to say that the Jews of Romania were not persecuted or murdered and sometimes even killed in pogroms (for example, between June 28 and 30, 1941, more than 3,000 Jews were killed in Lasi by the Iron Guard). Beginning in May 1941, the "Romanization" laws prohibited Jews from working as doctors and lawyers, owning stores and businesses, selling liquor, and owning motorized vehicles and radios. Jewish children were forbidden to attend school beyond the age of thirteen and the food rationing law stated that Jews could receive only what remained after food was distributed to the Romanians. Some of these laws were copied almost verbatim from the racist Nuremberg laws. But it must be noted that these laws were almost never enforced with excessive strictness or zeal. The Romanian ruler (or "the Counselor," as he liked to be called) at the time, General Ion Antonescu, was a fascist and a Romanian nationalist more in the style of Mussolini than of Hitler. He hated Communists, Russians, and Hungarians more than he hated Jews, as did King Carol II (who had reservations regarding cooperation with Germany and the Nazis and who, like most of the Romanian elite, was an admirer of both French culture, before France surrendered to Germany, and English culture).

The worst crimes against humanity and against the Jews committed by the Romanians actually occurred outside the borders of Romania when, in the summer of 1941, the Romanian army cooperated with the Wehrmacht and "liberated" the lands which were called "Transnistria" but were actually part of the Ukraine. These had been promised to Romania by the Germans as compensation for their participation in the invasion of the Soviet Union and for the transfer of part of Transylvania to Hungary. In Transnistria (today Moldavia) itself, Jews were placed in concentration camps along with Jews from Serbia and North Bucovina (areas with a mixture of Russians and ethnic Romanians) and anyone who was, or was suspected of being, a Communist.

It is important to remember that part of these regions were taken from "Greater Romania" a short time earlier and annexed to the Soviet Union following a Soviet ultimatum—an annexation that had originally been supported by the Germans themselves. Prior to the invasion, 300,000 Jews lived in these regions and about 180,000 of them, including most of the Jews of Odessa, were slaughtered by the Einsaztgruppen (who were recruited mainly from among ethnic Germans in the area and in Romania), the Jandarmeria and the regular German and Romanian forces. And if this was not enough, Ion Antonescu also initiated the expulsion of about 150,000 Jews from Romania proper to concentration camps in Transnistria. Approximately 90,000 of them were annihilated.

However, continuous internal pressure by liberal circles, including the Royal House and the Patriarchate, led to the cessation of the expulsions in October 1942, a fact that in effect saved the lives of most Romanian Jews, including us. Along with the fascist Iron Guard, Romania also had anti-fascist forces that were very active—and not only within the Communist party. The publicist Gregorio Gafencu led an intellectual-democratic faction sympathetic to the Liberal Party, and demanded that Romania strive to emulate the British political system that served as an example and model for him. Thus for instance, in March 1939, with the conquest of Czechoslovakia, the stormy anti-German and anti-Nazi protests held throughout Romania were also directed against Hungary and Admiral Horthy, who took advantage of the opportunity to annex parts of Czechoslovakia. On September 17, 1939 (a month before I was born), independent Poland surrendered to the Germans and the Soviets and most of the Polish leadership, together with 200,000 refugees, found shelter, at least temporarily, in Romania, including Turda.

The political fate of free Romania, however, had already been decreed a short time earlier. On August 23, 1939, the Ribbentrop-Molotov Pact was signed. The secret appendices to this agreement included the division of "influence" between the new partners. The clauses concerning Romania specified the return of a district of Serbia to Russia, from whom it had been taken following accords made at the end of World War I with the establishment of "Greater Romania."

On September 21, with German support, members of the Iron Guard legion shot to death liberal leaders, captured radio stations, and tried to bring about a fascist revolution. The king's response was immediate. The conspirators were arrested and put to death the same day and many members of the legion were rounded up and sent to prison camps. However, following efforts to reach "a general national reconciliation," when the requests of the Soviets to annex regions in Serbia and Bucovina became clear, the members of the legion were released and returned to the streets and to the political arena. Berlin coerced Romania to accept Russia's demands and even forced it to sign a "trade agreement" to provide oil and wheat to Germany without any clear compensation. Romanian statesmen such as Iuliu Maniu hoped that in this way they would at least earn Hitler's support against Hungarian territorial claims over Transylvania but even here, they were mistaken. In reality, they had no choice: Romania was geo-politically strangulated between Germany, Russia, and Hungary.

On July 4, 1940, a fascist government was established in Romania under the leadership of Ion Gigurtu and included the head of the Iron Guard, Horia Sima. All parties except the Nationalist Party were made illegal and emergency legislation prohibited strikes and included the first laws against Jews. All of this, however, did not guarantee Nazi Germany's support and at the end of August, Romania was forced to give up about half of the Transylvanian region (which included some 150,000 Jews) to Hungary. The surrender agreement caused a wave of anti-German and anti-Hungarian sentiment and brought about mass protests in most Romanian cities. The army that was sent to disperse the protestors refused to obey and soldiers and officers even joined them . An additional coup attempt by members of the legion of the Iron Guard also failed and on September 6, King Carol II, who gave them cautious support this time, was forced to give up his throne to his son Mihai (Michael) I and leave the country immediately with his partner, Mrs. Lupescu. Before his resignation, however, Carol appointed the Commander in Chief, General Ion Antonescu, as Prime Minister and in this way the process that transformed Romania into a fascist country in every respect was, allegedly, completed. This transformation included a military and economic alliance between Romania and the Third Reich and the stationing of German army bases in Romania.

In January 1941, the independent militias of the Iron Guard took over the prisons and massacred intellectuals and politicians who opposed the regime and had previously been imprisoned by Antonescu. They then captured the gendarmerie station in the capital, Bucharest. However, when they also tried to take over the army bases, Antonescu's patience wore out and on January 22, he ordered the army to exterminate the fascist militias, an order that the army carried out enthusiastically and efficiently. Within twenty-four hours, the Iron Guard legion was wiped out in Romania and its leaders, including Horia Sima, fled to Germany. Antonescu tried to form a new government, composed of the leaders of established parties (the Liberal and Farmers parties), but they refused to participate in it.

On June 23, 1941, one day after the Germans began their invasion of the Soviet Union, Romania also declared war on it. The Romanian army participated in the invasion and, together with the Wehrmacht, reached Stalingrad. It should be noted, however, that the Romanian public was divided in its feelings and opinions regarding both the war and the alliance with Nazi Germany. Objections regarding the logic of the war could be heard even within the army, although it was acknowledged that Romania had to regain control over the territories it had lost a short time earlier to the Soviet Union. Thus, for example, at the end of April 1944, fifty-five of the most prominent intellectuals and professors in the state requested that Antonescu stop the war immediately and cut off all contacts with Nazi Germany, an appeal that echoed throughout the educated community. In fact, since 1941, an anti-fascist underground, which primarily tried to sabotage strategic positions, was active in Romania. More than 300 of its members were executed and thousands more imprisoned.

But the real change in public opinion and among the political elite of Romania began with the crushing defeat and enormous losses that the Romanians suffered in the battle for Stalingrad between July 1942 and February 1943. When Field Marshall Von Paulus surrendered on December 9, this was also the end of the Second and Third Romanian Armies, which included 300,000 soldiers, most of whom did not survive. From that time on, King Mihai and his court searched for a way to extricate Romania from the German stranglehold and to join the Allies, perhaps also because they understood that the war would end with the collapse of Germany and the fascist order. However, what delayed them was principally the worry about the possible replacement of the Nazi conquest with a Soviet one. Helena, the queen mother from the Greek royal family, tried to persuade the Allies to land in the Balkans (that is, in Romania) before the Soviets arrived. Numerous secret contacts took place, but the attempt failed and in the meantime, the Red Army overran the country's borders.

Around May, 1944, a pact was made between the king and some of the commanders of the army, and a plan took shape inside the palace which was intended to remove Romania from the war and change its regime. On August 23, 1944, the plan was carried out: Marshall Ion Antonescu and his government were invited to the palace and placed under arrest by the king's guard. At 10:00 p.m., in a dramatic speech on the radio, the king turned to his nation and the world and announced the change of government and the declaration of war by Romania against the Third Reich. The German army present in Bucharest tried to recapture the capital and additional Romanian cities using massive air raids by German planes located in Romanian air fields. The following day, the U.S. Air Force destroyed the German bombers on the ground and after several days of heavy fighting throughout Romania, the German army surrendered, even though its remnants continued to fight heavily as they retreated, causing massive and deliberate destruction.

# Notes

1. The title was wrongly translated as "The Formaldehyde Vision" in the English edition of the "Haaretz" Newspaper. Formaldehyde is a gas and it is not a preservative: its aqueous solution, formalin, which was mentioned in the original Hebrew article, is.
2. Ahdut HaAvoda (*Labor Unity*) was a socialist, Zionist party that was founded in 1919 by Ben Gurion and went through several transformations until, in 1968, it joined Mapai and Rafi to form the Israeli Labor Party
3. *Tzvi* is the Hebrew word for deer.
4. Mizrachi Jews are Jews of Eastern, non-European origin.

# 5

## THE *TRANSYLVANIA* WAS NOT THE *ROSLAN*[1]

It is very difficult to say that a twelve-year-old boy made *aliyah* or "ascended" to Israel. My parents did not ask my opinion, and even if they had, I would have gone along with their wishes, especially knowing how much they suffered until they received a Romanian exit visa. This was also a wonderful adventure for me. Sailing on a ship. Perhaps meeting pirates. Who knows? It sounded to me like an interesting opportunity that was not to be missed. In retrospect, being uprooted from Romania added one more dimension to my identity that I have never been able to escape—that of a refugee and an immigrant. Not long ago, a conversation similar to the following took place between Dalia Karpel and me.

She asked: You grew up here, you were educated, studied, and raised a family and you taught and wrote books and read literature and research and perhaps poetry, all this while the state was being built. How does your biography, in your eyes, fit in with the formation of the state, if at all?

I answered: First of all, not being born here, I experienced, along with my parents, all the difficult stages of Israelization, from the transit-camp tent in Gan Yavne until… until some "here" (a "here" that I cannot exactly define) and there still remains in my identity some of the consciousness of an immigrant, perhaps even that of a refugee. Therefore, what many people cannot see is so obvious for me, namely that we are a state of immigrants and not a people indigenous to this land. A state of immigrant-settlers. Like North and South America, Australia and New Zealand, South Africa, and Algeria. This is my starting point in every discussion on Israeli society and it appears in many of the articles and books I published and has caused more than a little indignation.

I was asked in addition: How does this change the perspective?

I answered: This changes everything. Because internally, we are more heterogeneous than all the other "old nations" and hence there is a potential promise of multi-culturalism that we have not yet realized and which perhaps we never will. Instead, we crowd together under an umbrella of whatever "Jewishness" we invented and improved here. This is a mixture of secularism and religiosity—which we call "Judaism"—that includes nationalism and permanent existential anxiety accompanied by the worship of the Holocaust and a pathological ethnocentrism. This is the latest reincarnation of what is called Zionism and anyone who does not accept this syncretic identity is defined as "post" or "anti" Zionist. Outwardly, we are meant to live by the sword as if it were a self-fulfilling prophecy because we settled in a region whose residents did not want us and we did not have the power to "take care of them" in the way that other immigrant societies "took care of" indigenous peoples. We did so partially in 1948 without really solving the problem; perhaps we made it worse. This also changes the position of the Palestinians on the political, ethical, and cognitive map, at least for me. When we speak of rights of immigration, for example, we can't forget that we are the immigrants here, not them.

It must be added, at this point, that the fact that Israel is a non-native society of immigrants is a big impediment for it, especially in light of the presence of the Palestinians who consider themselves to be indigenous. On the one hand, we ignore the Palestinians in an attempt to make them conceptually, and even physically, disappear while we create a native Jewishness, like the "sabra," even for those that were not born in this country. However, the principal attempt to overcome this "immigrant-ness" is through creating a story about "the return after 2,000 years in exile" and emphasizing Zion and the longing for it as an important part of the Jewish religion, even though Zionism was originally a secular ethno-national movement. The idea of a return created a kind of imaginary historical "indigenousness" and granted rights and ownership over the land. An interesting method of denying the existence of the other, original, people is the claim in the style of Israel Zangwill that a land without a people waits for a people without a land. The central assumption nurtured by this statement is that the land was empty of Arabs or that most of them came into it at the same time as the Jews did in order to find work among them.

The journalist Joan Peters' detailed and supposedly well-documented book *From Time Immemorial*, which became a best seller in the United States and was translated into Hebrew, contributed to the successful attempt to disseminate this idea. Even Yehoshua Porat, an expert on the Middle East who is not known as a great sympathizer of the Palestinian cause, deconstructed the book into its parts and demonstrated that it was based on false data. This, of course, did nothing to convince many Jews of the unreliability of Peters' assertions. By the way, as a means of countering these Jewish arguments, a strange race for "primordiality" developed also among the Palestinians, a race which was supported by their claim, no less unfounded, that they are the descendants of the Philistines in particular and the Canaanites in general who inhabited the land before it was conquered by the tribes led by Joshua, son of Nun.

But the Palestinian culture developed a more concrete "return" which frightens Jews the most—"the right of return" for refugees of the 1948 and 1967 wars to their homes and fields, which long ago ceased to exist the way they were before 1948. And it is difficult to persuade them that history is not a time tunnel in which one can travel back to a country frozen in time, as in the story of Sleeping Beauty.

In any case, the Palestinian claim to the right of return is much more valid in light of generations (resulting in millions) of Palestinians living in refugee camps, with refugee status, here and now, than the Jewish return after two thousand years in the Diaspora. The Palestinian claim for the right of return is viewed by Jews as resulting from the desire to destroy the Jewish state, and it causes deep anxiety among the Jews living in the country, some of whom are even aware that their homes are built on villages or other populated regions which once belonged to Arabs. This fear, alongside the Palestinian claim for which it is hard to envision a compromise, constitutes one of the most important factors affecting the ability to find, at this stage, a solution to the Palestinian-Jewish conflict, which will be discussed later in the book.

Despite my self-image as an immigrant and a refugee, it's not that I do not feel that I belong here—just the opposite. The Hebrew culture and language are my only homeland. I grew up on the Nahal band, like everyone else. Even Naomi Shemer's songs (well, not all of them) play in my head. In poetry, I prefer the pagan and sensual Tchernichovsky over Bialik—except for the "The Diligent One." Leah Goldberg, Nathan Zach and Dalia Rabikowitz, Hanoch Levin (oh, *Queen of the Bathtub*), Yehoshua Sobol, Josef Mundy and even "HaGashash HaHiver" are more significant for me than Shakespeare. I named my eldest daughter Shira' after S.Y. Agnon,[2] who is an outstanding Jewish writer but not really Israeli, and even Uri Zvi Greenberg and Shimoni are a part of me. One of my favorite books was *A Castle in Spain* by Benjamin Tammuz. In my opinion, Amos Oz writes parochial fluff, but A.B. Yehoshua, Sami Michael, and Emile Habibi wrote works of universal value. I generally, but not always, identify with David Grossman's political writings. I never read Yona Wallach and Pinhas Sadeh and I have no intention of doing so. Don't ask why. I don't know. Because. When I was young, I loved Moshe Shamir, Medad Schiff, and Hasamba (and one more work of Mosenson's, *A Man's Way*) like everyone else but I was weaned long ago. I make an effort to read Yitzhak Laor, but I admit that I don't always understand the pattern of his associations.

I started to read Ephraim Kishon in the newspaper *Uj Kelet* while still in Transylvania and I have to say that I appreciate his ironic humor and his sharp insight into the different phenomena of Israeli society. His perspective was that of an outsider who desires to be integrated into the society he immigrated to; in consequence, he avoided real criticism in his writings. But in my opinion, his humor was preferable to the rough native Israeli one in the style of "Yalkut HaKazavim" by Dan Ben Amotz and Haim Guri. It's no wonder that Kishon—despite accomplishments in various fields and his winning of the Israel Prize—felt that he was not really appreciated in Israel. The images of Salach Shabati and Officer Azulai, however, were written almost entirely from a Hungarian perspective. The crazy Blumliech who turns Tel Aviv into "Venice" due to bureaucratic stupidity, and Arbinke, who is nobody's fool, dealt with the most sensitive issues in Israeli society using a gentle humor which softened his criticism.

I loved Jerusalem very much before it was unified. I would wander around the alleyways of the ancient neighborhoods with my friend Bella, absorbing the voices and the smells when everyone else was still asleep, before they got up and hurried to synagogue to worship the Creator. Those were the years before the 1967 war, a Jerusalem of reason, "in whose heart there was a wall"[3] while in our hearts there was pride and humanity. Since the city has become unified, I have withdrawn mainly to the campuses, longing for the bygone days when the crazy legionnaire was on duty.[4] Acre is wonderful too, and the Kinneret shore, especially when the lake is full. What else will you ask of me, homeland?

Meanwhile, the atmosphere in Romania had become more and more stifling and the evil winds began to blow there again. In March 1948, the liberal Foreign Minister Jan Masaryk was murdered in Czechoslovakia. Like his father Thomas, he symbolized the spirit of freedom and the Czech democratic tradition. I heard his name mentioned numerous times at home. This mysterious murder, which was presented as a suicide, opened the way to communist control in the country. A short time later, even more drastic steps were taken against central members of the Communist Party in Czechoslovakia, most of them Jews, who later were tried after being accused of treason and espionage on behalf of the imperialists and Israel. Already at the end of 1950, Ana Pauker, considered the iron lady of the party, a Communist who had been imprisoned for years and who allegedly benefited from Moscow's unreserved support, was dismissed from the Central Committee of the Party and from her appointment as Foreign Minister. It was hard to avoid the impression that her dismissal stemmed only from the fact that she was of Jewish origin. And there were also the "Prague Trials" and purges, in which most of the accused were Jews. Jews were also among those purged in local branches of the Communist Party. In contrast, members of the fascist military organization, the Iron Guard, had no difficulties changing from brown to red, and many of them became enthusiastic Communists when the party opened its gates for them during the process of Romanizing local Communism. The stench of anti-Semitism began to spread. It was no wonder then that tens of thousands of Romanian Jews began to leave the country and immigrate to Israel, not only after it was founded and had won the 1948 war, but even during World War II. Thus in February, 1942, the *Struma*, while trying to get to Palestine with 768 Romanian Jews on board, was sunk—apparently by a Soviet submarine—and only one refugee from it was saved. By the way, that small boat, which left the port of Constanza at the end of 1941, was chartered by members of the Beitar movement in Romania known as "Ha'apalah" (which means "overshadowing"). But the British discovered it immediately and the ship was forced to wander between different, mainly Turkish, ports which also refused to harbor the refugees.

As I said, the only Zionist in my family was my mother; I believe that my grandfather changed his mind about Zionism and the Jewish state after its successful establishment but he would still have preferred to immigrate to California. My father continued to believe in the future of communism and refused to hear about immigrating, although he never missed an opportunity to listen to the propaganda broadcasts of the BBC and Voice of America.

One incident, however, in the fall of 1950, changed my father's mind at once. One day, he was called into the branch office of the Party and given a task. He was required to go to the Sunday service at some Baptist church and to report on the minister's preaching, on the "atmosphere," and on whatever people said to each other. He was given a hint as broad as an elephant: "You yourself are allowed to be critical of the regime."

From my father's later recollections, it became clear that his world fell apart at that very meeting. He was convinced that the order was a loyalty test and that they were going to follow him to the church, but he also knew that he had not joined the party to be used as an "agent provocateur." On the designated morning, he dressed in his best clothing and went to the church. There, he stopped a man at random who was about to enter the church and asked him how to get to a certain place. After receiving a short explanation, he even asked him his name and departed from him with a handshake as if they were old friends. The next day, he reported to the party that he met a casual friend at the entrance and since this person knew he was Jewish, he couldn't enter the church. A short investigation could have revealed the deception and my father knew that he was entering a path that endangered him and his family. Within two weeks, the family submitted an official request to the Ministry of Interior Affairs to leave the country and to immigrate to Israel. That very week, my father's membership in the party was cancelled and he was fired from his job.

Since my father's job had been the only source of income for the family and because the war, the change in currency, and the acquisition of the house had eliminated all of our savings, we soon had to survive on bread alone. My grandmother, a proud lady, began to sell whatever household possessions it was possible to sell, including anything she had managed to salvage from the ruins of the war—carpets, silver, porcelain, crystal, and gold jewelry—at the flea market. At first, she tried not to bump into people she knew because she was so ashamed and my mother, father, and grandfather let her handle the situation by herself. But later on, she no longer cared if acquaintances and neighbors witnessed her destitution.

The situation got worse. Immediately after my family submitted the request for an exit visa, the state stopped providing permits and my family was sure that this was another anti-Jewish persecution by the regime. Only in recent years did I learn that it was actually Israel that delayed Jewish immigration from Romania. The country's economic situation was bad and there was international pressure to accept the return of the Palestinian refugees. Israel, therefore, decided to give preference to Jewish immigration from Iraq, which could be presented as an "exchange of populations" and also as an exchange of property. My friend and colleague, Yehouda Shenhav, even claims that the Jews from Iraq were promised equal compensation for their property there from those that were "abandoned" by the Palestinians who were either uprooted from the country in 1948 or became internal refugees. This promise, of course, was never kept.

Meanwhile, our situation grew even worse. Because of some law, we were not permitted to sell the house, but after a few months a "buyer" was found who paid about a quarter of its value. An unofficial agreement was made, according to which we vacated half of the house and the buyer came to live in it. My grandfather and grandmother moved to a small apartment nearby and we committed ourselves to moving out of the entire house within a year. Some years later, my parents received a notarized request to sign a declaration stating that the house had indeed been legally sold to the new owners and that they were entitled to register it in the estate books under their name. Without any hesitation, my father and mother signed, just as they had promised.

During the period we lived in Cluj, I continued to be a rather solitary boy. I formed a loose friendship with a Hungarian boy my age named Lachi, who was our neighbor. We made a concealed hole in the wooden fence, and, to our parents' dismay, crossed it into each other's territory. He told me that when he grew up he was going to be a dentist.

"Why a dentist?" I asked. "Because," he would say, without explaining. One day, he could not restrain himself anymore and he took me down to the basement of their house. He wanted to show me a secret if I promised not to tell. In the basement there was a fully equipped dental clinic. "You see," he said to me while carefully taking off the cover from the dentist chair, which was the first one I had ever seen, "I have everything ready for my clinic." When I told my mother the secret, she told me that it was known that before the war, the house had belonged to a Jewish dentist.

I didn't play with Lachi for about a month; however, after a while, our relationship resumed. He gave me a pair of domesticated pigeons and then another pair and helped me to build a pigeon coop. By the way, whoever designated the dove as the symbol of peace never saw a dove. Or perhaps he did. These are extremely aggressive birds, capable of pecking each other to death. Lachi also gave me a small puppy, to my mother's dismay since she was afraid of rabies. For the first time in my life, I entered into a bitter conflict with my mother. I cried, I screamed, I went wild until she apparently acquiesced. But one morning I woke up and the puppy was nowhere to be found. My mother denied all involvement in the puppy's disappearance but I didn't believe her and didn't forgive her for many years, although I never mentioned my anger and disappointment. Now, when three dogs wander around my house—each adopted from the street in turn by a different one of my children—I have mixed feelings about them. On the one hand, the noise, their hairs, and the terrible smells they emit drive me nuts. On the other hand, they provide me and my wife with a feeling of security and it's good to see their devotion to us. There is no doubt that they are part of the family. When we flew to Canada on a sabbatical, they flew with us and I don't think there is anyone who is as crazy about dogs as my wife is.

Aside from Lachi, the regulars in our home included Zoli (Zultan Frankel) who was a student at the University of Cluj and also the youngest brother of my first teacher, Magda. He taught me how to play chess, a game I played with anyone I could talk into it. I tried to teach my mother and father to play but to my disappointment, they did not have the patience. The only one who made any effort and even learned to play the game was my grandfather. Later, when I arrived in Ramat Gan, I tried to join a local chess club, but it soon became evident to me that I had nowhere near the kind of minimal level of ability required because I didn't even know about the existence of the widespread professional literature on the game and I hadn't learned or analyzed the games of the great masters. I have not touched a chess board since.

My father and mother had a couple of friends from before the war, the Markowitzes, who had a son a little older than I was, Utzu (Yitzhak). From time to time, they would send the youngster and his friend, Gershi, to play with me, but I always had the feeling that they did so because they had been forced into it. Years later, they both studied natural sciences at the Hebrew University and became faculty members at Ben Gurion University.

That was all the company I had in Cluj, but my really close friends were all the books that I devoured eagerly. I also loved listening to radio plays, to which I became addicted in Cluj and continued to be an enthusiastic listener in Israel, where, as I have already written, I realized my dream by becoming a writer of them.

On weekends, my father would carry me on a small seat that was mounted on the front of his bicycle and in the summer and fall we would go hiking. My father and I didn't speak much but I loved the heat of his body as he held me close to his chest while riding the bicycle. We would reach the bed of a clear stream, always at the same place I believe, spread out a blanket and eat what we could not eat at home—slices of pork with fruits and vegetables. My father tried to teach me to swim, something I have never been able to learn in my entire life, but I loved the clean sand and the small pebbles in the stream. We were usually alone there and it seems to me that those were my father's only moments of happiness. He was very relaxed and sang—perhaps to me, perhaps to himself but only when we were alone—sad songs about broken hearts ("your eyes bewitched me, your lips are inebriating, and you have left me alone in my desolation…"). It's possible that he felt miserable in his marriage.

Finally, near the end of 1951 and after waiting almost a year, we received an exit visa from Romania. We were permitted to bring with us two crates that were not very big and for nearly a month the whole family was busy dealing with the question of what we should squeeze into the crates and what would be useful and valuable in Palestine. It later became evident that, apart from the down comforters and pillows, the sheets and some of the clothes, only the crates themselves were really useful in our new country. One night, we left in a carriage for the train station from which we were supposed to travel to the port of Constanza where the boat *Transylvania* waited to transport us to Haifa. Accompanying us, overwrought and with tears in their eyes, were my grandmother and grandfather, who still had not received an exit visa, my Uncle Imre, and Lilly and Pityu Hausman, whose daughter, as previously mentioned, was named Eva. The latter immigrated to the United States about a decade later and became established there quite rapidly.

This wasn't my first train trip. Apart from the return trip from Hateg to Turda two years before leaving Romania, my parents and I had traveled by train while searching for "great doctors" who might be able to find a cure and a remedy for my handicap, a quest they were unable to carry out during the war or immediately after it. We traveled to Bucharest and stayed with my paternal aunt, Gisela, and her husband Gustav, who was an amazingly warmhearted fellow and with whom we maintained contact even after he divorced my aunt. We heard different and strange kinds of diagnoses and suggestions for treatments, some of them rather brutal. One doctor, for example, assumed that an otological problem affected my center of balance. He sprayed powerful torrents of water into my ear until he caused minor but irreparable damage to my hearing. Another doctor, who later became very famous in Israel, mainly as a result of his daring operations which made many people miserable, apparently found the location of the damage in my brain but fortunately and correctly (even for modern science) admitted that the brain damage could not be repaired. Nevertheless, as I grew up, I learned to control my body more and more and my physical condition continued to improve until, at the beginning of 1984, it began to deteriorate.

When we arrived at the train station in Constanza, my father pointed out the Pullman cars with an extreme know-it-all attitude left over from his earlier work as a traveling salesman. The train was already full of Jews and its only goal was to transport them to the harbor. The train was "protected" (it's not clear to me from whom) by tens of militiamen armed with frightening submachine guns. The atmosphere on the train was subdued and perhaps even apprehensive. People barely spoke with one another and it was as if they couldn't believe that they really were on their way out of the country until they actually reached the shore. I don't know how long we traveled or how many stops we made along the way—I just remember that my parents woke me up in order to see the Danube passage—but at the end, the train stopped somewhere and we could see from the window only wire fences and armed militiamen. After a while, militia officers began to pass through the cars with lists in their hands, calling out names. Families and individuals began to leave. Slowly the cars emptied out until we were apparently the only ones left on the whole train. My father tried to go out and ask what was happening, but the armed militiaman would not let him leave the car. He asked him to call the officer in charge but the militiaman refused. I had seen my parents in situations of overwhelming distress and fear more than once before, but I had never seen such terror reflected in their eyes. My father told me after the incident that he was convinced that it was "the end," and who knew what crime he would be accused of. At last, an officer appeared and ordered us to board the ferry that took us to the dimly lit ship which, in the foggy night, looked like a sleeping giant. "Just some bureaucratic confusion," the officer told us, maybe apologizing or perhaps just explaining. They didn't find our names on the list from Bucharest and it took a lot of time to check that everything was in order.

But before I separated physically and emotionally from Romania, I was exposed to the kind of meeting that cannot be erased from the memory of an adolescent. After we were given the right to receive an exit permit from the country, Magda, my teacher and great aunt, suddenly appeared. This was a rare visit. Unlike her brother, she had remained in Turda and in addition to being a teacher, she was very busy with Party matters, agitation, and propaganda among the "masses." Magda was an ardent Communist and in retrospect, I understood that her support for King Michael originated from the fact that Stalin, the initiator of the anti-fascist revolution, had himself decorated and praised the king more than once. But when Michael fell from grace in Moscow and obviously also in the Communist party of Romania, it was perfectly natural for Magda to change her views, a fact that was unacceptable in my opinion. This, however, was not why Magda came. She came in order to try and save me. She asked to speak with me alone and started approximately like this: "Have you heard of Darwin and his theory?" I confirmed that Professor Almashan had discussed Darwin and his theory of evolution (which he found exciting) with me, as well as Lamarck and Michurin, (whom he ridiculed and derided but, loyal to my promise to Almashan, I did not mention this fact to Magda). "You know, my Roby, the place your parents are dragging you to is a capitalist country disguised as a socialist one. Capitalism, like Darwinism, is based on natural selection, in which only those who are the strongest in every aspect survive. And you are not among the strongest and, on top of everything, you don't know the language and there you are going to be a foreigner, an immigrant, and forever a weak person, whereas in our socialist country, which is marching toward communism, equal opportunity will be given to all. You must stay here. I'll raise you and I'll take care of all your needs…"

Even to a twelve-year-old boy, this was an astounding offer, both emotionally and practically. Magda was single and no longer young. Indeed, thinking back, it seems to me that she needed a child of her own to raise and thought that perhaps my parents would give me up with relative ease (and in fact, research shows that parents of disabled children, especially of those with unaesthetic deformities, tend to abandon their children too easily). Perhaps she sincerely thought that this was an action that had to be taken for my benefit. I do not suppose that she talked about it beforehand with my parents. Apparently, she thought she would convince me first.

But Magda, who may have been a rationalist and a devoted teacher, probably had no clue about the thoughts, feelings, and desires of children. I never even considered separating from my parents, either emotionally or physically. My parents were everything I had in my world and at the age of twelve, it never occurred to me that I was taking part in a Darwinian struggle for survival, even though it seems to me that I understood her intention very well. Furthermore, I had never been raised as an "invalid." To this day, I am proud of the answer I gave to Magda. I did not enter into an ideological argument with her, but I told her that as a boy of my age, I didn't have the authority to make decisions about my destiny even if she was correct about my chances of survival. Therefore, I would go with my parents and when old enough to stand on my own, I would consider where I wanted to live. Magda argued that by then it might be too late and that my fate could already have been decided (and she was almost correct) but that in any case, I should know that she would always be there to help me. Poor Magda, who despite her talents and loyalty to the Party, remained stuck in a marginal job until she retired. Many years later, when I was with my family in Seattle, Magda asked her brother Zoli, with whom I remained in sporadic contact by mail, to write to tell me that I had been correct. However, I did not feel any joy.

Micha Zachs was probably right. In the eighth grade of the primary school "Matmid" in Ramat Gan, where I was the only new immigrant—*ole's*[5]— from Europe in the class, he said to me, with the candor that characterized him: "You will never be one of us. You are not like us. You are so similar to the people from the Diaspora. Polite. Gentle. In short, not a Sabra (native Israeli). Aside from this, your disability will always come between you and us." Micha was a little more developed for his age and in my eyes he was the embodiment of the "Sabra" species: he was, like most of the boys in my class, intelligent but not educated. Studies were never his top priority and apparently he didn't need them since he belonged to a very affluent family. Micha was a good sportsman in spite of having a large body. He was very self-confident and very authoritative. Along with this, he had a great heart and was happy to help his friends. Therefore, he gave me an older brother's protection (Micha's older brother was killed when an El Al passenger plane crashed over Bulgaria)—even though he knew that I was older than him by several years—and made sure none of the children harassed me. Ours was a brotherhood of opposites and apparently Micha valued my erudition. For several children, and certainly from the perspective of the school, which was located in an area where well established residents lived, I myself became a national project for the absorption of new immigrants and the living proof of their willingness to accept those who are different.

Micha's assertion that I would never be "one of the guys" did not stem from malice or from an intention to harm. For him, this was a statement of fact and perhaps even an indication of praise. Looking back, his words did hit me, an immigrant child, in the most sensitive spots. At that time, my dream was to be "like them" and perhaps even more, to be "like everyone else." In my eyes then, not being a Sabra was a social handicap more burdensome than my physical disability. My ultimate desire was to be accepted into their company and to talk, behave, and feel like them. And indeed my whole world fell in on me because in my opinion no one was as much of an authority on this matter as Micha. But in spite of this, I decided to fight my bitter fate and to prove to Micha and everyone else that I could indeed be—at least a bit—part of the magnificent race of "Sabras."

Yael Zisman sat next to me in the eleventh grade at the Ohel Shem Secondary School in Ramat Gan. Yael was a tomboyish girl with short hair and freckles and she was the best athlete in the class. During boring lessons, I would write her limericks and Yael would burst out in restrained laughter and her whole body would quiver in the attempt not to arouse the anger of our dreadful teachers. I was in love up to the ears with Yael—and perhaps even more so with her being a "Sabra." Only the beautiful, blond Naama Kolton, who was also considered an outstanding student and the queen of the class for all four years at high school, was superior and more desirable in my eyes than Yael. Toward the end of the year, I revealed to Yael that I was a "new immigrant" while I braced myself for her verbal response and facial expression. "You?" she said, giving me an inquiring and unbelieving look, "I always thought of you as a "Sabra"." No one on earth was happier than me at that moment. Yael thought I was a "Sabra." She, who no less than Micha, and perhaps even more than him, symbolized in my eyes the "Sabra" species, did not sense my foreignness.

However, I did not have time to prove anything to Micha himself because he was killed on the sixth day of the 1967 war which, with the arrogance typical of our place, is called the "Six–Day War." In any case, a great many years passed before I understood and accepted the fact that not being a "Sabra" did not necessarily constitute a cultural or social handicap. At the same time, my identity as an immigrant and refugee slowly but surely grew stronger. The perception of myself as being located on the threshold of this society and experiencing it both from the inside and the outside became increasingly sharp. Perhaps not really from the outside because for most of my life I lived here, almost since the beginning of the state, with all of its ups and downs, even though I had never really been accepted into it but only into some place between the elitist-center and the margins where people are at times rejected and at times also attacked or hated.

*   *   *

The ship the *Transylvania* was not the *Roslan*. Unlike the seventh *aliyah*,[6] my parents' immigration was never counted among the heroic ones. They were the "human dust" about whom Ben-Gurion spoke. Late in the morning on January 10, 1952, the news spread through the terribly crowded *Transylvania*: land had been sighted. This was my brother Adam's fifth birthday. My father tried to protect me with his body so that I would not be trampled by the crowd that surged toward the stern of the ship like a wave. He lifted me onto his shoulders while my mother clutched my little brother to her chest. The shore drew closer and in a short time, we were able to see the green peak of Mount Carmel, the roofs of houses scattered about in no clear order, and a few high, smoking chimneys. There was a deathly silence on the crowded deck—a kind of awed reverence. Somebody started humming "HaTikvah" and everyone who knew the national anthem joined in. I felt my father's warm tears on my naked legs. I tried to sing what my mother had taught me and for the first time in my young life, I felt the intoxicating elation of being part of a mass. We then waited and waited for long hours, apparently until it was our turn to enter the port. My memories of disembarking from the ship are hazy but many years later, when the issue of the insult that was inflicted by DDT spraying was raised publicly, something dimly emerged from the depths of my memory. I asked my mother and she indeed confirmed that before we disembarked from the *Transylvania*, we were all sprayed with disinfectant. In Israel, there was a justifiable worry about epidemics.

The next clear memory I have is that of the transit camp in Atlit, called "the gate of *aliyah*" which was originally a British army base. Years later, I greatly loved hearing Chava Alberstein's song about the dreams of the gate of *aliyah*. This song contained a vestigial recognition of my parents' "*aliyah*" as part of the Zionist epic even though, by this time, the epic had begun to fade. The barracks we were sent to live in looked gigantic to a boy. Two rows of beds were arranged lengthwise and there was always a hustle and bustle, day and night. The pungent smell of Lysol that penetrated my lungs has never left me to this very day. We were lucky that the beds assigned to us were placed near the entrance to the barracks. This meant that everyone who entered or exited the barracks passed by us, but on the other hand we had no neighbors on one side since my mother's bed was placed in the corner together with mine, while my father's bordered us on the opposite side. Thus some semblance of privacy was retained. The small family was euphoric and my father's eternal optimism swayed my mother as well. As for me, if I can indeed reconstruct my feelings, I experienced the already familiar sense of insecurity we felt when wandering in order to escape the Germans.

We were placed under quarantine because of the worry about the spread of epidemics and diseases. I don't remember exactly how long we stayed in Atlit, but my parents did a good job of taking advantage of the chaos that prevailed there. When we arrived at the camp, my Aunt Yoli, Aunt Margit, her husband Shlomo (the "Pole"), and Uncle Leichi were already waiting for us on the other side of the high barbed wire fence. "Pass the children over. Pass the children over," yelled Margit to my parents in a strangely accented, non-fluent Hungarian. She was already an established resident in Palestine. In a spur of the moment decision, my father tossed my five-year-old brother over the fence and Uncle Shlomo caught him. "Pass Roby over too," yelled the aunt. "We'll take good care of them until you get settled. They'll have the best of everything. You don't have to worry." But my mother refused, whether out of consideration for the relatives who would have had to care for two children, one of whom disabled, or because of her inability to part from both her children at once. Adam stayed with the aunts and uncles for about four months.

I don't know what went through the mind of a five-year-old child whose entire world had obviously been suddenly disrupted as a result of being uprooted. My perception is that he felt abandoned by my parents and that he was never able to—and perhaps never wanted to—overcome this feeling of insult and misery. He had, after all, been born after the war, and the feelings of insecurity and upheaval that I experienced at his age were unknown to him. I had lived through that period in the arms of my parents while he suddenly found himself in a foreign and unknown world in which he was unable even to understand the language spoken by the people around him. We never talked about this because my brother was very reserved in his interactions with us and didn't like to talk about either himself or his feelings. After his death, his friends described him as warm, sensitive, and open to his surroundings—a person I barely knew.

Within a few days, my father "sneaked out" of Atlit and began wandering around in Jaffa. With a mixture of Romanian, broken Yiddish, a little Hungarian, and a few words in Hebrew, he began "making connections." To him, everything was rose-colored and full of promise. The sky was the limit. The people he met were, in his eyes, all wonderful and full of good will. After all, they were all Jews. The opportunities were endless, the country needed everything, and he was ready to provide it all, to build and to be built in it. He introduced himself as an electrician, as an electrical engineer, and as an expert in the molds used to manufacture metal parts for electrical products. I think that he really believed he was all that. With what remained of the money we received from the Jewish Agency and my aunts Margit and Yardena, my father bought various kinds of samples of electrical devices: switches, sockets, lightbulb sockets, fuses and other strange products. He would return to Atlit, hide his purchases under the mattress as if they were a precious treasure, and under the light of an oil lamp he would take them apart with a screwdriver, the first tool he acquired in the Promised Land. He would calculate the cost of the parts, compute how much the "market" could absorb, and how much profit he could make from each item. Mother would listen to his enthusiastic stories and calculations with a great deal of skepticism, but since, in any case, she didn't know how to respond, she let herself be swept away by his creative enthusiasm.

My mother's hopes were channeled into a different direction. Her goal was to be given an apartment as a reward for her Zionist activity before and after the war. My mother had been a member of the Gordonia movement since the age of fifteen. She collected money for the Jewish National Fund from a mostly hostile Jewish community, attended "activities" in the movement, and prepared herself for "training." After her younger sister, who was less active in the movement, left home to live in Palestine, my grandfather was furious and prohibited my mother from continuing her membership in the movement. My mother continued anyway, although less actively, even after she married my father about a year later and became pregnant almost immediately. After the war, she renewed her Zionist activities, almost clandestinely, when the Communists rose to power. Therefore my mother thought it was time to claim her rights as an activist in the movement.

And indeed as soon as the rumor reached her that Zionist activists from the Diaspora could obtain benefits in Israel, among which was a priority in receiving housing, my mother began her odyssey. Immediately after we left Atlit, she ran around from person to person and from office to office in order to prove her eligibility. Most of her expectations were focused on three people. Israel [Rudolf or Rezso] Kasztner had been her counselor in Gordonia. But Kasztner had his own problems at the time and even if he remembered my mother, what power did he have other than to write a polite letter confirming that Mrs. Chana Kimerling, nee Lazslo, was indeed an outstanding trainee in the movement? Yet it seemed to my mother that this letter would be the key to our new home in Israel.

Another person she requested help from was Erno Marton, another Zionist activist who had been like a comrade in the movement and, if I am not mistaken, also the editor of the daily Hungarian newspaper *Uj Kelet*. The third person was a mysterious man my parents knew—how I don't know—who had been active in the illegal *aliyah* from Transylvania. Rumors about him suggested that he was an agent in the Israeli secret service. For days or weeks, my parents tried to locate him in order to "be helped by his connections" but to no avail. Finally, however, our small family obtained a tent in the Gan Yavne transit camp after we left Atlit.

The winter of 1952 was one of the most difficult in Israel. The taxi driver who took us to Gan Yavne with our suitcases could barely find "our" tent within the sea of black, ugly, crowded canvas. Many years later, in entirely different times, I came across a photograph of the Deheishe refugee camp from exactly the same period and it looked precisely like "my" transit camp. I hastened to include the photo of Deheishe in the book on the history of the Palestinians that I wrote with my American friend and colleague Joel Migdal.

There was a powerful storm accompanied by flooding on the night we arrived at Gan Yavne. The tent collapsed and a powerful torrent of water rose and began to sweep us and our belongings away with it. My father leaped after me, took hold of me, and pulled me out of the stream. We finally found refuge in the tent of a neighboring Iraqi family already established there. The tent was equipped with a smoky kerosene heater that burned the eyes but provided enough heat to dry us off. The next day, my mother packed my clothes and my father took me to Aunt Yardena, who lived in Ramat Gan.

My Aunt Yardena had an exciting apartment. She lived in a basement room, but it had a big porch and a bathroom outside, which she shared with another family. My aunt was afraid of this family since she sublet the room from them. However, what was really magical at Yardena's was the fenced-in garden surrounding the apartment that was actually the remains of an orchard which had been swallowed up by the city of Ramat Gan as it expanded. In the garden next door, there was a nursery school and I was forbidden to disturb the toddlers and the two nursery school teachers. After the children were picked up to go home, however, the orchard was entirely at my disposal. I could climb the trees, trying to reach as high as I could, closer to the treetops, or sink once again into the fantasy that I was Superman. I wove stories in installments with myself at the center as the omnipotent child who fought fearlessly against the German invader in the Russian steppes, or returned to hike in the Carpathian forests. And when I climbed the wooden stairs from the basement, I found myself in the midst of a noisy and tumultuous street, almost at the center of the big city. A bus stop for Dan buses was adjacent and the buses were always completely full. It seems to me that the first combination of Hebrew words I learned in Israel was "Nobody else gets on," while the door squeaked shut on those who didn't manage to squeeze in.

Just down the road was the chocolate factory and farther away, a plant producing citrus juices and jams. When the wind blew in the right direction, wonderful smells of chocolate and bonbons reached me and sometimes my aunt, or the children next door, would bring me some. The children in the neighborhood discovered me quickly. The Stiassnie family lived next door. My aunt had a good relationship with them since the mother was of Czech origin and spoke some Hungarian. Their son, David, was two years younger than me, but apparently he was required to extend his protection over me, to teach me Hebrew, and to help me to be accepted into the group, roles which he fulfilled with the utmost seriousness. But I learned more from the neighborhood children, who revealed great curiosity about me, than I did from David. My characteristics as a refugee and as a disabled person blended together and generally caused no aggression or derision. During most of their games, however, I was usually a spectator on the sidelines, and they let me participate out of politeness only during games of marbles and "bandoras" and at times they even let me win worthless bandoras. Only David knew how to play chess a little, but after he realized that he would always lose, he showed no further interest in the game. However, I occasionally played checkers with him and a few of the other children. Here, the abilities were more evenly distributed.

At my aunt's house, I lived for the first time without my parents, although they would "drop by" from time to time to visit me. Most of the time, my aunt wasn't home either. Unlike my brother, I apparently did not feel abandoned; however, it must be remembered that I was six years older. I left the paradise of Ramat Gan to return two years later to almost the same area and the same children.

We managed to receive a completely new Swedish hut in the Nes Tziona transit camp. It rested on a cement surface but the two rooms lacked the partitions they were supposed to have. It had no running water, electricity, or bathrooms. The hut was furnished with four Jewish Agency beds and a small refrigerator my father got from I don't know where and which was our pride and joy. We also received four thin blankets made of excellent wool, a gift from Mrs. Eva Peron to the Jewish nation. This caused me to be impressed over the years by Mrs. Peron's kind heart and to wonder about the mysteries of her country, Argentina, whose marvels I had heard about years earlier from my grandfather. On a little stand inside the Swedish hut, there was a new kerosene burner for cooking, a gift from Aunt Yardena. Mother was never able to manage with this burner though, so that all of the pots were sooty and the hut always needed to be aired out every time mother tried to cook. More than once, the food had the aftertaste of a smoking wick. Our Iraqi neighbors looked with noticeable scorn at my mother's desperate attempts to operate the complicated instrument and even tried to show her how to do it, but to no avail. Instead of closets, we used the two crates in which we placed all the belongings we were permitted to take out of Romania. Instead of a toilet, we had an outhouse that stood about fifty meters from the hut. The filth and smell emanating from it prevented me from getting close to it without feeling sick and I used a chamber pot for my needs instead, which my father or mother would empty.

The hut, which stood on the periphery, was located in what was considered one of the transit camp's most prestigious neighborhoods. Further on, in the direction of the road that connected the orchards to the city of Nes Tziona itself, there stood a crowded tent city. This transit camp also had something called a school but after my mother visited it once, she returned depressed and resolved that "this is not a place for the child" and that it would be better if she herself taught me at home—that is, at the hut. My mother did not have an opportunity to teach me much, although my aunt sent "appropriate" books; nevertheless, I was able to acquire some command of basic Hebrew reading.

Our hut was located at the back of the camp, next to the foot of a hill. On the top of the hill, hidden amidst a grove of cypress trees, stood a large building. The house seemed to me to be a gloomy and mysterious palace. No one ever saw or heard any sign of life coming out of it such as people's voices or cars or wagons entering and leaving the side facing the camp. I understood from my parents that this was a sanitarium, "a crazy house." This just increased the mystery, anxiety, and fantasy. I would go on long hikes alone, between the fields and the orchards, all the way to Moshav Beit Oved, the closest settlement I could reach. In the transit camp, I was completely cut off from any company and from the world, and aside from the palace at the top of the hill and the people in the camp —all of whom apparently spoke Arabic, Persian, or Kurdish, none of which I understood—I was afraid of nothing. Only many years later did I learn that the area had been breached by Palestinian infiltrators and that some members of Beit Oved had been victims of a brutal murder during that same wonderful summer in 1952.

We traveled to Haifa for a visit and mainly to bring Adam home. I was shocked and I must have envied my brother. We found a warm family with two children younger than my brother, almost babies, named Naomi and Tzvika. Apparently, they too envied Adam since the aunt complained a lot about her children's wild behavior in comparison to Adam's exemplary conduct. They bestowed on my brother much love, warmth, and toys. They offered to adopt Adam as their son, perhaps seriously, perhaps in jest. These were the days of austerity, with serious shortages and food rationing, but in their home there was abundance such as I had never seen before. Apples from Italy, juicy vegetables like those I remembered only from Romania, and a variety of Swiss cheeses and cold cuts. Since our arrival in Israel, we had eaten nothing but bread spread with Blue Band margarine and marmalade. In my relatives' home, they put fresh butter on the table as if it were completely normal. They knew about the rationing of eggs, meat, and bread, as well as about "the war" on the black market only from the announcements made by the Allotment Minister, Dov Yosef. Adam didn't speak much but when he did, it was with a Hebrew that was almost that of a sabra, like the children of Ramat Gan. We returned with Adam to the hut. The trip from Haifa to Nes Tziona seemed much longer to me than the trip from Nes Tziona to Haifa. My father talked about business the whole way and my mother talked about housing.

# Notes

1   The *Roslan* was a ship carrying almost 700 Jewish immigrants to Palestine at the end of 1919. These immigrants increased the Jewish population at the time by 1%. That voyage marked the beginning of the third *aliyah*, during which large numbers of young pioneers immigrated and contributed greatly to the building of the country.

2   S.Y. Agnon wrote a book entitled *Shira'*, which is the Hebrew word for "poetry."

3.   These are words from the song "Jerusalem the Golden."

4.   When the city was divided between East Jerusalem, which was under Jordanian control, and West Jerusalem, which was under Israeli control, Jordanian soldiers occasionally fired from the eastern parts of the city into the western ones.

5.   An *ole'* is a person who immigrated to Israel under the Law of Return.

6.   Immigration to Israel by Jews is called "*aliyah*" and means "ascent." Periods of widespread immigration to Israel are often numbered. For example, the first *aliyah* occurred between 1882 and 1903. The seventh *aliyah* occurred between 1946 and 1948. The seventh *aliyah* included many people who later became prominent members of Israeli society.

# 6

## THE LIBRARY

My father's business began to take off. He discovered a kibbutz somewhere in the north which had established a firm called Neeman that manufactured plates, cups, and other household items from ceramic. My father was able to persuade the factory manager, who was among the senior founders of both the kibbutz and the factory, to add electrical products to their lines. Like a certified economist, my father warned him that the market in plates was limited and not profitable enough. The industry required a good deal of raw materials as well as investments in new lines, product finishes, marketing and storage: that is, a substantial capital was needed for a slow, and low, rate of return. My father suggested that rather than putting all of its eggs in one basket, the factory should instead diversify its product line. I remember him repeatedly practicing what he would say to the manager of the factory. With his somewhat clumsy appearance and his awkward and strange Hebrew, my father succeeded—amazingly, in my opinion—to gain the trust of people and that was perhaps a vestige of the abilities he had acquired during his original occupation as a traveling salesman. At times when I think of him, he reminds me of a character out of one of Arthur Miller's plays. When my father suggested that the kibbutz factory should begin to produce electrical devices, he was able to convince the manager that these products would be much more profitable than plates and cups, that the investment would be gradual, and that large sums of capital would not be required. My father proposed that this established kibbutz enter into a partnership with him. The kibbutz would supply the ceramic components of the electrical equipment and my father would supply the metal parts. My father assumed the responsibility for assembly and marketing and he and the kibbutz agreed that they would divide the profits afterwards. Apparently, I must have inherited my father's wild imagination.

As a start, my father suggested that the kibbutz manufacture just two products, "plugs" and light bulb sockets. Today, almost every apartment and house has a device which immediately cuts off the electricity if there is an electrical short circuit, thus preventing electrocution and fire. In the 1950s and 1960s, such a device did not exist. Instead, a plug, which is still known today as a "fuse" (which was said to "jump"), was installed. This was an element made of ceramic with a very thin conducting wire inside, the thickness of which depended on the intensity of the current that was expected to flow through the electrical device. Metal caps were located at the two ends of the plug. A thin, sensitive wire made of a silver-like material stretched between the two caps. When an electrical short circuit occurred, the wire burned, thus stopping the electrical flow through the device and preventing electrocution. A skilled person could replace the wire in the ceramic element by himself, but generally even experienced electricians preferred to throw away the fuse and use a new one. I have described the fuse and its function in detail since my family members and I assembled thousands of them in different sizes and amps and, in addition, because this was the main product that my father introduced into the Israeli economy, eliminating the need to import them and enabling our family to establish itself in Israel quite  quickly. It was, if you may, my father's primary contribution, not only to his family but also to the building of the nation, a contribution he was proud of until the end of his relatively short life.

The people of the kibbutz listened with interest to my father's offer but at the same time they found it difficult to accept the idea of a partnership with someone from the "private sector." Their counter-offer was to accept my father, together with the family, into the kibbutz (for a trial period only, of course), so that he could develop his ideas within the kibbutz framework. My Zionist mother, with her Gordonia background, loved the idea but my father did not. This was one of the few times my father won an argument with my mother. "Did I lose my mind?" argued my father, the former Communist, with great logic. "I'll bring the kibbutz a lot of money that will be divided among its members and what will we be left with? A place at the table in the dining room? And you'll have to work shifts doing laundry and washing dishes for other people? No thanks." He touched one of my mother's sensitive spots because she was an individualist by nature. It was finally agreed that the kibbutz would manufacture a certain number of ceramic elements for the fuses and my father would pay for them within a set period of time. More than once I wondered what would have happened to my family—my father, my mother and myself— if my father had accepted the offer to join the kibbutz, which in those days was rather tempting. I have no doubt that I would be a different person with different experiences and perhaps with a different view of life.

At about the same time, my mother succeeded in her efforts. As a Zionist activist, she was given priority in receiving housing in the Dora neighborhood near Netanya. It seemed as if all our dreams were coming true. The two-story, cube-shaped house contained four apartments. Our apartment had a sort of entrance, a kitchenette, two small rooms, a toilet and shower, and a tiny porch which could be accessed through one of the rooms. Behind the house there was a large yard which my mother and grandfather—who had come to Israel in the meantime, along with my grandmother—transformed into a vegetable garden with trees and even a chicken coop. It was almost like a small farm. My grandfather was about seventy years old but healthy and strong in body and soul. The hard red sandy soil did not frighten him. He put up a fence, removed the rocks, and plowed this quarter-dunam of land. He arranged garden beds, one after the other, and sowed different types of vegetables, tomatoes and sweet potatoes. He forced me into hard labor whenever he came from Ramat Gan, where he lived with my grandmother in the home of the daughter from whom he had previously been estranged. They arrived about nine months after us and were accommodated by Yardena in her small room.My grandfather didn't know what to do with himself. He was too "old," didn't know the local language, and was thus unable to acclimate professionally. So he spent his time reading Hungarian novels that my aunt found in a run-down library in the neighborhood. In contrast, my grandmother adapted well and quickly. With the little German she spoke, she began working as a maid and a cook in two homes, three times a week at each. One belonged to the widow of the poet Yitzhak Lamdan. The second belonged to the family of a civil servant who worked at the British Embassy, the Vincents. My grandmother and Mrs. Lamdan developed the usual relationship between housekeeper and employer, one of cold correctness. My grandmother and the British woman, on the other hand, developed a close friendship. For years after she returned to Britain following her husband's death, and even after my grandmother died, Mrs. Vincent kept in contact with the family. She sent us parcels of mostly worn-out clothing as she continued to think of Israel in terms of the past austerity and because her own pension must have been very modest. My grandmother's economic contribution to the household was not much less than that of my aunt, who was an established resident of the country.

Within a short time, Yardena's dream was realized too. From the time she left the kibbutz, Yardena had been saving up, one coin after another, in order to buy her own apartment and when the state was established, she even signed up for the housing lottery for long-term residents. In 1953, she won the lottery and bought an apartment with two rooms and a living room in Giv'atayim. Her parents joined her and all three of them lived there until they died. My grandfather Adolf died in his bed at the age of ninety-five, lucid and mentally sharp. My grandmother, Esther, could not endure his loss and died shortly thereafter. Cancer killed Yardena five years later. The cause was bureaucratic negligence on the part of the health insurance organization which resulted in a delayed diagnosis, a series of operations, and much suffering. She died old, single, embittered, and at odds with the world after having spent more than two decades taking devoted care of the parents who had severed contact with her when she ran away to Palestine. My mother used to say that Aunt Yardena lost her trust in men following a stormy relationship she had, while still living at the kibbutz, with a man who later became well-known in Israeli politics and in the security establishment. It was a story of love, passion, and infidelity such as those found in cheap novels, except that this one happened in real life. Later on, I studied in high school with this man's daughter until she dropped out of class. Years later, Yardena's apartment provided a portion of the money which helped me acquire my own home in one of Jerusalem's suburbs.

In 1954, however, everything was completely different. Our family moved from the Swedish log cabin to the housing complex and everything progressed smoothly. My father turned the apartment into a small-scale factory. Deliveries of ceramic and metal parts arrived. My father, when he was not running around, my mother, and even little Adam and I began to assemble the "merchandise," and soon we were able to distinguish between a five amp fuse and one of ten or twenty-five amps. My father even paid an hourly fee to the Barda family, who lived next door to us, for the services of their adolescent children, who helped with that task.

During this period, the Mesilot School opened in Dora. As one might guess, it was not a pedagogical marvel. I don't believe that any of its graduates ever attended an academic high school. The head teacher there was Mr. Eliyahu, who taught basic arithmetic in sixth grade, which was the highest grade, but his primary task was to keep law and order by means of the corporal punishment he inflicted on the pupils. Mr. Eliyahu was actually a pleasant man with a good sense of humor as long as he was not irritated. Originally, he had been trained in Batzra as a paramedic but since there were no opportunities in this field, he retrained professionally to be a teacher.

The Mesilot School did, however, have one great advantage. Somebody, I do not know whom, had donated a wonderful library to the school with about two hundred books for children and young people. The library was housed in a large, new Swedish hut and equipped with real shelves. Since I was the literate child of the school, the library and its key were deposited in my hands. Not many bothered me to borrow books, but for me this was a great treasure. I entered the library, closed the door, and spent as much time there as my mother allowed. It was there that I found my old friends like *Emil and the Detectives*, the stories of the brothers Grimm, Baron Munchausen, *The Heart, Pippi* (Bilby in Hebrew) *Longstocking, The Adventures of Tom Sawyer, Nils Holgersson and the Wild Geese, Aba Gurio, The Count of Monte Cristo, Don Quixote*, and even *Les Misérables*. I also discovered that the book that I had known as *The Children of Paul Street* had been translated into Hebrew and been given the creative name *Double Camp*. Most of the books were outdated translations by the publishers Omanut and Shtibel, but in any case they were in Hebrew and I knew most of them by heart in Hungarian, Romanian or both. It was there that I also discovered Nachum Gutman, Uriel Ofek, Anda Amir-Pinkerfeld, volumes of the newspaper *Davar for Children* and even the beginning of the Hasamba books. However, I missed other books very much, like *Dashanke the Dog, The Young Guard*, and especially *The Amputee Pilot* (in the Soviet version by Boris Polevoy), along with his motto "nothing stands in the way of the will" on which I was raised. Today I know there are plenty of things that stand in the way of all the determination you might have. But the one crucial thing the library at the Mesilot School gave me, besides the pleasure of reading, was that when I had finished reading nearly all of the books for the second time, I knew Hebrew almost perfectly, even though I mixed up "stockings" and "socks" and made other similar errors. To this day, however, I still make a few spelling errors and reverse the genders—male and female—in a strange way when my writing flows rapidly.

My father's business was successful and we were soon able to buy a new apartment. It was not large but was comfortable by the standards of the time.

The apartment was in Ramat Gan, in exactly the same neighborhood in which my Aunt Yardena had lived before. This was a leap, not only into the heart of Israeliness, but also into the tiny but older and more established bourgeoisie of Israel. My mother hurried to register me at the Matmid School in the neighborhood and went to speak with the teacher of the class in which I was supposed to study. The teacher had serious reservations about admitting me into the class: a new immigrant, and particularly a disabled one, would not fit into the class; the children were cruel and would abuse him; it would be better to find him an appropriate institution. My mother begged and finally the teacher, Ofra Ofir, agreed to admit me into her class for a two-month trial period. My mother disclosed to me all this only many years later.

My integration in the class was, however, quick and easy, so much so that not only did I become an outstanding student, but I had in addition been man-euvered into the uncomfortable position of being the teachers' pet. Both the teacher, Ofra, and the principal, Mr. Brand—as he continued to be called even though he changed his family name to "Or-Raban"—showed an excessive fondness for me until I finally decided to take action. In one of the science classes, when none of the other students had prepared their homework, Mr. Brand went from bench to bench and yelled at everyone. In order to demonstrate that I was like all the other children in the class, I declared in front of everyone that I too had not prepared the homework. Brand did not yell at me, as I had hoped he would, but asked that I go to the principal's office after the lessons, a very threatening request since a child was summoned to the principal only in the most serious cases. I wondered what serious punishment awaited me and anxiety took hold of me until the end of the day when I reported to the principal.

To my surprise, Brand let me into his office, asked me to sit down, and sat next to me rather than on the other side of the desk. "Is it true that you did not do your homework?" Brand both asked and stated in a soft voice. I was forced to admit that indeed I had prepared the experiment as we had been asked to. "You wanted to win the approval of those irresponsible and empty-headed children?" he challenged. Afterward, he delivered a speech in favor of individualism and personal achievement—Ayn Rand style—and about the disgrace of collectivism. "What you will achieve in life will be achieved only by yourself and for yourself; none of them will help you get ahead. Don't try to win the approval of your friends and don't ever be part of the crowd. Remember that you are better than all the rest and you owe nothing to anyone but yourself…" This speech remains engraved in my memory almost word for word, even though I didn't agree at the time with part of what he said and I don't agree with it today either. Being ambitious and elitist does not necessarily mean being egoistic and anti-social.

However, my finest hour at the Matmid School was during a mock public trial which a teacher decided the class should hold for Joseph ben Matityahu (Flavius Josephus). The trial would last for two hours and at its conclusion, the class would serve as jury and rule on whether Flavius Josephus betrayed his people or not. Ron Bar Sever (later known as Ben-Yishai) was happy to take on the role of prosecutor. With no other volunteers (who would want to defend a traitor to his people when his verdict had already been decided in the school books?), I assumed the role of devil's advocate. At that time, there was a personal hostility between Ron and me and I have the impression that it has not dissipated to this day. Both of us were vying for the attention of a wonderfully cute girl, Yehudit Ben-Shmuel. This fact turned the merely "legal" confrontation between us into a much more serious matter. I walked home, accompanied most of the way as usual by my friend Eitan Gorni. Eitan advised me to give up the role of defense attorney as well as the competition for Yehudit's heart since, he argued logically, I had no chance in either case. Roni was indeed wild and hasty, but he was also charismatic, very articulate, and very popular. But the harder Eitan tried to bring me down from the limb I had climbed out on, the more determined I became to face the challenge.

Instead of two hours, the "trial" continued for two days and drew the attention of all the teachers, who came to listen to it during the recesses. The rest of the students in the class were also fascinated. My idea was to transform the trial of Joseph ben Matityahu into a trial of the hopeless and irresponsible rebellion that brought about the destruction of the Temple. As my star witness, I called Rabbi Yochanan ben Zakai, thanks to whom Judaism was preserved, while due to Joseph ben Matityahu himself, historical documentation of that period still exists. My claim was that although an act may appear as a betrayal at the time in which it takes place, it sometimes has a different meaning when considered later on from a broader historical perspective. I challenged the prosecutor, asking whether he would also be ready to try Rabbi Yochanan and his scholars, who betrayed and left the besieged city too. Perhaps, I asked rhetorically, those who should be tried are the fanatics Rabbi Akiva and Bar Kokhba. Roni was not prepared for this counter-attack and stuck to his routine claim that a traitor is a traitor. Consequently, a large majority of the class found Flavius Josephus not guilty. I did indeed win the trial but not Yehudit's heart.

About twenty-five years later, when I was living on French Hill, Yehoshafat Harkabi would give me a "lift" home and during those short trips would tell me secrets from the "pit" about wars, armistice negotiations, the "Night of the Ducks," Ben-Gurion, and Moshe Dayan, whom he fiercely hated. I also told him all sorts of stories. Once I told him about the "trial" and I saw how his eyes lit up. Sometime later, I found the idea at the heart of one of the books he wrote following his change from predatory hawk to predatory dove. I feel no resentment toward Phati. Perhaps he inadvertently made a more important use of the idea, a use I was not capable of at the time.

Since I was about two years older than the other children in the class, Mr. Brand tried to move me ahead to high school at the end of seventh grade (at the time, junior high school did not exist). He introduced me to the principal of the "Ohel Shem" High School, Mr. Artzi, but the latter did not agree. And thus I lost another year of school.

"Ohel Shem" high school was supposed to be a prestigious institution and despite the impression given by its name, it was not a religious school. But it was perhaps the only revisionist high school in the country that was not a military school. I am almost sure that we were the only school in Israel during that period in which Uri Zvi Greenberg[1] was taught alongside Alterman,[2] who (what could be done?) was required. In addition, along with Moshe Shamir,[3] they taught Jabotinsky's "Shimshon" and they loved Brenner, who was filled with hatred for the Gentiles (and the Arabs), together with all the rest of the Jewish classics, Agnon included. And this wasn't just a coincidence. The student body in my class alone included Uzi Landau, Yossi Achimeir, the twin grandchildren of Avraham Krinitzy and the daughter of a well-known Zionist leader at the time. The Rivlins studied in higher grades.[4] Aside from them, most of the students in my class came from families that were already solidly established during the pre-state period, and they even considered themselves an elite, albeit a scorned and persecuted one.

The teachers too were an extremely varied collection of people, very erudite but quite eccentric. Perhaps the most influential figure in the school at that time was Mr. Yochanan Sephardi who, as far as I know, was of Lithuanian origin and who was both the English teacher and the person in charge of discipline. Sephardi was consumed with hatred for David Ben-Gurion (whose original surname was Green) and the whole Bolshevik gang of Mapai that controlled the Jewish community (the *yishuv*)[5] and the state. He even wrote a book, the only copy of which I later found in the National Library, under the pen name Y.S. Phardi. The book's main character was Ben-Gurion and it dealt with the leadership of the *yishuv*. It was in the style of the better-known work by Y.H. Yavin (*Jerusalem Waits*, if I recall correctly) in which the leadership of the Jewish community is described as profit- and power-seeking lecherous impostors. In class too, he never missed an opportunity to propagandize against the government. (In time, I came to accept some of his criticisms.) Suddenly I found myself opposing him and defending Ben- Gurion and Shertok. It seems to me that he too was happy that there was a young person in the class who challenged him and allowed him to expand the scope of the argument which, at least towards me, was conducted in a very polite way. Obviously, we didn't learn much English under these circumstances.

Nevertheless, since Mr. Artzi was determined that we would be the best school in the country, we competed constantly with Herzliya High School, the Reali School of Haifa, and the New High School in Tel Aviv. The criterion, as well as the lofty aim, was that no student from the Ohel Shem High School would ever fail in any matriculation exam. The means of achieving this goal was not necessarily high-quality teaching but rather the expulsion of any student who did not have a high probability of passing all of the matriculation exams. Thus when we began to study at Ohel Shem in ninth grade, there were five full classes, but we ended twelfth grade with three surprisingly shrunken ones. This method placed a great deal of emotional pressure on the students and in almost every incoming class, there was a student who committed suicide before graduation. Years later, by chance, I rode a bus with one of our teachers and I told him that I would never have sent my children to a school like that. He was deeply offended. But at that time, for me, Ohel Shem was a challenge I had to meet. Any other option was considered a failure. From conversations with my students today, it is evident that the atmosphere at Ohel Shem has changed beyond recognition since those days.

Nevertheless, we learned a lot and, most importantly, we learned how to study. We also had a number of exceptional teachers. First and foremost, I have to mention Dr. Boshvitz, the philosophy and classics teacher. He couldn't control the class and there was noise and turmoil from the time he entered the classroom until he left, but the noise and the lack of attention did not bother him, or at least he made it appear that way. Boshvitz had immense knowledge and had conducted his own research, some of which had been published in international journals. His teaching always reminded me of Almashan's approach, and I'm almost sure that I was the only one in the class who listened to him. A number of years after I finished school, I heard that Dr. Boshvitz had committed suicide following a family tragedy. I mourned him.

My hero was the math teacher, a great mathematician but one who had no patience for, or interest in, average and weak students like me. The assistant principal was certified to teach chemistry but as an administrator, he had no time or desire to teach. Dr. Rauchberger preferred to talk to us about his exploits during World War II when he served in the Red Army as an intelligence officer. According to him, he was among the first to enter Hitler's bunker.

Principal Artzi was supposed to teach biblical studies but he turned almost every lesson into a sermon—"behave modestly," "always tell the truth," "help others." I believe, however, that the prevailing feeling among us, the students of my graduating class, was that the man who demanded such high standards was far from "practicing what he preached." The Talmud teacher was a religious man who taught the subject using almost the same curriculum and methods used in a yeshiva. We all detested him and he made us hate a subject which could have been fascinating. Years later, his daughter, who was a year ahead of me in high school and with whom I was friendly, came to my apartment in Jerusalem and told me with tears in her eyes that her father had suddenly died and would be buried in a plot he had purchased in Jerusalem. She asked me to come to her father's funeral because she was afraid there would not be enough men to form a minyan.[6] Obviously, I couldn't refuse and I went. And, in fact, none of his colleagues or former students was present. The situation was saved by a boisterous truckload of eleventh-grade students who arrived with the gym teacher from Ramat Gan. As I said, I didn't like the man; nevertheless, my heart turned sour because of this unpleasant event. Mr. Artzi was not even able to pay his last respects to one of his teachers and I was furious with him. When I was invited to the ceremony for the celebration of the thirtieth anniversary of the school (or something similar), I threw the invitation away.

\*   \*   \*

Although my handwriting was at that time fairly legible, my father decided to give in to my repeated requests and bought me a typewriter. My first one came in the form of a used Hermes-Baby, black in color. In order to prevent it from falling apart, it was mounted in a kind of wooden box, hand-made by an amateur carpenter. At about the same time, the newspaper *Maariv for Youth* began to be published. At home, along with the Romanian *Viatsra Nuestra* and the Hungarian *Uj Kelet*, we—at least my mother and I—also bought and read *Maariv*, which was at that time the most widely read newspaper in the country. Since I had always wanted to be a writer and a journalist, I was happy when *Maariv* announced that it would be publishing a newspaper for youth, and I decided to participate in the "competition" held to choose writers for young people in that paper.

Composition was the one subject in school at which I really excelled. Gideon Katznelson (nicknamed "Katzi"), who was my teacher for Hebrew, literature, grammar, and composition never understood how I, who had zero knowledge of Hebrew grammar in its many facets, was able nevertheless to write compositions with almost no mistakes and also mastered a different kind of writing skill. This happened when I stumbled upon two books which, I believe, largely changed my way of thinking. One book, with a soft and crumbling cover, contained the essays of Ahad Ha'Am. Its style was polemical but based on a combination of facts (or pseudo-facts) and processes which were analyzed as if a razor-sharp scalpel had been used. The rational assertions resulting from those analyses captured my imagination and my heart. I was particularly impressed by the articles "Priest and Prophet" (which I still regard as an exemplary sociological article) and "Truth from the Land of Israel," which constitute the genesis of Hebrew critical writing (I discovered Yitzhak Epstein's article on a similar subject only during the course of my academic studies). *This is how I want to write too*, I decided in my heart, even though Katznelson taught Ahad Ha'am's work (which was, in any case, included in the curriculum) as an example of writing that was both demagogic and factually erroneous. However, Asher Ginsburg's[7] arguments actually convinced me while Katznelson's counter-arguments appeared to me quite weak. I told him that in my opinion he didn't fully understand Ahad Ha'am. After a moment of embarrassment, he asked me to explain myself; it seems to me that it was then that I gave my first public lecture, including quotations. To my surprise, the class listened to me attentively and with interest. When I finished, Katznelson said to me "write this down." At home I wrote a well-reasoned essay and gave it to him the next day. I never received an answer. Perhaps both of us preferred to end the dispute this way.

The second book was a volume containing research by Yosef Klausner on the Second Temple period. Although I was less attracted to the subject matter, I did find it interesting, especially when I compared it to the historical novel by Moshe Shamir, *The King of Flesh and Blood*, which I read avidly a number of times. What particularly caught my attention in Klausner's book was the meticulous "scholarly structure." From it I learned the difference between *ibid.* and *op. cit.* and how to cite sources and prepare bibliographies. During the same period, I also tried to tackle the volumes of Yehezkel Kaufmann about *The History of Israeli Faith*, but I found it too exhausting and dull and many of his claims were unintelligible to me, apparently because I lacked the appropriate background. Only many years later did I understand his broad Zionist context and his tendency to connect the creation of knowledge and values with a particular geographical location.

About a month after I sent two short articles to the editorial board of *Maariv for Youth*, I received a very impressive letter in which I was informed by the editor himself that I had been accepted as a "youth correspondent" and was asked to send a photograph to be displayed on the "journalist's press pass" issued by the weekly. Unrestrained joy and pride flooded me. I sat down immediately and typed several articles, one of which was even printed after substantial editing. But who cared? I could come to class with the newspaper and most of the students would gather around me to read what I had written. This way, my status there as a writer and a journalist was officially established even though my position in the school continued to be quite marginal the whole time I was there. This situation stemmed not only from my strange handicap but was, I think, primarily a result of my inability to participate in the Scouts, a youth movement in which almost all of the students of my class were members and which constituted one of the central social activities. In addition, I didn't participate in class trips or in sports, and physical education classes were free periods for me. All of this would have made me an outsider even if I had not been disabled. In hindsight, I don't understand why, actually, I could not have participated in at least some of these activities.

I developed a close relationship with some children in Ramat Gan. Most of them were socially marginal like me but for different reasons. Talia Vardi, an orphan who grew up in her uncle's home (while suffering emotional and perhaps even physical abuse by him, as was disclosed years later) was an outstanding student in grammar and Talmud and volunteered to help me in these two subjects, which were difficult for me. My mother, who loved Talia, always hoped that we would marry at some time in the future. Talia later completed a doctorate at the Hebrew University but was neither accepted by that university nor by the Israeli academia of the 1970s despite her talents. She married Yochanan Thorion, a professional colleague and an exceptionally pleasant man and their son Yotal (a combination of Yochanan and Talia) was born on the same day as our first child, Shira. In time, they both found quite respectable academic positions in Germany but were killed in a car accident which Yotal miraculously survived.

A number of months before she was killed, Talia wrote me a letter and asked that we adopt Yotal in the event that something happened to them. Talia loved me very much and Yochanan was in love with my wife, Diana. After consulting with my spouse (even though I thought that raising a fourth child would further complicate our already complex lives) I agreed, primarily because I thought that it was an absolutely hypothetical situation. I wrote to Talia what she needed to do legally and then I forgot about the whole matter; I didn't even save her letter. When we were informed about the terrible accident, Diana felt a moral obligation to adopt Yotal but in Germany, no will or other written proof could be found to support our claim. We participated in meetings about the topic with the rest of Talia's and Yochanan's families and with the official in charge of adoptions at the Israeli Ministry of Welfare. None of the family members wanted to take in the youth, while the senior supervisor of adoptions was of the opinion that we were not fit to adopt him.

Yotal remained in Germany in his neighbor's home and became a very talented young man who apparently followed a career in music. We tried to maintain contact with him, but his German guardians prevented us from doing so.

The reason for having been ruled out had been revealed to me, years later, by a senior Hadassah Hospital physician who was a very close friend of the Turion family and was a member of the board that decided about Yotal's fate: my handicap had been considered an impediment. He told me on that same occasion that, with time, he regretted very much that decision especially because the neighbors, with whom Yotal remained, did not encourage, to say the least, any contact with the Israeli family friends who, like us, strove to stay in touch with him.

A second friend was David Keller. He too, like Talia, found refuge in our home from the pressures and constraints of having a seriously ill mother. On the pretext of helping me in math, which was also difficult for me, we became good friends but when he dropped out of the Gymnasium, our friendship suffered, apparently because his pride was hurt.

A third friend, who also preferred to spend many days at my home, was Rafi Heptka. Rafi was considered the mathematical genius of the school. No one was at all able to understand his discussions with the mathematics teacher, Mr. Abiri. But it wasn't only his genius that separated him from the rest of the class but also his ambition, the likes of which I have never encountered in anybody else. Rafi, almost from the time he was born, had suffered from anxiety about death and aspired to become immortal. He developed two alternative theories for this purpose. One theory assumed that if a person moves at a certain speed through the space-time continuum, he would be able to avoid biological aging and be spared the effects of old age. The second theory was to freeze the person's body, putting him to sleep until medical technology became advanced enough to insure a significant, even if not absolute, increase in life expectancy. Rafi was aware of the enormous difficulty which would be encountered in explaining his approach to the public and politicians and convincing them to add this project to their agenda. Therefore, when he discovered my ability to express myself, he tried to recruit me for the task of explaining and disseminating his idea. In exchange, he promised me immortality too. I had ethical, social, and practical reservations about his plans, even though I understood him very well. The plans for the space race and the development of ballistic missiles apparently worked in Rafi's favor and even without my intervention, enormous budgets were allocated for those plans. Rafi himself became a highly acclaimed aerospace engineer who conducted research for

NASA and served as a professor of space sciences at the University of Florida. As I was preparing to write this portion of the book, I found him on the internet and asked him if he is still troubled by death and still believes in the same approaches. "Yes," Rafi answered me, "although it will not be realized in my present lifetime. Therefore I'm a member of an association that will freeze my body after death until, perhaps, genetic and other solutions will be found for my resuscitation and the healing of my illnesses." Rafi stunned me with his counter-question: "And are you still worried about the prospects of Israel's future survival?" Thus we continued the conversation and the argument that we had engaged in almost forty-five years earlier.

I had other friends at the Gymnasium, such as Eitan Gorni and Dov Mishor. Our friendships had begun while we were still at the Matmid School and continued even through the university, but in our relationships—at least this was my feeling—they did not regard me as an equal and there was at least a hint of arrogance on their part. Besides them, perhaps my most unusual friend from my days at Matmid was Meir Palermo. The Palermo family had a small restaurant near our home and Meir was busier taking care of the family business with his older brother than studying. Meir was not a learned and sophisticated youth, but he possessed the deep wisdom that comes from life experience and he radiated warmth. Meir was the first young person I met in my new homeland who did not want to join the army. "Why enlist?" he asked. "In the army, you either kill or get killed." He said that he would inflict some injury on himself if he had to in order to get an exemption from the military, and it seems to me that he did just that. I was shocked but I didn't argue with him. I felt that Meir was made for friendship, not arguments, and I found great power in the simplicity of his words.

\*    \*    \*

My uncle Berko was considered an adventurer without a conscience. Many stories were told about him, his misdeeds, and his strange and dubious ways of earning a living. One of them was advertising himself as a "magician." He would pass through Romanian villages with a partner and deceive simple farmers. He would pick up an object in his hand and call his partner (who was unable to see the item), supposedly by his name, when he was actually using the Yiddish name of the object he had in his hand. The magic worked until one day the pair came to the home of a farmer who had worked for years in a Jewish home. The two were severely beaten and kicked out of the house in disgrace while their mothers and their Jewishness were mentioned. Berko also became famous for his escapes from police officers and even for a daring escape from a military train after being drafted to work as a civilian for the army. Grandpa Herman would, from time to time, rescue him by paying generous bribes and my father would occasionally smuggle cash to him. Many years later in Israel, Uncle Berko was one of the causes of my family's collapse, thus entirely confirming my mother's fears.

Berko, the scoundrel, had also immigrated to Israel. My father, without my mother's knowledge, of course, decided to help him and perhaps also to benefit from his assistance. The details were never made clear to me. Apparently they agreed that my father would engage in the production and Berko in the whole-sale marketing of the merchandise. Meanwhile, my father's factory, which was situated on Chelnov Street near the old central bus station, expanded and began to manufacture new products. My father transferred the merchandise to my uncle, trained him, and gave him leads. But my uncle, as it became evident, had other plans, or perhaps he became entangled in other businesses. Like a bolt from the blue, our world fell about us in ruins: a small report on the first page of *Maariv* carried the headline "Industrialist Marco Kimerling Entangled in Debt, Flees Country." The reporter mixed up the names—Berko, Marco, who cares?—and didn't check the accuracy of the report he published. My father, of course, had not fled the country but my uncle disappeared, together with all the merchandise my father had given him. My uncle's flight caused a domino-like avalanche in my father's business; however, Berko wasn't the sole cause of it. The rapid expansion of the small factory was not based on personal capital but rather on credit and loans with exorbitant rates of interest. From the moment the report was published in the newspaper, all the creditors began to request the immediate return of their money. My father, who was left without most of his merchandise and whose money was invested in machinery, raw materials, and molds, was not able to repay the debts, which continued to swell.

And then the creditors began showing up at our home too—angry and aggressive people, shouting and threatening. This was my first encounter with "real life." They called my father, who was a Romanian, a thief, a cheat, and a liar (as I mentioned earlier, "Romanian" was at that time a synonym for thief). Most of them were convinced that my father had cheated them. One man, Mr. Plesner, made our lives particularly difficult. He was an elderly man who made his living as a loan shark. Today, I can understand that he was just a man who was witnessing part of his wealth going down the drain in his old age but back then, I hated him. He raged all over the neighborhood and with frightful shouts announced that my father had stolen the last of his money. Mr. Plesner sat in our home and declared that he would not leave until he received his money back, including all the interest to which he was entitled.

Father disappeared and we did not hear from him for several days. My mother feared for his life. I don't know where he went but when he returned, he was slightly encouraged and said with frightening calm to Plesner: "I don't have the money now. I will pay you when I will have it. But know that if you continue to harass my family, I wouldn't mind cutting your throat." Apparently Plesner became really scared because he did not appear again at our home, but I continued to hear his name for a long time afterward. Creditors tried to foreclose on our home and what remained of the factory. The matter went to court and, when my father was declared bankrupt, was put under the supervision of the Official Receiver. Since the apartment was also in my mother's name, it could not be sold to satisfy the creditors, although a lien was placed on it.

During the course of the nerve-wracking trial, the creditors and my father reached an agreement for the payment of the debts that would continue for years.

All of this took place during the end of eleventh grade and continued into the twelfth grade. There was tremendous tension at home although my mother understood that this was not the time to settle scores with my father who was now, in any case, a broken man and even more withdrawn. And although he tried for the rest of his life to support the family—even after he became partially paralyzed following a stroke he suffered a few years later—the sparkle in his eyes was extinguished. My mother became an expert at preparing meals from groats, two potatoes, a carrot, an onion and once or twice a week even from chicken wings. It was difficult for me to prepare my homework, study for the matriculation exams, or invite friends over. Instead of going to school, I would escape into the thick woods of the Monkey Park. This spacious area extended from the top of a hill, which could be reached by climbing many steps via an alley where embassy villas were located, and was then swallowed up in the trees down toward the center of Ramat Gan. Benches were scattered along the winding road and in the morning, the park was usually empty unless a flock of young children from some nursery school passed by on the way to the monkey cages and the peacocks. Since I didn't feel well either at home or in school, I would sit down on a bench, read a book, or just sink into day dreaming and wait for the time to pass. The next morning, I would stand by the door of the school doctor's office in order to receive a "note" for being sick the previous day. The doctor was a pleasant pensioner who never questioned me or preached. With an understanding smile in the corners of his mouth, he would write the requested certificate.

Somehow, I passed the matriculation exams, albeit with very modest grades, and I registered at the Hebrew University of Jerusalem. This was not a simple affair since an extension of the university had been opened at Sheikh Munis that year and my mother was afraid to send me all the way to Jerusalem. But I didn't want to be at home anymore; in addition, I wanted to study at the real, respectable institution, and not at some extension. The previous year, I had visited Givat Ram with my class. The university left a huge impression on me with its many students running around and the professors, who were walking legends for me, hurrying between buildings, libraries, and the beautiful auditorium. I took a copy of *Pi HaAton*[8] with me and threw a coin into the small pool at the entrance. "Whoever throws a coin in will return here," one of the teachers told us half seriously and half in jest. I swore to myself that I would return.

## Notes

1.   An Israeli writer and politician who was a member of Menachem Begin's Herut party and an advocate of Israeli control over the West Bank.

2.  Nathan Alterman, the poet.
3.  An Israeli author and political figure, who was originally a Mapam activist but became a proponent of Greater Israel after the 1967 War.
4.  These references are to prominent Israeli political figures, mostly identified with the right side of the political map, or their offsprings.
5.  The word *yishuv* designates usually communities of Jewish settlers founded in Palestine prior to the establishment of the state of Israel.
6.  A minyan is a quorum of ten men needed to conduct some Jewish religious services.
7.  Ahad Ha'am (which means 'one of the people') is the pen name of Asher Ginsburg.
8.  The name of the student newspaper which means "the mare's mouth."

# PART TWO

## CAMPUS

# 7

## AT THE DORMITORIES

In any event, I entered public life. One day, a quite tall, thin, mustached, and muscular young man suffering from a very mild case of cerebral palsy (C.P.) showed up at our house. I don't remember how he learned of my existence, but he introduced himself as follows: "I am Uri Brill. I am studying agriculture at Rehovot and I served in the Nahal."[1] Uri was the only child of a couple, German in origin, who lived in one of the cooperative settlements (*moshavim*) in the Sharon region. They were rigid, stubborn people who, apart from earning their living by working the land, made it their life's mission to train Uri to "overcome" his disability. My parents, especially my mother, dealt with the situation indirectly by adjusting their attitude towards me and my disability: they mainly avoided overprotecting me and treated me like a "normal boy" as much as possible. The Brill family's way of confronting the problem was tough and blunt. They did daily gymnastic exercises with Uri as if they were preparing an athlete for the Olympics and they demanded uncompromising physical achievements from him. We became friendly with Uri and his parents or, to be precise, he almost forced their friendship on me and my family, and the visit to the *moshav* was a fascinating if embarrassing experience. Besides educating Uri to persevere in overcoming his disability, the Brill family, together with other people who had family members afflicted with C.P., tried to establish an association whose purpose was to fight for the rights of people with this disability and their families.

I think the main goal was to be accepted into Ilanshil-polio, a large, well-known organization that was established following an epidemic of polio which hit the country in the 1950s. The foundation acquired legal status and, thanks to the March of Dimes, collected a substantial budget. The parents of children stricken by C.P., a disability that was still not understood at the time even in professional circles (I remember that I had to sit with doctors many times and explain the nature and cause of my disability), asked that the veteran foundation give them sponsorship too, but it refused. In response to this refusal, those parents, primarily on the initiative of the Brill and Raz families (Herzliya Raz was quite a well-known educator and children's author whose beautiful daughter Noa was seriously stricken by C.P.), established the *Shtelem* organization. Within that framework, I met two people besides Uri with whom real friendships developed.

Dr. Joseph Putter was an agricultural statistician who worked at Beit Dagan. Yoske, as everyone called him, was wise, pleasant, and full of humor, a man who always saw the comic side of whatever happened around him. It was difficult to understand his speech, but it was always worth investing the effort since he was a person who had much to say. Dr. Putter was run over in a road accident a few years later and died after a great deal of suffering. Chava Landau was also a very erudite woman. Her lower limbs were completely paralyzed and she almost never left home unless her brothers drove her in their car. She depended on her elderly parents for her daily needs. Chava earned a living by giving English lessons to high school students. She had a charming personality and many of her pupils became her friends. She was the only one in the *Shtelem* group with whom I had conversations that had nothing to do with being handicapped. We talked about poetry, literature, and philosophy. She did not like politics. After I got married, we lost touch, as happened with many others.

Before I started at the university, Putter, Brill, and I were the "assets" of the new association and a kind of consolation to parents who had "impaired" children and often tried to get rid of them at any cost. We were living "proof" that despite disabilities "it is possible to go far" and to function in every respect as well as, or even better than, a completely normal person. But this is not the whole truth because some of those afflicted with C.P. are mentally retarded in varying degrees. For still others, the physical and aesthetic deformity constitutes a growing emotional burden which prevents them from having contact with the outside world and with reality. Uri was also the first and almost the last in this group who married a woman who wasn't disabled (at the time it was expected that a disabled person would marry another disabled person). He had a great job as an agronomist at the Jewish Agency and he had a daughter. All his dreams came true. Over twenty years later, without any connection to his disability, he developed the rare disease, A.L.S. (a progressive and fatal neurodegenerative disease). One day when his family wasn't home, he climbed into an empty bathtub, put a gun in his mouth, and shot himself "so as not to become a burden to you," as he wrote in his farewell letter to his wife and daughter. I understood him well. Before pulling the trigger, he even called a friend and asked him to clean up and remove his body before his wife and daughter returned home. Once a Yeke, [2] always a Yeke, even up to the moment of his planned death. Unfortunately for him, his hand was already unable to obey him and the bullet missed the spot at which he had aimed. Uri hovered between life and death for almost a week before he breathed his last.

For a while, I was a very active participant in the association and represented the disabled in the "administration." I spoke with parents who wished to get rid of their children and lectured in front of various audiences about the significance of being a young disabled person. However, most of my activity involved preparing the newsletter for the association with the pathetic title "We Shall Overcome." Even though I sometimes received material from other members of the association, in practice I wrote and distributed it all by myself. When I moved to Jerusalem the "editing" was passed on to Chava Landau, however the newsletter stopped appearing. Actually, there was no more need for it since the association accomplished its original goal and merged with *Ilanshil-Polio*. A new foundation for the handicapped called *Ilan* was created and, I believe, is still active to this day.

My acquaintance with the Caspo family also belongs to this period of my life. They had just immigrated from Romania and their adolescent son was studying at the Be'er Sheva High School where they had settled. Being troubled about the future of their only son, Dan, who had moderate C.P, they came to consult with me and my family. I quickly realized that Dani was a youth with well above average intelligence and I convinced his parents, who saw no point even in his finishing high school ("He needs a profession," they decided), to let him take his matriculation exams and then study at the university. A few years later, when Dani came to the university with his Hebraized name "Caspi," we became quite close friends and he did very well in his studies. Today, Professor Dan Caspi (author of a children's book, *Inbal's Father*, about the relationship between a disabled father and his "normal" daughter) is the head of the Communications Department at Ben-Gurion University.

Even before I came to Jerusalem, I decided to stop working for the foundation. It did not seem to me that I could, on my own, be of any use to an organization that was now dealing primarily with politics and internal power relationships.

I carried a big, heavy suitcase with me to Jerusalem. When I arrived at the dormitory office in Givat Ram, the supervisor received me with noticeable cordiality. "Baruch Kimmerling, right?" she both asked and stated. She had probably already been told about me. I received the keys for Room 3, Building 7 and was told how to get there. "I'll find you a great roommate," she promised. When I got there and tried to insert the key, it refused to go in. "Nobody is going to disturb me!" someone shouted from the inside. Alarmed, I hurried back to the office and explained that there was someone in the room who wouldn't open the door for me. The dormitory supervisor checked her lists and declared that it was impossible since the room was empty. In spite of that, she sent her helper, Ahuva, with me to check the situation out. Ahuva, in a very assertive voice, forced the intruder to open the door. There stood a plump young man in his underwear who seemed to be afraid of her. He pleaded to be left in peace because he had a final exam for a second history degree and needed to study quietly (this in itself evoked great respect in me for that worried individual—a final exam for a second degree! When will I reach that point, if at all?). But that did not make any impression on Ahuva. "You always have a final exam," she sneered at him and ordered him to vacate the room immediately. However, she also promised to find him another room and, at the same time, called the cleaning woman, Mazal, to clean both the room and the closet well.

Mazal was a red-headed woman in her early forties with a strong Moroccan accent and a youthful beauty that was still partially preserved despite her wrinkled face. She was strong-minded, loquacious, and curious. While cleaning the room, she conducted an in-depth investigation of me. She was very vivacious and although her questions annoyed me and were highly intrusive, I answered them. Not only did I not want to offend her, but she also radiated a warmth which overcame barriers. Within days, we became friends. She was also my housekeeper for a few years after I bought myself a small apartment in Kyriat Yovel. After a while, the reason for her special interest in me became clear. Mazal Cohen was a single parent who had raised two children by herself: a son, who was on the fringes of the criminal world, and a daughter, Ilana, who was disabled by C.P. Mazal was very concerned about her and what she did when not at home. Eventually, Mazal married off her daughter and brought up Ilana's several children by herself.

Within a few days, a roommate was found for me, John, an American Protestant teacher who arrived in the Holy Land for a year of advanced study. That was the first time in my life that I had met a WASP. Our relationship was correct and distant and we tried not to disturb each other. In my second year, I shared with Ilan, who resembled the eternal student and who was, in my opinion, eccentric. His only interest was Rudolf Steiner's theosophy and he tried, without success, to interest me in it as well. Ilan was a burdensome roommate because of the constant attention he demanded, but he was also a good and dedicated friend. Once when I spilled boiling oil on myself while frying an omelet and suffered in bed for about a week with terrible pain and a high fever, Ilan took care of me faithfully and even carried me on his back to the bathroom and the shower.

In my third year, I lived with Arale Deutch (Dishon), a pleasant and colorful person who was proud of the fact that he came to Israel on the *Exodus* when he was a child. Arale (who was also one of the participants in *The Song of the Neighborhood*, which was a hit at the time) was registered for many years at the Department of Geography, but I never saw him study anything. He played the accordion and was the official dance instructor at the dormitories; however, he had other mysterious occupations. Rumor had it that he was an agent for the Security Services. Once I asked him and he denied it with a large smile. Arale was a great roommate; he only bothered me on those nights during which he made love with his girlfriend Shosha, who later became his life-long wife, and I would pretend to be sound asleep.

My arrival at the dorms and the university changed my world completely. For the first time, I was accepted more or less as an equal among equals into a quite heterogeneous and varied community of young people. This was not exactly one happy family, but it did contain a great many young men and women, some of them fascinating and others definitely unusual. In those days, in 1962, the city of Jerusalem was small and intimate and I could meet almost the same faces in the dorm's restaurant (where a cashier named Gohar reigned), the Kaplan Building's cafeteria or the National Library as I did outside the university at Ta'amon, Atara, and the Yemenite restaurant, "The Magic Carpet," which I particularly loved. During my first year, I used to go home every weekend, but as the years went by—and I lived in those dorms for about six years—my trips home became less and less frequent.

The campus overflowed with political activity. Although I never joined any of those groups in Jerusalem from which the new Israeli left, with all of its colorful figures, was born—long before the phenomenon became known in Europe and the United States—I did participate in the heated arguments that took place there at the time. However, these groups—Mazpen people, Trotskyites, Maoists, etc.—were like closed castes with their own language. The differences between them, which were accompanied by passionate debates, seemed extremely insignificant to me. In retrospect, I can say that I was influenced only by their consciousness and analysis of the Jewish–Arab conflict, an influence that found expression a few years later. Even if these analyses were not accurate in their details, in principle these groups had the closest understanding of the causes and results of the conflict and some of their predictions proved to be correct. Their point of view on history, including the course of the 1948 War, was closer to reality than the official historiography, and the first to tell me about the massive expulsion of Arabs from the country in 1948 was Israel Shahak.

An event that proved quite traumatic was West German Chancellor Konrad Adenauer's visit to the campus. Groups of students from the right and left tried to prevent him from entering. The university administration asked for police intervention and large numbers of policemen, including some on horseback, entered the campus. Many students were beaten with clubs until they bled. Sometime later I understood that the policemen were only too happy to beat students in response to the ethnic and status conflicts in Israel.

In the dorms, however, there was a remarkable absence of hierarchy. There were a number of doctoral candidates who were not interested in associating with mere mortals—students working on their first and second degrees—but most of the dorm residents were ready to hold open and free dialogue with each other. There were also overseas students who kept to themselves at first but soon developed friendly relations with the Israelis. An example is my warm friendship with a girl from the "American group," Sidra DeKoven, who remained in Jerusalem and within a short time married Yaron Ezrachi. This friendship, despite its ups and downs, has endured for a lifetime. Sidra stood out on campus from the time she was an "American student" until now when she is a professor, because of her intellectual acuity and her appearance. For the first time in my life, I even met Arab Israelis, but I will talk about this later. Because the new world I was busy discovering absorbed me completely, I didn't focus on the reason I came to Jerusalem and my investment in my studies was minimal.

As far as I am concerned, the most fascinating encounters at the dorms were those with girls. I didn't have a sister and my contacts with the representatives of the opposite sex in my high school class were minimal since I was never the kind of boy that was sought after by them. Hence my attitude toward girls was very romantic as they seemed to me pure and holy, something like the Sabbath candles whose light could be enjoyed but not actually used. Furthermore, I thought to myself that if I were a young girl, I would not be interested in a man with an unaesthetic appearance like mine. At the university, and particularly at the dorms, I slowly recovered from my complexes as I realized that girls were interested in me and wanted to be close to me. But it was actually a new friend of mine who influenced me on this matter and many others and who brought about a change in my self-image and did a great deal to boost my self-confidence.

At first, I heard only his voice in the hallway as he sang in the shower of Building 7. It was a powerful bass-baritone, very similar to that of Paul Robeson. Soon afterwards, a bearded man appeared in front of me, leaning heavily on crutches. Azriel had been a sailor, a "Hebrew seaman," he used to say pedantically. A number of years before, he was injured on the job: he had tripped and fallen into the ship's boiler. His life was miraculously saved since he was taken out in pieces (as he described it) from inside it. He was sent to France for a series of operations and for rehabilitation, a process that lasted a number of years. Even after his rehabilitation, though, he remained severely disabled. His lower limbs were completely paralyzed and he couldn't move his neck to change the position of his head. However, the muscles of his hands and chest were powerful because of the time he had spent in his previous job. His penetrating and authoritative eyes held a spark of mischief and, as far as I could tell, he made a huge impression on everyone around him, especially women. It seemed to me that although he was self-taught, he was erudite and had a vast knowledge of many fields. He had an exquisite style of speech filled with apt retorts as well as a large and rich Hebrew vocabulary peppered with juicy slang that he had apparently acquired during his seafaring days. He had definite opinions about almost everything and I don't think I was ever able to convince him to change any of his plans, but I didn't argue with him much either. From my point of view, Azriel was like Meir Palermo—good for friendship but not for arguments. What we mostly had in common was a sense of humor, a lust for life, and a rare capacity for empathy. I assume that in his previous life he was not a little macho man but the catastrophe which befell him made him more refined, tolerant and open to his surroundings and to himself.

During his rehabilitation, he married Sarah, a divorced woman from a kibbutz up north and the mother of an adolescent girl. Sarah was a bitter and very unhappy woman. She helped Azriel get through the most difficult time of his life; however, it didn't seem as if they had much in common, especially after Azriel developed intellectually in his new environment. On the other hand, Azriel loved his step-daughter, Bat-Sheva, very much, even after their own daughter, Sarit, was born. Azriel's love for Bat-Sheva would, years later, have repercussions reminiscent of a Chekhov tragedy.

Azriel had a deep love of nature and after he acquired a Volvo that was adapted to his limitations as a driver, we would go out for long trips in the mountains around Jerusalem. Sometimes, it was just the two of us and, on hot summer days, a big container of ice cream which we would happily finish off. At other times a girl or two accompanied us. Usually, those young women were not students. Sometimes, they were volunteers or foreign tourists. Occasionally, they were soldiers. The young women (and the not-so-young ones too) would be enchanted by Azriel's charm and would follow him as though he was the Pied Piper of Hamelin. I didn't always accompany him on those trips since he sometimes wanted to be alone with himself or with one of them. Even so, to the best of my knowledge, Azriel didn't share his adventures with any other man besides me, either because he didn't trust them or because he had "adopted" me as a kind of educational project. His attitude towards women was totally practical. It was not that he didn't respect and love women, but my whole romantic-naïve approach seemed ridiculous to him. His attitude could be summarized as follows: women need men emotionally as well as sexually, just as men need women.

Years later, Azriel and Bat-Sheva left the house one morning in the Volvo. Azriel, who couldn't turn his head and drove with the help of an elaborate set of mirrors, was not paying attention when he crossed a junction near his home and crashed into a tractor. Bat-Sheva was killed immediately and Azriel's body was again smashed into pieces. Sarah took care of him devotedly once again, even though, as she put it, he "killed" her daughter. When I visited him several times in Beit Levinstein, he spoke only of Bat-Sheva. He spoke to her as if she was in the room with us, sitting on his bed. When there was nothing else they could do for him at Beit Levinstein, they sent him back to his beautiful home at the *moshav* which, in the interim, had become a wonderful suburb of Tel-Aviv. When we came to visit them, he whispered to me that he wanted to die. About a week later, I heard Sarah's choked voice on the phone—Azriel had breathed his last. Of course we went to the funeral, where plenty of people talked nonsense about Azriel, as it is customary on these occasions.

Although I invested no effort in my studies during the first year, my interest in sociology grew as time went by. I arrived as a student at the sociology and political science departments quite by chance. I had planned a career as a journalist and an author and those subjects seemed the most useful to me. When I met my sociology advisor—who was later considered to be an outstanding expert on education—he looked at me and said "Sociology is a difficult subject. Perhaps you should content yourself with political science. It will be easier for you there." I, who had already grown accustomed to such situations said: "Let me try." He smiled and signed my schedule form. There was a long line of people waiting for him outside. The years 1962 and 1963 were years of great expansion and an unprecedented number of students flooded the country's only university. Except for a few subjects like medicine and psychology, the only requirement for admission to the university was successful completion of the matriculation exams.

The institution was not prepared—either in terms of physical facilities or teaching staff—to absorb so many students. Lecture halls like Kaplan A and B were packed and in order to be able to get a good seat and actually hear something of what the lecturer said, one had to come early or rush into the hall as soon as the previous lecture was over.

As mentioned, I was not especially interested in my studies during the first year. Nevertheless, there were two classes I loved very much and which fascinated me. The first was "Introduction to Sociology" and the second was "The Israeli Society." The assigned textbook for "Introduction to Sociology" was the most unreadable book I have ever tried to read. The sentences never ended and it was impossible to understand what the subject, object, and verb were. However, the lecturer was a not-so-young doctoral student (by the way, most of the teaching staff was composed of people who hadn't yet finished their third degree, something I became aware of only a few years later), and a good teacher—Abraham Zlotchover, whom everybody, including the students, called Zloch. Zloch would translate *Introduction to Sociology* into understandable Hebrew for us and explained what the two authors, Professor Shmuel N. Eisenstadt and Dr. Joseph Ben-David, meant. Zloch was a colorful man and a Communist who agreed with none of the ideas or statements that appeared in the book. Therefore, he taught the way Almashan did: this is what is written in the book and this is what you will write in the exam. The truth is different and I will reveal it to you. I actually liked what was written in the book, especially after I discovered an introductory book in English. This was Kingsley Davis' book, which was written in the clearest way and more or less overlapped with the one in Hebrew. In both books "society"—a kind of mysterious-metaphysical entity—was described as functioning like some kind of elaborate machine or living organism that has well-defined goals to meet in order to continue to exist, which is in fact the primary objective of every society. This entity was even depicted as having self-correcting mechanisms in response to the failures and mutations that occur all the time.

Since I had never thought before in terms of the concepts of structural-functionalism, which supposedly could provide immediate and comprehensive explanations for any phenomenon, I was fascinated both by the doctrine and by its scientific character. Zloch, on the other hand, was an orthodox Marxist who disagreed completely, and rightly so, with the approach he was forced to teach. His alternative theory which, at least superficially, was familiar to me and explained all social phenomena in terms of economy and class conflict, was unacceptable in my opinion. As a result, almost every class turned into an argument between Zloch and me. Once, I sat in on a different section of the same course taught by Ms. Rivka Bar-Yosef, an intelligent woman who had mastered correct and very sharp answers. She lectured "by the book" and I was bored, even though I agreed with what was said.

Rivka was from our home town, Turda, and studied in the same class with my Aunt Eva. She immigrated to Israel at about the same time as my Aunt Yardena. I think that after a number of years in a kibbutz, she ran away and went to study in Jerusalem, but I don't have factual biographical details about her. My mother heard that she was teaching in the department of Sociology and went to Jerusalem, without my knowledge, in order to understand what sociology is and whether I should study it. Rivka apparently didn't recognize my mother and confused her with her sister Eva, but she received her coldly and was openly reserved. I imagine today that, as a teacher, my response to being approached by a parent of a potential student of the department would have been the same, if not even harsher. It seems to me that Rivka thought, perhaps justifiably, that my mother was seeking some kind of favoritism for her problematic son and she dismissed her with a few vague statements. After I found out about this, I was angry at my mother, but I said nothing to her. Throughout the whole year, Rivka and I ignored each other. In the second year, I took a course with her on relations in the workplace and we formed a proper teacher-student relationship. I even participated in a modest ceremony when she received her doctorate.

However, at two points in time, Rivka played a crucial role in my academic career. The first time was after I finished my first degree. I was already in love with sociology then and I was looking for a field of specialization. I thought a useful and important field to develop would be the sociology of disability. Since no one in Israel dealt with this subject, I came to the conclusion that it would be possible to attack the subject from the point of view of the sociology of work, since real rehabilitation for a disabled person is achieved when he is employed in a job that honors its holder and is capable of supporting himself and perhaps even his family without the help of charity and other outside assistance. Rivka listened to me attentively and said that it was a really important subject but that she did not recommend that I deal with it myself. "You could be the best sociologist in the world in this field, but people will still treat you as a cripple first and then a sociologist," she said. For many years, I thought she was right and that she had saved me from a trap. Today, after many years of work in even more sensitive and charged fields than the sociology of disability, I'm not sure that there exists any field at all where the sociologist doesn't bring himself and his own identity into his own work, for better or for worse, and is not also perceived in terms of that identity by others. I will write later about the second time that Rivka played an important role in my life, probably without being aware of it at all.

The second class I loved was Shmuel N. Eisenstadt's crowded class on Israeli society. The class covered various subjects, most of which, theoretically, I should already have known about; however, during the course of this class, I found out how fragmented, incomplete, and lacking in historical context my knowledge was. I was especially fascinated by the connections that Eisenstadt made between different subjects and fields and his ability to make an overall analysis while using the concepts and the approach I had learned in the introductory class. His lectures were much clearer and more understandable than his writings and he knew how to adapt himself to the level of his listeners. A long time passed before I gradually discovered his weak points and the gaps in his approach, but there is no doubt that he laid the foundations for the investigation and the analysis of Israel in those same pioneering classes. Whoever really followed him could "hear" the development of his thoughts, even though he lectured fluently. Eisenstadt was not only a great teacher with an amazing breadth of knowledge, but participating in his classes was a real intellectual experience. Throughout all the years of my formal studies, I took every class or seminar he taught, and even though he repeated himself in some of his lectures—especially his jokes—he always brought a new idea or a fresh approach which made it worth investing the time listening to him. However, his lectures were not easy, not only because of their level of abstraction but also because of the amount of reading he required, and demanded, that we do between classes. Despite his limitations, about which I will talk later, I have never met a person of such stature in my life.

During the second year, Joseph Ben-David taught us, in particular, social psychology. He was sharp-witted and gave pointed, correct answers but he lectured against his will, with obvious carelessness, and displayed a complete disregard for the students. As time went by, I had a number of clashes with him about his attitude toward science (especially natural science) and its innovations, a field in which he was then considered an international authority.

I did not understand Eric Cohen's lectures at all, and today I have doubts as to whether he himself understood them. But all the female students were head over heels in love with the handsome young man. In contrast, Chaim Adler's complementary class was clear and relatively easy.

My first class at the university, "Introduction to Statistics," was taught on Sunday afternoon by Professor Roberto Baki. Baki was a pleasant person and a competent instructor who did a good job of teaching a subject that most students find difficult. You could see that he loved to teach. A few minutes before class started, a young woman, of below average height and dressed with simplicity—unlike most of the other female students who were rather well-dressed—came up to me, offered her hand, and asked, "Baruch Kimmerling, right?" "I plead guilty," I answered. "And with whom do I have the honor?" "Drora Cohen," she replied. "I am Uri Brill's pen-pal and I promised him I would help you." "How would you help me?" I asked curiously. "Bring carbon paper to all the sociology classes and I will make a copy of all the lectures for you. You will not have to write yourself. I know it's hard for you." And, indeed, throughout my undergraduate studies, I sat next to Drora and was given notes that were so thorough and detailed they could have been provided by the instructor himself. Drora's handwriting was clear and neat, she understood the material well, and she also knew how to distinguish between what was essential and what wasn't. For years I used her notebooks, even when I started teaching myself.

Drora was already a married woman at that time, but she later divorced and remarried. She met Uri Brill through correspondence—a phenomenon that was common among teenagers even then, before the internet era—when she served in the Pioneering Fighting Youth. Sociology was a minor subject for her, her primary one being the more prestigious psychology. Drora faithfully kept her promise to Uri, but kept a rather paternalistic (or should I say maternalistic?) distance from me. Throughout all my studies for the first degree, Drora received higher grades than I did except in the Introduction to Sociology class. It seems that later on, when my academic career began to take off, this came as a surprise to her, a fact that she didn't try to hide.

I really began to understand sociology as a profession only toward the end of my undergraduate studies, which at the time required a focused effort to read extensive and integrative material. I studied with Amiram Vinokur, who was considered the best student in our class, until we graduated. After graduation, Amiram left to continue his studies at the magnificent University of Michigan, married an American woman, and stayed there.

During my undergraduate studies, I understood that there is something that I called socio-logic, which does not contradict the logic I learned (for example, from Professor Yehoshua Bar-Hillel), but which has some additional content that does not exist in conventional common sense. Thus, for example, Emile Durkheim, one of the founding fathers of modern sociology, examined statistical data and found that people tend to commit suicide more frequently during both economic recessions and expansions than they do during ordinary times. You do not need to be an outstanding sociologist to find out that people commit suicide during periods of recession, but why do they also commit suicide during times of general prosperity? It was necessary to find a theoretical explanation that would interpret what is commonly shared by periods of depression and those of prosperity, a task which requires vast knowledge and a special sociological imagination. What Durkheim suggested, and was found to be correct and valid to this day, is that in times of both economic lows and highs, the norms and laws of society lose much of their validity and uncertainty develops regarding the expected behaviors of its members. Durkheim called this social condition "anomie" (lack of law). It is necessary to add that anomie is not the immediate cause of suicide but it does increase the chance that a person who suffers from whatever problem—let's suppose, a disease, emotional distress, or disillusioned love—will carry out the most extreme act of separation from society. Of course, it is not only rapidly changing economic conditions that might cause anomie. The first research I initiated, implemented, and even published on my own while I was still a student was the examination of the connection between the suicide rates in Israel and salient fluctuations in the Jewish–Arab conflict, a relationship that was indeed found. And from this I deduced that the conflict creates a condition of permanent anomie, albeit to a variable extent, in Israeli society. All of this was in contrast to the accepted theory that wars and external pressure increase social unity.

My awareness of the "Arab problem" and my curiosity about it developed gradually. I met Dabach in what used to be the kitchen of Building 7. He was the first Arab I had met in my entire life. We did not become friends because he didn't seem to be interested, but we would engage in meaningless small talk. Dabach studied law and was close to finishing his degree. One day he disappeared for a considerable length of time and when he showed up again I was happy to see him. "Where have you been? Were you sick?" I asked. "No," Dabach replied, "the (military) Governor did not give me an exit permit." "Why? What did you do?" I asked. "I didn't do anything," he said, "their usual abuse." I didn't believe him but didn't say a word. Bachor Dabush, a blind student of political science who later changed his name to a bombastic and patriotic Hebrew one, was in the vicinity, heard the conversation, and butted in. "He should be grateful that he is allowed to study at the university. They should have expelled or killed them all." Bachor had been blinded on an annual school trip when the bus struck a mine hidden by the Fedayeen. A number of children were killed and others injured. Dabach did not answer. He just left the kitchen. I was shocked. That was the first time I had encountered this kind of hatred in my entire life. I thought that Bachor hated Arabs because of the mine that blinded him but after I knew him better, I got the impression that he had felt that same hatred even before, long before. Later on, I discovered Sabri Jiryis's book, *The Arabs in Israel*, at the faculty library. I didn't attribute much credibility to Jiryis's book at first because it was difficult for me to digest the fact that Jews can inflict such injustices on a minority. The book described the means of expropriating land from Arabs, their mistreatment by the military government, and other discriminatory practices carried out against the Arabs in Israel, all under the pretext of protecting the security of the State. In due course, I understood that even this bold book did not reveal the whole picture, maybe because it was written from a lawyer's point of view and the author was not sophisticated enough.

## Notes

1. The Pioneering Youth Brigade.
2. The word *Yeke* is used in Israel to designate German Jews and also to indicate a rigid and even obsessive behavior in keeping everything neat and in place.

# 8

## ADAM

My brother Adam skipped a grade and at the age of seventeen finished the science track at the Ohel Shem Gymnasium. He was accepted into the military's academic reserve and registered for mechanical engineering studies at the Technion. He was very disappointed when he found out that he was only on the Technion waiting list and that it was not certain he would be studying there that year. I had never seen my brother as depressed as he was when he received this news. Having friends who studied economics and statistics in Jerusalem (Azriel, for example), I thought these fields suited his abilities. At first, my brother was not willing to consider the idea at all and claimed he had no interest in economics. Since this happened during the summer vacation, I was at home and kept telling him what can be done with economics and statistics and finally I convinced him, perhaps because not many choices were left.

And indeed Adam started his studies at the Hebrew University and soon fell in love with economics and did quite well. During his third year, he was even asked by one of his professors to help students by tutoring them in what was considered the most difficult class in the entire profession, econometrics. Adam also lived in the dormitories and our relationship continued to be good yet somewhat distant. We had neither friends nor many interests in common, and each of us was busy with his own affairs. At that time, I had already moved to Building 12, a modern building where every handicapped person was allotted a separate, spacious room (probably because not many students were willing to live with handicapped people) and he would come twice or three times a week for short visits. To the best of my recollection, we didn't even talk about the problems that still existed at home. Adam too, while he was a reservist, supported himself financially. However, a major change occurred in his status at home because my mother began to be proud of him and his achievements and not just of me.

In any event, the 1967 war had broken out and Adam joined the Jerusalem brigade. He sustained minor injuries near Nebi Mussa yet managed to arrive in Hebron with his unit. He told me afterwards that his most difficult "fight" was the one he had with his soldiers when he prevented them from looting. When the battles were over, he was assigned to build a camp for prisoners and to prevent their abuse by the staff.

After finishing his undergraduate degree, Adam was conscripted into the army and was transferred directly to the army's manpower department. From the beginning, he excelled there too. To the best of my knowledge (and this is a very general description), he was required to deal with statistical models of manpower recruitment and was allowed to continue his studies for a second degree at Tel-Aviv University. As his discharge date approached, Eitan Bergles and Chaim Ben-Shachar suggested that he continue for the doctorate but at the same time, he received an offer to join the research department of Bank Ha'poalim. I don't understand why the two offers were mutually exclusive— maybe because Adam wanted to do everything perfectly and was concerned that two demanding jobs would interfere with each other—but after a short period of indecision, he chose Bank Ha'poalim. At the bank, he created models used to predict market behavior, for example, by forecasting the consumer price index. Within a short time, he became the favorite of Ya'akov Levison, the omnipotent manager of the bank, and was soon promoted to the international business department.

While he was in the army, Adam met a slender brunette soldier who was both incredibly beautiful and bright, by the name of Sophie Shamia. As far as I know, it was love at first sight and not long after being discharged from the army, Sophie and Adam got married. I do not know what Adam's previous experience with women was or if he had any girlfriends before Sophie, but their marriage was amazingly successful. Sophie was the daughter of a large, warm, and—so it seemed to me—quite matriarchal family of Iraqi origin, and Adam was warmly welcomed into it. Sophie showed warmth, closeness, and concern for my parents; however, Adam and Sophie's relationship with me was one of distance and cold correctness. The relationship became more and more distant and was severed almost completely after my brother died, when we would meet only at my parents' and Adam's memorials and later on, not even on those occasions. I was not happy about this situation, especially because I wanted to remain in contact with my brother's children. I wanted to be an uncle but my lack of mobility also contributed to the disconnection. However, when Sophie found out about my disease, she came to visit us in Jerusalem with Gil, the oldest of their two sons, and the former correct relationship was re-established.

Adam continued working in his chosen field and was sent to London and then to New York to run the bank's affairs outside Israel. After a while, Galit, Gil, and Tal, who are a little younger than my three children, were born. Sophie herself had a career as a manager in hi-tech industries and they were a perfect and wealthy couple. When Adam felt that the affairs at the bank were not conducted properly, he left it for the private sector and mainly brokered deals between international hi-tech companies, providing them with financial funding when needed. In a way, Adam followed in his father's footsteps, even though he did not deal with production and the extent of his business was completely different. He also succeeded in areas in which our father failed or had been caused to fail. But that was in a different world and the skills he had at his disposal were never available to my father. Even though he wasn't born in the country, he was not only a second-generation Israeli but was among those playing a part in the initial formation of the global and trans-national world order.

Adam helped Aunt Yardena who, for many years, was sick with cancer and went from one surgery to another. As much as he was able, he helped our father, whose health deteriorated continuously, our mother, and Uncle Imre, who was now an old man, by giving them the assistance that I, for obvious reasons, could not provide.

I grew really close to Adam for the first time when we sat *shiva* in my mother's house after my father died. My father had suffered stroke after stroke and died in a kind of sanatorium for the terminally ill. My mother did not want me to visit him at all, claiming that he wouldn't recognize me anyway. When we drove there from Jerusalem, we got caught in the traffic around the Bnei Brak industrial area and when we arrived, the visiting hours were already over. I said my final farewells to him only at the Holon cemetery, where my mother bought a joint burial plot, and they rest there today next to each other. Besides receiving those who came to comfort us, I took advantage of the time spent sitting *shiva* and, for the first and last time, had a heart-to-heart talk with Adam. Suddenly he felt a need to talk about himself, his actions, his family, and our family. He was a different Adam from the one I knew. At a certain point he made a remark whose significance I understood only after a few years: "I have accumulated enough assets to provide for my children and Sophie for the rest of their lives."

In September 1978, I arrived in the United States for my first sabbatical, with a two-year-old and a baby. We landed at La Guardia with numerous suitcases, and we knew that nobody would be waiting for us since both Adam and Sophie were at work. We took a taxi to their apartment in Manhattan and the doorman let us in. Two weeks before our arrival, Adam had gone to Boston, at my request, to rent us a cheap apartment about a fifteen-minute drive from my office at MIT. He even purchased for us a small but very efficient and reliable car. The next day, the holy Sabbath, we loaded all our belongings into the car and Adam drove us from New York to Boston with very few stops. The New England landscape and the colors of the trees were wonderful in the fall. After unloading and bringing up all our stuff, Adam flew straight back to New York. After about six months, I thought that if we were in the States, we ought to visit and get to know a little about the "Big Apple," and I planned a three-day trip. When I asked Adam on the phone when it would be convenient for him to host us, he was exceedingly reserved. It was clear that he wasn't happy about our upcoming visit. I thought that Sophie was responsible for this lack of enthusiasm and I was quite angry because I knew that they hosted members of the large Shamia family many times, and I actually forced our visit on Adam. We arrived in New York on a train which broke down on the way and we had to wait many hours for another locomotive to arrive. In addition, I felt sick during that trip, probably because of some stomach virus.

When we arrived at Adam and Sophie's apartment and I told them what had happened on the way, Adam shut himself up in the bedroom and we stayed by ourselves in the living room. Sophie said Adam wasn't feeling well and that we shouldn't go into his room. Adam stayed there for about twenty-four hours and we mainly played with little Galit and our children while Sophie prepared meals. In the meantime, I recovered from the virus and Adam came out of his room and asked what we wanted to do. The question surprised me a little since I had hoped that Adam would take care of tickets for some Broadway show, which was a must for every visitor to the city. "To visit the Guggenheim," I answered, referring to the well-known Museum of Modern Art. A quick phone call revealed that the Museum was closed for renovations. That same day, Adam took us for a car ride to Central Park and a few other places, like Wall Street (disappointing and surprising in its squalor) and the Twin Towers (Bin-Laden was still an unknown nightmare). The only attractions we managed to see in the Big Apple were the ones we saw during that strange drive. Diana tried to hide her disappointment and I pretended as if it was just rain and nothing more. We returned to Boston tired and humiliated.

The mystery was solved, in all its cruelty, after a decade. On the morning of January 10, 1989, a phone call woke me up. Adam called because he knew that I wanted to wish him a happy birthday, like every year. He told me, by the way, that he was hospitalized in London because he needed some sort of treatment, that he didn't feel "great" but he hoped "to overcome it." A thousand alarm bells went off in my head—Adam never talked that way. He also asked me not to tell our mother in order not to worry her. He said that Sophie was with him and the children were fine. "Take care of yourself," he said and I had a terrible feeling that this was a farewell blessing. This fear was confirmed quickly. Sophie called after a few days from London and said she had a request that was contrary to Adam's wishes. She told me that Adam had become sick years before with Hodgkin's disease (a type of blood cancer) and that the chemotherapy had stopped working but not before destroying his immune system. Therefore, he urgently needed a bone marrow transplant that could save his life. Indeed, a donation from me had the smallest chance of being rejected and would perhaps save his life but Adam refused to endanger me in view of the severe spinal cord injury I had already suffered. The next morning, I went straight to the Hadassah Ein Karem Hospital in order to have a sample taken from my spine. The process of sending a sample to London and analyzing it for compatibility was supposed to take about a week, but my little brother Adam's time had run out. Ruti, Sophie's sister, called after three days to announce that Adam had died and Sophie was making arrangements to fly the body back to Israel. I will never know whether donating at an earlier stage could have saved my brother's life. He was only forty-two at the time of his death. I felt like an orphan.

# 9

## MY BODY'S BETRAYAL

If there is anything new I have taught myself over the last two decades, it is to be tolerant and patient with myself, my body, and all the people around me and to accept my almost absolute dependence on them, especially on Diana. From the beginning of the 1980s, my physical condition deteriorated slowly but perceptibly. Not only free movement in space but even actions previously taken for granted like holding a book and leafing through it or picking up an object that has fallen on the floor have become difficult and require time and patience. My body is already almost non-responsive to me and even my ability to speak has diminished. My buttocks are often painful because of bed sores, the result of constant sitting or lying; sometimes even just sitting down hurts. However, I have learned to bear the pains well and they do not disturb my peace of mind, even if typing itself is accompanied by considerable soreness in my fingertips and is very slow (which is frustrating in itself) and full of mistakes, a fact that obliges me to rewrite several times the words I have already typed. However, it seems to me that my thoughts have never been as lucid and organized as they are now although one can never really know, and much less give an account of himself—especially not about his own clarity of mind.

I even have to be fed by Diana if I don't want to get myself and my surroundings dirty. I am also forced to depend on her for my most basic needs. I used to think that if I ever reached this state or a similar one, it would be the end of the world. But now I realize that it is not yet the case, thanks to Diana's devotion. This situation, however, has created a growing mutual dependence between me and my spouse. Thus since I am dependent on Diana, she has become dependent on me too. This dependence exacts a high emotional price from both of us, and perhaps more from Diana since she is the one obliged to "give the service" while I am the one who receives it. We have tried a few foreign workers to help Diana care for me and maintain the house, but the idea of having a stranger walking around the house most of the time and intruding on our privacy was uncomfortable for us.

As long as I am still able, although with increasing difficulty, to type with the fingers of my right hand—even if it entails substantial pain in my fingertips—I do not regard my physical condition as a complete disaster. Even so, I am afraid that soon I will become even more paralyzed and that it is possible that this book will be my last.

And then, suddenly, the disease that everyone dreads so much—cancer—struck me too and changed my life almost completely. Diana did everything she could for many years to prevent this: a healthy, balanced diet and all sorts of supplements meant to prevent cancer. For her, the illness itself and her "failure" in preventing it were a double blow. A reporter who interviewed me asked whether I became angry when I found out that I had cancer. Did I feel that this was a direct continuation of the same interminable process of my body's betrayal? I replied that I really did experience some kind of anger since I felt that it is "too early" and that I still have things to accomplish. However, I did not regard it as a "direct continuation" but rather as an accumulation. She continued to ask "how do you cope with the illness?" I answered something like: "Since this is a new situation for me, I am still figuring out what to do and how to act and if it's at all worth continuing to 'cope.' Life is not a goal in itself. A minimal quality of life is also needed." After having gone through seven months of chemotherapy and side effects too difficult for me to bear, I derived some practical conclusions from this approach. At a certain stage I decided to cease the cancer treatment since, in any case, it could not cure me but would only prolong the pain and the time spent at the hospital, which is a very difficult place to be in. I want to leave this world in my own bed, at home, surrounded by my loved ones. Nevertheless, I refused to receive guests, even my closest friends, because I do not like "farewell visits." I allowed only Sidra Ezrachi to visit me for twenty minutes after she actually begged to see me. The meeting was extremely emotional. My relationship with her lasted from the time I arrived at the university until now and was unique in its closeness.

For nearly a year before my terminal diagnosis was made, I did not feel as well as in the past. I would tire quickly, at times to the point of total exhaustion. My ability to concentrate and to work productively decreased. It was sometimes more difficult for me to speak and to make myself understood. After dozens of medical tests which shed no light on the matter, a hematologist suggested the possibility that it could be a rare form of blood cancer. I immediately underwent (twice to make sure) the appropriate tests and the suspicions were confirmed. That was the diagnosis. When I asked about the prognosis, the doctors looked at each other and said that there was no way to know but that half the patients have a life expectancy of less than five years while the other half have more than that. They also said that it is impossible to know in advance how my body, with its many problems, would respond to the treatment. The chances for a recovery were only "theoretical," as my personal physician said, and the only questions were how long life could be prolonged and what its quality would be.

Within a few days of receiving the diagnosis, I started chemotherapy. The treatment was extremely difficult for me. I was almost entirely unable to function for over a week and often had a high fever. The fever led my doctors to suspect that I had an infection somewhere in my body. It is well known that cancer weakens the immune system and most patients die from secondary complications rather than from the cancer itself. Once again, I went through a series of unpleasant tests but no infection was found. Nevertheless, I was "privileged" to receive large doses of intravenous antibiotics. All this went on until a doctor found out that "my" type of cancer is sometimes accompanied by bouts of high fever. My entire way and quality of life had suddenly changed. It was clear to me that in spite of my love for both the students and my role as a teacher, I would not be able to teach any more under these circumstances. I asked to retire and started planning what I could research and write about on those days in which I would be able to work.

As I mentioned earlier, I was born with cerebral palsy, whose main manifestations were involuntary movements, speech impairment, difficulties in walking, and unaesthetic distortions of the face which sometime seem like a sneering smile that has more than once hurt people who were unfamiliar with me. However, in the first stage of life, up to about the age of twenty-five, my physical condition improved and I gained more and more control over my body. For example, until the age of seventeen, I would pee in my pants every time someone or something made me laugh or touched any sensitive part of my body. Afterwards, my physical condition improved and remained stable, and I could function almost like any "normal" person. I never perceived my disability as my own problem but primarily as a problem that some people have in dealing with me, the "different," while my role was to help them do that. The range of responses I got from people who didn't know me intimately was exceedingly varied. There were those who regarded me as a martyr who possessed almost supernatural qualities, while others treated me like a mentally retarded person and spoke to me slowly, loudly, and using simple language to help me understand. There were also those who feared that my condition could be contagious. I remember that I once went to see a popular movie at the cinema in Ramat Gan; however, when I arrived, the box office was already closed since the tickets had sold out. A woman showed up at that point to sell tickets and many people thronged around her. As usual, I stood off to one side and was not part of the crowd. The woman looked around, caught my eye, and turned to me. "Would you like a ticket?" I indicated that I was interested and then a complicated process started. She asked someone from the crowd to pass me the ticket and to take my money and pass it to her, lest there might be any physical contact between us. Another time, I stood by the display window of a bookshop and a kind woman came up to me and handed me a ten lira bill, not a small sum in those days. It took me a few seconds to figure out what she meant. People who already knew me were curious to know if my disability was of genetic origin or the result of some epidemic disease like polio. I was already trained to lecture about cerebral palsy and its causes, which originate mainly from the lack of oxygen supply to the brain at the time of a difficult or early delivery. In my case, the damaged area was the one responsible for the control of motor coordination. Until the mid-1970s, I still met doctors who showed an amazing ignorance about the condition.

In the poorer neighborhoods of Jerusalem, groups of unruly children would follow me calling "Abu, Abu." To this day, I do not know who or what this "Abu" was but most likely, they knew someone with cerebral palsy whose name or nickname was Abu. In general, people used to identify me with any other person they had ever met who had C.P. and not always for the better. Once I almost got beaten up by a taxi driver who was convinced that I had given him a bad check. Another time, someone felt deeply offended when I didn't recognize him as a traveling companion on a trip to Australia (which, unfortunately, I never visited). What made him lose his temper was my ingratitude, since he had helped "me" so much during the trip.

But even people who knew me would fall into the generalization trap and I don't blame them. Several years before I attended the Gymnasium, a pupil with C.P. named Joshua studied there. Joshua, who lived with his widowed mother and in the shadow of his deceased father, who had been a prominent man, apparently caused the teachers serious trouble because of his eccentric and aggressive personality. Some of them decided by analogy that I was like him and were, at least initially, reserved and hostile towards me.

I met Joshua later on at the university dormitory. Upon his arrival, he became the laughingstock of the dormitories when he demanded emphatically from the supervisor to have his degree (B.A.) marked next to his name on the door, a request that was actually carried out on the spot. Joshua had studied at Bar-Ilan University, where he had been a "protégé" of Baruch Kurtzweil. The two were probably very much alike. A big fight broke out between them, the reasons for which I don't know, and Kurtzweil refused to grant him the degree. Joshua and his mother took legal action and a compromise was reached—the Ministry of Education bestowed the title "university graduate" on Joshua—which, it seems to me, is the only such case in the history of higher education in Israel. He arrived in Jerusalem with his degree in order to study library science and to prepare a comprehensive bibliography of Kurzweil's writings. Maybe he wanted to take revenge on him too. There is no doubt that for Joshua, whose degree was achieved with great difficulty, it was appropriate that this achievement should be recognized and honored. However, in a place where some students had already finished their second degree while others were close to finishing their third one, his was a ridiculous demand. They could not understand Joshua and he was incapable of understanding them. He didn't form any relationships with any of the students living in the dormitory and after a year or so, he disappeared from the Jerusalem scene and I don't know what happened to him. The only time I tried to enter his room and talk to him, he looked frightened and shouted at me to leave. His mother subsequently contacted the residence director of the dormitory, complaining that I had tried to steal something from her son and requesting that I be removed from the dorm.

I introduce the story of Joshua as an example of the difficulty many people who suffer from C.P have in functioning in their social environment, a phenomenon which I had encountered many times when I was engaged in "public activity" on behalf of the organization for the disabled. Since people are either deterred from having or do not know how to have "normal relationships" with the disabled, who themselves may not have learned how to function socially, a vicious cycle is created. Some of the disabled withdraw into their own emotional shell and create a strange inner world which is significantly disconnected from reality. This world vacillates between self-pity and feelings of inferiority and megalomania accompanied by arrogance or any combination of these. However, there are also quite a few disabled people who break out of this cycle and their disability does not become the main trait characterizing them.

I have no idea when or at what stage I began to understand that I was different from others and not a "normal child," but it seems to me that this was a gradual process of discovery, drawing conclusions, and of trial and error. I had nobody to discuss this with until Uri Brill showed up and I became active in Shtelem. At the university, I used to initiate informal conversations with young people when I saw that the subject was on their minds or bothered them. From my arrival there, I consciously decided to be ready to converse openly and freely on every subject related to my disability, but I made an effort not to unnecessarily embarrass people. From those conversations I also learned a lot about myself and about how people view me and my condition.

I decided to behave the same way also in regard to the cancer. Before handing in my request to retire (after about forty years of service at the university), I sent an email memo to all the department staff and explained the reason for my decision.

It is almost self-evident that my political and ideological opponents tried to use also my physical condition as a pretext for de-legitimizing my ideas. Thus, for example, on February 7, 2002, someone using the name Ian posted the following comment in a discussion group on the Middle East and Israel: "Kimmerling is badly disabled and as expected in this situation, he is a bitter man. Unfortunately, he pours his bitterness out on his people and has created for himself a reputation as a quisling and a self-hating Israeli Jew. I can understand why he hates himself, but he risks the lives of innocent human beings with his hatred for his nation and his people." In response to the remark of someone in the discussion group that not all disabled people are like that, Ian agreed and added that indeed it would be better if I were to direct my efforts toward assisting doctors who favor mercy killing. Seldom have I come across such vituperative writings, which even appeared on university walls, but it has to be said that I am not the only one who is frequently attacked and not the only one at whom unrestrained hatred is flung (they have lists with addresses for hate-letters spread via the internet), especially by religious Jews of American origin and fundamentalist Christians. Almost from the beginning, I decided not to respond to these kinds of attacks, a fact that usually throws them more off balance.

I also heard about colleagues who circulated the opinion that I was retained and promoted at the university only out of compassion. I decided not to respond to these slanders either, in spite of the fact that they probably did cause some damage to my reputation. However, they did not really harm my local and international reputation in the long run. Still it can be assumed that if I had not had to invest time and energy coping with the challenges posed by my physical handicap and had pursued a career in academia and research while being in a normal condition, my achievements in both fields could have been much greater, because I would have had more resources at my disposal. In addition, my ability to participate in international conferences was limited and, consequently, so was my opportunity to create the networks of acquaintances and connections which are some of the prerequisites for establishing a reputation and succeeding. Yet, this argument and its contrary are mere conjectures.

The development of virtual communication through the internet was, for me, an efficient but partial substitute for mobility. There is no doubt, however, that my disability badly damaged the "public" part of my activity since it prevented me from appearing in the electronic media (television and radio) and I had to content myself with writing newspaper articles (especially in *Haaretz*, whose circulation is low but which has considerable influence).

Menachem Friedman arranged for me to teach two classes at Bar-Ilan University during the 1983–1984 academic year. Although they did not keep their initial promises and my salary was paltry, my growing family—our third daughter Na'ama was two years old—demanded additional income. I was also happy, considering the institution, to teach two "subversive" subjects at Bar-Ilan, namely, the Israeli–Arab conflict and sociobiology. I would get up early in the morning and take the bus—via Bnei Brak—to the station opposite Bar-Ilan, cross the upper bridge, and arrive at the department. The trip was quite exhausting and the bus was full of ultra-Orthodox families with lots of screaming children. After teaching two courses almost consecutively, the trip back was difficult for me and as time went by, I noticed that I was barely able to move my legs or stand on them. My physical difficulties increased with time and we decided to examine the cause since it was no longer possible to explain it as simply the result of fatigue.

Almost a year went by before we discovered the reason for this serious decline in my physical abilities. It became apparent that two vertebrae in my cervical spine were displaced and pressed on my spinal cord. It was clear that if this trend continued, I would be completely paralyzed within a short time and consequently all of my physiological functions would cease, one after the other. This problem was probably unrelated to cerebral palsy. However, my basic disability was definitely relevant to the fact that it wasn't possible to fuse the vertebrae firmly together since my involuntary movements could break them and leave me completely and immediately paralyzed. We could not find a doctor in Israel who was willing to take the risk and operate on me. One of them said to me in the bluntest way, "If you were a nobody, I would cut you today, but you're Kimmerling…"

Then we started an international search. My brother Adam took the x-rays to a number of centers in the U.S and in Europe and in every place they looked at them, the response was the same: we can try and operate, but the risk is much greater than the possible benefits. Japanese articles raved about impressive successes in the field. However, Yoram Diamant, a friend of the family and professor of medicine, cooled our enthusiasm when he told us about the common Japanese habit of reporting in medical journals astounding successes which never actually happened.

With the complete encouragement and support of Diana, I decided not to give up hope. With Aliza Olmert acting as mediator—at the time, she was still a family friend—we contacted Dr. Rapoport, who was then the deputy head of the Department of Neuro-Surgery at the Hadassah Ein Kerem Hospital. Rapaport suggested an intermediate approach: not to join the vertebrae firmly but to cut their back part, the lamina. In this way, at least part of the pressure on my spinal cord was supposed to be relieved. This surgery, if successful, would slow my physical deterioration. By how much? Rapaport either did not know or refused to commit himself, but he too was not particularly optimistic. If I had been told, in the summer of 1985 when this discussion was held, that more than twenty years later I would still be as active as I am today, even affected by cancer, I would have been a happy person then. It seems to me that this awareness helps me now to accept the cancer as I do or hope to do. Nevertheless, it dismays me when I still have so many projects to complete and I am about fifteen years short of attaining the average life expectancy for Israeli men.

I awoke from my spinal surgery in unbearable pain caused mainly by the rigid cast in which my head and neck had been placed. I asked that the cast be removed but the people around me refused. I asked for pain medication but they refused that too. I begged and cried. I asked to see Rapoport, but he was in no hurry to come. The only thing I remember from those hours is the pain. After what felt like an eternity, my surgeon arrived and agreed to give me a pain killer. However, he announced that I would remain in the cast forever in order to prevent sudden jarring of the head. I told him that I had not been informed about this beforehand and we hadn't agreed on it and I would not be able to live while encased in it. He claimed that I had no choice. The argument between us continued, I don't remember for how long, but finally Rapoport gave up, disavowing all responsibility for the results. In any case, I lay there as unable to move as if I had been tied up. I was convinced that my life had ended. I was wrong. All this happened during the 1985 summer vacation and by that autumn, I stood in front of my classes teaching, although I leaned on a tri-legged metal walking stick I nicknamed "Dreyfus."

About a week after the surgery, I was transferred to the rehabilitation department of the hospital on Mount Scopus. Thus, at least physically, I was closer to the university. There, the staff almost forced me to stand on my feet again. At first they brought me miniature crutches, but those did not help me since I didn't have enough strength in my arms. Nurses, physiotherapists, occupational therapists, and also a lovely volunteer for the national service would support me as I walked along the hospital corridors. It was exhausting, not only for me but for them too. Once a week, the medical staff and senior nurses would gather and discuss the therapeutic plan for each patient. Moreover, most of the patients undergoing rehabilitation would encourage and challenge each other.

I remember two particularly sad cases there. The first case was that of Ambassador Shlomo Argov, who had been shot in London. His attempted assassination had served as a pretext for the First Lebanon War, just as the kidnapping of two soldiers was used as grounds for the Second Lebanon War. He stayed by himself in an adjacent room. Sometimes, he was taken outside the ward to the small but amazingly well-tended garden and I would follow him there once I became able, although with difficulty, to walk. I tried to communicate with him but he would stare into space and didn't appear to be aware of anything. The second case was that of a young policeman who suffered from the same neck problem as I did. He had undergone almost the same surgery with another surgeon the same week that I had mine. In spite of his young age and the fact that he didn't suffer from cerebral palsy, they were not able to get him on his feet, at least not while I was in the ward. "A matter of bad luck," the nurses whispered to each other, and they seemed to be referring to a surgeon's error.

Meanwhile, a drama occurred at home. I demanded that Diana stay with me almost all the time; I preferred to be taken care of by her rather than by the nurses. Naturally, I was focused on myself and the difficulties I was experiencing and I was not able to think about or be aware of anything else around me. My son Eli', aged seven, asked Diana if father was going to die and Diana didn't have an answer. She was afraid that if she denied it and said I would be "okay" and it didn't happen, she would lose her son's trust forever. Shira', my nine-year-old daughter, tried to cook, clean, and take care of her younger brother and sister but the task was too big for her. Diana expected my parents to come and help her, but my father was already half-paralyzed and my mother wasn't young any more. In despair, she turned to Adam, without knowing that he himself was incurably ill, and asked that he and Sophie take the children for a few days since they had a spacious villa in Herzliya. Adam came and took the children but they returned within a day. They were scared and Shira' even started throwing up, frightening Sophie. They couldn't find anything in common with Adam's children or adjust to Sophie's rigid rules. They demanded categorically to return home.

Eventually, I was released from the hospital and even the prolonged tenure process ended successfully when I received a position as a senior lecturer, mainly due to my new book which described and analyzed Israeli society during wartime. It seemed as though life had returned to a normal and stable routine.

In any case, I decided to accept my friend Joel Migdal's invitation and in the summer of 1987, we left for a sabbatical in Seattle. Seattle was a comfortable and pleasant place in every respect and I was asked to teach only one class there. As opposed to Boston, even Diana felt comfortable in Seattle and fell in love with the place and its people. However, there was a catch. The long flight damaged my spine and there was a significant decline in my physical condition. I partially overcame the problem by purchasing a scooter. The tiny vehicle, similar to a motorbike and powered by rechargeable batteries, significantly improved my quality of life. It was quite amusing to find out that even perfectly healthy people envied my ability to "gallop" between and within buildings on campus in Seattle and, later on, in Mount Scopus. The immediate problem was that ramps were often non-existent in spite of clear laws on the topic and my scooter was unable to navigate stairs and curbs. In the long run, since I used the scooter too much, I "forgot" how to walk by myself and my muscles atrophied more quickly than expected, which led me to use a real wheelchair because it was safer. The fact that I was almost always sitting continuously caused bed sores which seriously affected my quality of life. However, my physical condition didn't matter that much to me because I could still use my mind. During that same sabbatical, I completed one book and sent it to the publisher and also started research for another one which, in time, marked a turning point in my professional career, while positively affecting my status in the Israeli and global academy.

# 10

## DIANA

Fanny was actually my first real girlfriend. She had a quiet, classical beauty, fragile and gentle. Her left hand was partially paralyzed from polio. She was of Columbian origin, lived in the opposite corridor of the dormitory, and studied library science. We met many times in the dormitory kitchen, but it was difficult to start a conversation with her. At first I attributed this to the shyness of a girl who grew up in an aristocratic home. After she finally responded to my courtship, I even took her home for a weekend and my parents liked her a lot. However, within a short while, it became clear that Fanny was carrying a heavy secret that she never told me about and didn't know how to deal with. One night at the dormitory, I was contacted and told in a very emotional way that Fanny had climbed out onto the roof of a building and was threatening to commit suicide. By the time I got there, someone had already brought her down and I walked her back to her room. As soon as we went in, Fanny attacked me, grabbed my throat, and started strangling me. I began losing consciousness. This delicate and quiet girl had terrifying strength. Just in the nick of time, her roommate walked in and forcibly took her off me, practically saving my life. An ambulance had already been called since the residence director knew more about Fanny's mental state than I did. She suffered from schizophrenia and was taken straight to Talbieh hospital. At first, I wasn't allowed to visit her and was told that she was in the closed ward.

After two weeks, I started going to the carefully tended hospital garden and would bring her different things that she liked, but Fanny was still under the influence of strong medications. She did not know and did not remember what happened, but she felt ashamed that I was meeting her in such a place. And in reality, those visits were very difficult for me and not only because of Fanny. There were many faces there which I knew from the university—students and lecturers—some of whom were catatonic. I felt committed to Fanny but when she came back to the dormitories, I didn't know how to relate to her. Fanny herself solved the problem by distancing herself from me on her own initiative, apparently because she was embarrassed by the fact that she hadn't told me in advance about the problem, although there may have been other reasons too.

Another young woman who didn't tell me about her condition (but her brother, a friend of mine who really wanted to "fix us up," did) was Ilana. Ilana was a petite young woman with a perfect figure. Her face, however, did not match her beautiful body. She was amazingly intelligent and a master of sharp-witted responses. Ilana suffered from epilepsy (which even then could be controlled by medications), accompanied by bouts of depression which led her to a number of suicide attempts until, finally, she succeeded. Ilana was quite erudite and more than once she tried to persuade me to commit suicide with her. "A person in your condition doesn't have a chance to survive in this world anyway. Who will offer you a job? Who will marry you? Ultimately you will end up in an institution. Precisely because you are so clever and erudite, life will bring you only suffering." Ilana placed a cruel mirror in front of me and asked existential questions which, although they stemmed from her mental state, could not be ignored, at least not then, when I myself was also bothered by those same questions. However, I tried to give them an optimistic response. The question "Who will offer you a job?" would be on the agenda years later in my more serious relationship with another woman.

Ruthie was a young, shapely woman, blonde and brimming with the joy of life. I met her in the dorms too. Although she had no interest in intellectual pursuits and even despised them, I still had a lot of things in common with her because of her humor and deeply ingrained non-conformity. She was the most liberated woman I had met until then—this without any feminist ideology and long before this term was used in public discourse. Ruthie would hug and smooch me in public; it seems to me that she was defying the whole world. Later on, we lived together for a while in my apartment in Kiryat Yovel. I was very fond of her but neither of us wanted our relationship to be too serious. In 1985, while I was in the Hadassah rehabilitation center after undergoing the difficult surgery on my spine, Ruthie would wait until my wife left. Then she would come to me, force me out of bed and onto my feet, and let me lean on her while I walked along the hospital corridors.

The two women I "almost" married were Sarah and Rivka. Sarah was my first research assistant at the university. She was my height—I mean short—and a beautiful brunette, born in Tunisia and raised in Paris. There was a story about two men in Paris who had fought a duel because of her. With her beauty, it was difficult not to fall in love with her, which is indeed what happened. Sarah loved me but with reservations and claimed that the only thing that bothered her and made her hesitate to marry me was the future problems our children would have as a result of my being so disabled. I suggested that we consult a psychologist about the subject and we chose a well-known professional in the field. He listened to Sarah and told her what I myself thought but didn't dare say: "Children who are born and grow up in a certain reality know how to deal with it well. You are projecting your own concerns on the children who haven't been born yet…" However, what I didn't know was that Sarah was romantically involved at the same time with a handsome neurologist, a Canadian Jew who was doing his residency in Israel. One day, Sarah disappeared into thin air. A little while later, she called me from Toronto: "Baruch, I'm sorry. I am going to marry Peter. We will stay friends." And for years we actually did stay friends. In the spring of 1979, while I was in Boston, Sarah and Peter invited me to Toronto and were wonderful hosts to me. On that occasion, I was introduced to Sarah's doctoral tutor, a brilliant and productive sociologist by the name of Robert Brim. Later on, I developed a close friendship with him until I severed it because of a number of important promises he failed to keep. Sarah herself was accepted into the Canadian academia and eventually ended her relationship with me.

Before I explain how I opened a marriage file at the Rabbinate with Rivka yet never married her, it seems proper to write about Rina and the strange connection between these two women and a third one. Rina also lived in the student dorms. She was not only beautiful but aristocratic too. As the daughter of a well-known and wealthy gynecologist from Tel-Aviv, she did not associate with ordinary mortals. She radiated the self-confidence of someone who was sure that she was the perfect woman. I had met "princesses" at school but none even came close to having Rina's royal airs. At a certain stage, Udi and I were competing for her heart. Udi, who later became a prominent politician, was in those days a law student, who was desperately in love with Rina. I courted Rina too, but almost only for sport since I assumed that my chances of winning her were nil. Rina, perhaps sensing my cavalier attitude toward her and maybe also because she enjoyed torturing young Udi, came to my room late one evening and suggested that we start going steady. During the next two days, no one on campus was happier than I was. The next morning, we had breakfast at the cafeteria together, all cuddled up. On the third day, before we consummated our "relationship," Rina announced that it was over, that we were no longer boyfriend and girlfriend but rather just friends, and she refused to explain why. But Udi too failed to win Rina's heart and as partners in defeat, a certain friendship developed between us.

Several years later, when my articles appeared on the editorial page of the newspaper *Haaretz* more frequently, Udi, who was at the start of his political career, would call me with his comments, objections, and sometimes even agreement. From time to time, these were delivered on behalf of Shmuel Tamir, for whom Udi was the parliamentary assistant.

One day he called me because he wanted to tell me that not only had he married but he also had a newborn daughter. He invited me to visit. We set a date when he would come to pick me up. And Udi indeed had much to be proud of. His wife Aliza is a charming woman with a well-developed sense of humor, a social worker by training, artistically talented, and open-minded. We found a common language immediately. This friendship lasted for a number of years. When a sewage pipe burst in our house, Aliza suggested that we bring the babies to her for a number of days, and she even nursed our son Eli'. Over time, the contact between us ended, maybe because as Udi became more politically prominent, we no longer fit into their social milieu, with their social status, or with Udi's position in Israeli politics. At that time, I was already beginning to be labeled a "radical leftist." But it is also possible that Aliza was hurt by my criticism of the manuscript of the play *Piano Fantasy* which she sent me before it was presented at the Cameri Theatre. In academia, when one asks for a critique, one gets it. In inter-personal relationships, it is probably different—it may be that one is expected to approve and praise.

For a while, Aliza "adopted" me and it was within this context that she played matchmaker. Rivka, a young woman of American origin, was writing her doctorate on Judaism. She was intelligent and had a sense of irony; however, she also suffered somewhat from low self-esteem accompanied by status-consciousness about her family pedigree. Her father was a professor of Judaic Studies and at that time a well known academic public activist. He was highly respected in Jerusalem and people were in awe of him because he controlled scholarships and sabbaticals in the U.S. Rivka admired her father and was seeking a partner who would be like him in status, perhaps because she did not believe she could ever achieve it on her own. I started dating Rivka and even meeting her friends from the various departments which dealt with Judaism. Most of them didn't make a great impression on me. After a short time, Rivka moved into my apartment in Kiryat Yovel and the next month we decided to get married. Rivka informed her parents in New York about the engagement and within days her father landed in Israel to inspect his prospective son-in-law. That was a truly surrealistic and grotesque scene. After a short conversation, her father asked to see my scientific "output." He stayed up all night reading, possibly because of jet lag, and the following morning decreed: "He has potential," as if he was a professional committee at the university. He told me that he was not happy that his daughter had chosen such a disabled man but that he respected her decision. I thanked him for his sincerity. After consulting her father, Rivka and I decided on a date for the wedding and went to register with the Rabbinate.

When Rivka's friends realized that our relationship was serious, they organized a committee to rescue their impetuous friend from the bitter fate of marriage to a cripple. Her friends knew how to play on Rivka's weak spots: he may be the cleverest person in the world but forget about him having an academic career or any career at all. Rivka withstood the incessant pressure heroically for about a week. However, she wanted me to help her repel the attack by promising her that I would be an outstanding professor at the Hebrew University. But how could I make such a promise to her when I didn't even have a doctorate yet and I myself wasn't sure that I could have an academic career or even that I wanted one? Rivka packed her things and announced that the wedding was off. Within a short time, Rivka married another doctoral student whose thesis, as far as I know, was on Dutch Jewry. He never did receive a position at the university and eventually became a professional photographer and a right-wing propagandist. For years, Rivka avoided running into me in the corridors of the Mount Scopus campus and her husband attacked me personally, accusing me in a number of articles that he published in Jewish journals of being an anti-Zionist.

One good result came out of the broken engagement. During that summer of 1974, I channeled my fury and frustration into the writing of my doctoral dissertation. By the beginning of 1975, I held the honorable degree I had longed for and about which I will write more later.

However, I did more than write my doctoral dissertation that summer. After the end of my relationship with Rivka, who escaped from me almost from under the wedding canopy, two additional "options" presented themselves. Zili was a plump but very feminine and pleasant girl who had no sense of humor. We dated a number of times and I felt her hesitation and puzzlement, even though she did not talk about them. In any event, one day when I went to the Kaplan library, the monitor on duty stopped me at the entrance. Her job was to make sure that no one "pinched" books from the library and she asked for the newspapers I had with me, assuming that I didn't come to the library to read them. I gave her the newspapers and as I left, we started talking and I invited her for coffee at my house. The truth is that I already had my eye on her. She almost always wore a red miniskirt which emphasized her chiseled legs and her overall femininity. She introduced herself as Diana and it became clear that she was newly arrived in Israel. She came from Italy and was born in Libya. She was Yeshayahu Leibowitz's doctoral student and was trying to formulate a dissertation topic in the field of the philosophy of biology. Previously, we had had some random encounters, mostly on the bus, and she had asked for my advice about how to preserve the modest savings she had accumulated from inflation.[1] I also learned that we were neighbors—she lived at the Stern Dormitories, while my apartment was located a few hundred meters from there.

I prepared chicken thighs cooked in wine with pears and various side dishes for her visit. About half an hour before the appointed time, Diana called to announce that she wouldn't be able to come since she still needed to study for an important exam for which she didn't feel adequately prepared. To this day, I have never asked what happened with that exam. I replied that it would be good for her to take a break for half an hour, to come and have a cup of coffee, and I also promised that even if she wanted to stay longer I would kick her out. Neither of us kept the promise and Diana actually remained with me from the moment she crossed the threshold of my apartment until the writing of these very lines more than thirty years later. This was on March 23, 1975, and for years we celebrated that day as a family holiday which we called "Coffee Day."

Diana revealed herself to be a warm, open, amazingly intelligent woman with a sense of humor matching my own. She had acquired a broad classical education and a vast knowledge in natural science while her main love to this day is mathematics. She has a natural opposition to anything that smells of religion or nationalism. In Libya, she vehemently refused to learn Arabic since the teacher used to say "You are under Arab rule now and you must speak Arabic, not Italian!" although she regrets it now. She knew almost nothing about Judaism or Jewish and Israeli history and never showed any interest in learning more about them, except for the Holocaust, by which she is profoundly affected. Perhaps her opposition to religion and nationalism is related to the fact that in her original family, religious precepts and festivities were imposed on her while she was still a child, after she had already consolidated her insights about atheism and her attitudes toward religion, race, and ethnic differences.

We talked through the night and as morning approached, we fell asleep together. A few days later, she brought all of her few belongings to my place and we began to live together. Later on, when I told Diana about my failed relationships with Sarah and Rivka, she knew even then to answer promptly that those were their failures, not mine. After about two months, we set a wedding date in August.

Diana Aidan's background had a very tough story woven into it, most of which I heard on our first night together. She was born in 1945 to an Italian family near Benghazi, Libya. Her grandfather was an Italian army officer who lived in that former Italian colony. His son, Diana's father, became a very wealthy local merchant. Her mother was a Libyan orphan. In those days, domestic violence was not discussed publicly and Diana told one of the most terrible stories of abuse I have ever heard. Her father, a physically huge man, would beat his slim, fragile, and unusually beautiful wife until she lost consciousness. He also beat his three children. He had total control in the house. He allocated a minuscule budget for the family while he lived a life of ostentatious luxury outside the house and squandered money on his many friends. He claimed his daughter for himself by declaring "When your mother dies, you will replace her." He tried to prevent Diana from studying, and she had to invent ingenious ways to overcome his opposition—such as studying at night on the outside stairway when everyone else was sleeping. When I tried once to question my brother-in-law Angelo, who is one year older than Diana, on his opinion of what happened in their house, he was not inclined to talk about it and said unwillingly, while both confirming his sister's story and defending his father, "Look, that's the way things were in Libya then." I was not totally convinced by this explanation.

When Diana finished elementary school, she wanted to attend high school. This required going to another city as no Italian secondary schools for girls were available in Benghazi. Because her father opposed this, she took the initiative—a trait that characterized her throughout her life—and with her mother's encouragement, went to the house of one of his friends and threatened her father to reveal to all his friends and the members of the Jewish community what was really going on at home. That was her father's most vulnerable point because the family had to reflect an image of perfection since he was regarded as a consummate gentleman.

Thus the child-adolescent was sent to study and live among strangers six hundred miles away from home. At first she lived in a convent outside town, bicycling to school. Then she wandered from one rented room to another, living on a meager allowance and studying at the Italian Scientific Liceum in Tripoli. It was there that she acquired her excellent classical and scientific education. When she finished high school, she returned to Benghazi, but then her father decided to transfer his money to Italy. According to Libyan law, he could only do so if he had family in Italy to send the money to. This is why he sent his wife and children to Italy while taking care, of course, to keep his money away from them. He himself remained in Benghazi in the meantime.

During that first night, Diana talked about her departure by ship as one of the happiest times of her life. The radiant young woman danced to exhaustion while all the young men on the ship courted her. "But you won't be able to dance with me," I teased her. "Do you really think that this is what is important to me?" She pierced me with a reproving look.

When the family arrived in Naples, they supported themselves with great difficulty from "donations" that her father would sometimes send them. Since university studies in Italy were free for her, Diana began studying biology. She also practiced fencing at the university armory and became an excellent fencer and a member of the university fencing team. The team was preparing for an international student competition in Hungary when she was asked during a political discussion if she was not a Demo Christian. She explained that she was a Jew and a socialist. Her trip was immediately cancelled and she never managed to have fencing lessons again. Diana was used to fighting. When Arab children in Libya attacked her, she would pull out a heavy ink bottle encased in a long sock and defend herself. But when it came to this kind of racism and anti-Semitism, she didn't know what to do and she had no one to complain to either. When the 1967 war broke out, the Israeli victory reverberated even in Naples. She learned more about Israel while fervidly reading—like everyone else—Leon Uris's *Exodus*.

Suddenly, her father announced that he too was leaving Libya and joining the family. Diana did not want to return to living under the terror that her father inflicted on their household and she made a crucial decision for the whole family. She turned to the Jewish Agency and asked them to help her and her family immigrate to Israel because "There, certainly, after all that the Jews have been through, there will be no racism." Needless to say, her disappointment later on was boundless.

On July 23, 1967, Diana, her mother, and her two brothers arrived in Israel and received an apartment in one of the ugly, squalid housing projects in Kiryat Yovel.[2] That winter was a very cold one. They had no heating or interior doors and Diana's mother, who already had asthma, collapsed. Diana and her older brother worked at odd jobs. Diana worked at the archeological excavations of the Southern Wall and later on at the botanical gardens of the university. She wanted very much to continue her studies and was even sent to learn Hebrew. Since her grades for the courses she had completed in Italy were not recognized by the Hebrew University, she was forced to study everything from the beginning in order to complete her first degree in biology. During the "pursuits" in the Jordan Valley, helicopters on their way to the Hadassah Hospital flew over their heads night and day. Her mother, who did not understand a word of Hebrew nor anything about the strange culture she had suddenly encountered, understood precisely the meaning of the helicopters: this was not a place in which to live, only a place to die. She took both her sons and returned to Italy. Diana preferred to stay and finish her studies since she had discovered by then that the Hebrew University was much better than the one in Naples. In addition, she did not want to give up the apartment, believing that her mother and brothers would eventually come back and would need a place to live in.

In Italy, her brothers Angelo and Enrico worked on a farm to support themselves and their mother whose health, and especially her eyesight, continued to deteriorate, most likely because her husband's beatings had caused her retinas to detach. In June of 1969, Diana received the terrible news that her mother, Julia, had been hit by a truck. It seems to me that, to this day, she has pangs of conscience for abandoning her mother and perhaps even feelings of guilt for her death. Her two sons buried her in Naples and returned to Israel.

Diana finished her studies in neurophysiology with honors; however, in spite of the fact that the subject fascinated her, she gave it up, partly because of the turbid atmosphere prevalent throughout the research community at the Hebrew University and Hadassah Hospital, but mainly because of the animal abuse it involved.

The younger brother, Enrico, became successful: he was in Kibbutz Givat Brenner for a while, volunteered with the paratroopers, and learned many languages by himself. Today he is the manager of several casino hotels in Greece and Morocco. Since he is located on the extreme right wing of the Israeli political spectrum, we do not have a close relationship with him.

The older brother, Angelo, remained without a profession and stability, even though he married a "woman of valor" and had four daughters. Angelo is self-taught, and has mastered an amazing though very selective amount of information. He is a member of one of the tiny political parties of the ultra-radical left and over time his ideas have become more extreme and even eccentric.

Immediately after her mother died, a special friendship developed between Diana and one of her fellow students, David (Dudu) Avrahami. During the 1973 war, he was killed and his buddy lost all four limbs. Diana decided that if they sacrificed themselves that way "for her," she had no right to desert the country which, even then, she had preferred to leave. This was a macabre and naive patriotism from which she has long since recovered.

On August 12, 1975, Diana and I married in a ceremony followed by a very modest family luncheon, in a private room at the faculty club ("Beit Belgia" in the Givat Ram campus). My parents, brother, uncle, aunt, Diana's brothers, and Tamar and Menachem Friedman, who were close friends of mine at the time, were present. Menachem also served as the photographer. Two days later we held a reception in our new apartment on French Hill for "everyone and his brother" and, indeed, everyone came. It seems to me that the highlight of the occasion occurred when I asked Yishayahu Leibowitz to install a silver *mezuzah* which was a genuine work of art we received from our friends Sidra and Yaron Ezrakhi as a wedding gift. If my memory does not deceive me, that was the last *mezuzah* which was installed on our doorframe because I saw in the *mezuzah*, and especially in the habit of kissing it, an expression of the paganism that still exists in Judaism. When I moved into my new office on Mount Scopus—I guess that was in 1985—the first thing I did was to remove the *mezuzah* from the doorframe of my office in a sort of private ceremony.

Diana spoke a lot about her desire to be welcomed and accepted into my family so that she could have a family to replace the one she had lost. She and my father developed a relationship of love and mutual appreciation. Diana also liked my Uncle Imre. The relationship between my brother and her was correct and since his death, she speaks of him fondly. However, she was not as successful with Aunt Yardena, a bitter and aggressive woman. My mother, who grew up and lived in a different world with other norms, believed that the man's role was to support the family financially while the wife had to do everything else. She refused to even acknowledge the extra burdens that fell on my wife as a result of my disability. Diana, on the other hand, expected my mother to help with the children, especially when I was hospitalized or whenever we moved to meet the needs of my decreasing mobility. At the very least, she expected some empathy from her. The whole situation was extremely painful for me.

\* \* \*

As the birth of our first daughter Shira'—whose name I had suggested a few months before—approached, Diana prepared everything that it was possible to prepare. I still suppose that there are very few babies whose arrival was prepared for so meticulously. In the wake of Israel's Independence Day, May 6, 1976, Shira' came into the world after a prolonged and difficult labor. I stood, unable to help, next to Diana's bed during the whole time. I was in the delivery room also but I wasn't allowed near her. The second time, when my son Eli' was born, they let me hold my spouse's hand and on the third delivery, when my youngest daughter Naama' was born, I was already almost part of the staff and even photographed her immediately. The reader doesn't have to believe me if I say, as a proud father, that Naama' was extremely beautiful, but the fact is that many of the Hadassah employees—nurses and doctors—came to look at her since the rumor about her beauty had spread in a flash. When she was five, we took her to a professional photographer on King George Street and later discovered that the photographer had enlarged her picture, framed it, and displayed it in the middle of his shop window.

The trouble with Shira', our first born, was that when Diana had to wean her at seven months of age, she refused to drink regular milk from the bottle and if she did drink a little, she had diarrhea. The scariest thing was that instead of gaining weight, she lost it. Diana, who was anxious by nature, worried even more because of the baby's condition. We went from one expert to another until I didn't know what I should worry about more, my child's life, my wife, or both. I too was not ready yet for these situations and perhaps my impatience contributed to Diana's stress and, indirectly, to that of the baby. The head of the pediatrics department decided that Shira's condition was a result of Diana's "stress." He hospitalized the baby and forbade Diana to come near her. That was just what we needed to make the situation intolerable and it went on for days. At home, Diana would pace back and forth endlessly, unable to calm down. My helplessness increased and I didn't know how to behave and what to say to her. When I complained about the fact that she wouldn't accept the situation more calmly, she decided that I either didn't or couldn't try to understand. I tried in vain to explain to her that no one is born a perfect partner, not even me, and this is something we learn over the years, if at all.

The mystery was finally solved. Diana's nerves were not the cause of the baby's condition. Shira' was simply allergic to milk. The doctors recommended a milk substitute called Nutramigen. From the moment we started feeding her this formula, she gobbled up the bottles with great appetite, quickly reached the proper weight, and started blooming. The substance was not only expensive but also difficult to find and the pharmacies selling it limited the amount each customer could buy. Thus began a race for the round containers with the white stuff. Diana went from one pharmacy to another in Jerusalem, Ramat Gan, and Tel-Aviv and she was not satisfied until we collected a stockpile of the precious powder. When Shira' moved on to regular baby food we donated the rest of the formula to others in need. It seemed like the crisis was over and we were again one small happy family.

Our son Eli' was born on March 6, 1978, while Naama' was born, not from the sea, on June 12, 1981. As already mentioned, I was present at the three births and I will never forget Diana's difficult labors as well as the wonderful moments when the babies burst into the world.

All of my three children were born with varying degrees of dyslexia and suffered until quite a late age from learning disabilities. This problem made life difficult for both the children and the whole family, especially for Diana, who helped them study every day since at the beginning, neither we nor the teachers understood or knew about the existence of this impairment, which even today is not easy to diagnose. Shira', a sensitive child, dealt with the situation courage-ously and achieved quite a good matriculation certificate. Having an inclination toward the arts in general and drawing in particular, for which she has a remarkable talent, she studied at the Bezalel Academy of Art and Design for about a year and a half until she grew tired of its regimen and quit. Later on we found out that, to this day, many students leave that institution for the same reason. And for a long time afterwards, she was not able to draw. Shira' also studied art history at the university, therapeutic yoga in India, and learned to be a tourist guide all over the world. Like all her contemporaries, she loved to wander around the whole globe and fell in love with India in particular and even learned to speak, read, and write Hindi and studied Buddhism. Today Shira' works hard with autistic children and is completing a degree in social sciences, apparently following in my footsteps, but actually she is mostly interested in the psychological aspects of it.

My son Eli' suffered even more than the girls because of dyslexia. He was classified at school as "a bad boy," "lazy" and lacking talent in every school he attended. I do not think that he actually spent more than a few days in any of the schools we sent him to. What he liked to do instead was to look for snakes and different kinds of weird animals which made me shiver. We did not even dream that he would pass the matriculation exams, despite the long hours that Diana invested in him. During his army service, he became a staff sergeant and made us proud of him when he absolutely prohibited his subordinates from abusing the Palestinians in any way. When Eli' ended his military service, he was a completely different person and began to study seriously natural sciences at the Open University. It became soon evident that he has exceptional talents in those fields. When we arrived in Canada for a sabbatical, he was accepted to study biology at York University, where he did so well in his first year—while learning English at the same time—that in recognition of his excellence, he was sent to Mexico for an internship. In his second year, Eli' decided that he was not going to spend his life exploiting nature and switched from biology to a more practical profession, sound engineering and production, which is closer to his first love, music. In the end, we found a common language in our shared concern for the environment and fate of the earth.

Naama', who was born physically small like me and remained that way, was the child we doted on. She was always close to Diana and spread a kind of "protection" on her and took care to keep the family unified. Everyone claimed that Naama' inherited my coloring and sense of humor, but Naama' inherited her love for the sciences and her talent in those fields from Diana, and she latched onto marine biology. This small and fragile child left, like all those of her generation, to travel the world by herself, scuba dive in deep waters, and jump off planes. She paid for most of her own expenses by working with young children. She loved them—and they loved her—so much that she thought she would become a preschool teacher. More than once I have wondered about the question—and it seems to me that it is the same in other families too—of how three children who are "created" by the same mother and father and receive the same education (more or less) become nevertheless so different from each other, not just in their appearance but also in their talents, tendencies, and temperaments.

At first, Diana thought she would be the ultimate mother and provide her children with everything that she herself had missed in her own childhood. She purchased every book in Hebrew or English about raising children and developing their skills and abilities and any toy that could contribute to this task. In Boston, our apartment looked like an elaborate kindergarten and we enrolled Shira' at the Harvard University preschool. Later on in Israel, she dragged me to parenting classes that I did not particularly like and in which I saw little point. However, as time went by, Diana realized that the children were not responding behaviorally "by the book" and that my condition was growing worse. Being exhausted, she set aside the theory and invented her own methods to solve the problems that popped up from time to time.

By this time, I had already lost all of my original close family but had managed to start my own family of which, in my very biased opinion, I can be proud. When we discovered that I had cancer, Diana handled it with supreme bravery. She did everything she could so that the treatment would be effective and I could remain at home as much as possible since the hospitalizations were terrible for me (and also for her). In addition, I couldn't work at the hospital and I was disconnected from my virtual world despite the somewhat preferential treatment I received as a "professor." For Diana, those were difficult days for another reason. Her best friend, Gavriella Safriel, with whom she had been in daily contact for twenty-six years, died of cancer after several years of suffering, so that one sorrow was bound up with the other.

## Notes

1.  During those years, the inflation rate often hovered around 100% annually.
2.  Kiryat Yovel is a neighborhood in Jerusalem.

*Baruch as a baby.*

*Baruch in the lap of his parents.*

*Baruch with his baby brother.*

*Baruch in his teens.*

*Baruch at the Hebrew U dorms.*

*Baruch and Diana on their wedding day.*

*Baruch with Diana, Shira' and Eli' in Boston, 1979.*

*Baruch as a young lecturer in 1982.*

*Baruch in his Hebrew U office.*

*Baruch in 1999.*

*Baruch with his youngest daughter, Naama'.*

*Baruch with Shira' on her wedding day.*

*Baruch with his son Eli'.*

# PART THREE

## THE STRUGGLE OVER THE PARADIGM

# 11

## MARCH 6, 1969

During the 1967 war, I stayed in the dorms. I convinced my parents that it was safer in Jerusalem and I promised them I would be in a bomb shelter the whole time (a promise that of course I did not keep). My parents were more worried about Adam's fate than mine, and rightly so. Adam was called up almost at the beginning of the big military mobilization. Thinking back on it now, I should have been at home to calm them down, but I preferred to stay with the young people at the dorms. Indeed, women, foreign students, and the disabled were almost the only people who remained there and it seems to me that the Arab students fled and went home. The tension and anxiety that was felt by the general public was less evident there, even after the Jordanians opened fire with their mortars on the Israeli part of the city.

As soon as the fighting was over, Azriel and I started looking for access to the side of the moon that had been hidden until then. We went to East Jerusalem as soon as it was occupied. We saw, off in the distance, the Western Wall, where throngs of people were dancing and singing, a mixture of traditional Orthodox, people wearing knitted skullcaps,[1] soldiers, and secular Jews. Still before Yeshayahu Leibowitz made his famous comment,[2] the event looked to me like an enormous wall-disco, even if I lacked his ability to summarize that feeling in one pointed expression. However, the joy felt at the liberation of the site holy to the Jewish people took hold of me too, and since I was studying to become a sociologist, I certainly understood the need that people and nations have for symbols. Nevertheless, the way in which this happiness was expressed seemed quite pagan to me since we suppose that the Lord is found in a still small voice. From there we made our way to the mosque. The place was almost empty. The Muslims had sequestered themselves in their homes and the Jews were not yet interested in the Temple Mount—at least those who knew about the prohibition against going up there. We took off our shoes as we were requested to do by some kind of guard or supervisor who stood there (we may also have washed our feet, but I'm not sure about this) and we entered structures of amazing beauty. That was the first and last time I went there.

Then we drove towards the mountains extending from Jerusalem to Jericho, all the way to the Allenby Bridge. The road was blocked by convoys of refugees moving east toward Jordan, some by car and some on foot while others rode on donkeys or in mule-drawn carts. The refugees were very quiet and withdrawn. We didn't exactly understand why and from what they were escaping. We tried to establish a conversation with them in English to convince them that there was nothing to fear or flee from. I was still in my naïve stage and those convoys of refugees brought back memories from another place and a different time. We merged into those convoys. Azriel drove one car while, if I remember correctly, Shlomo Reich, a friend disabled by polio and possessing a macabre sense of humor, drove another. It is strange that it did not occur to us that there may be something to be afraid of. The Israeli army was nowhere to be seen. Only the remains of mostly civilian cars, crushed and completely flattened by tanks which passed over them, and a few skeletons of Jordanian tanks by the side of the road reminded us that only two days previously, a war had been fought there. After many hours of slow progress as part of the refugee convoy, we arrived at the Allenby Bridge, which had been destroyed. However, a sort of very narrow bridge had been improvised among the ruins. Tired and nervous Israeli and Jordanian soldiers helped the families heading east with the belongings they carried. Suddenly, a fight broke out among a few families, probably over who would cross the bridge first. An Israeli soldier responded with a burst of gunfire into the air and quiet was restored. I had never seen so many people in a state of submissiveness and defeat—the complete opposite of the pictures we are used to seeing today on television from the cities in the West Bank and the Gaza Strip.

The great victory also benefited the sociology department immensely. Before the war, two pretentious research proposals on the causes of modernization and its obstacles in developing countries had been submitted to the Ford Foundation. One proposal, coordinated by Dov Weintraub, was in the field of agriculture, and the other, coordinated by Chaim Adler, was in the field of education. The lead author of both studies was, of course, S.N. Eisenstadt, who was then at the height of his worldwide fame as one of the greatest theoreticians in the social sciences. Matya, the energetic department secretary, got hold of me and told me that Dov was looking for me. Dov Weintraub was a lovely man, wise, very open, and straightforward. The department was his second career, after the one he had at the Settlement Department of the Jewish Agency. He was happy to meet me, said that he had heard that I was an "excellent student," talked generally about the goals of the study, and asked me whether I would be interested in being a research assistant. This was a somewhat strange question because, as I asked him, "What do I know about agriculture and developing countries?" He replied: "I'm sure you don't know anything about it, but you'll learn." This did not exactly fit my career plans, but, as it is well known, every project is an opportunity for change. "Look," Dov said, as though guessing my thoughts, "We will pay you at the state employee's rate, including benefits. What do you want the extent of the job to be, full-time or part-time?" I thought that being in the middle of my master's degree, I couldn't commit to a full-time job and I said "part-time." But while skipping down the stairs of the Kaplan Building, I thought to myself: *You fool, if they make an offer, take it.* I promptly returned to Dov and told him that I had changed my mind and would prefer a full-time position. I had already worked a little for the department as a teaching assistant for Professor Elihu Katz, who taught the kind of class which was fashionable at the time and was called "Communication and Modernization," or something like that, and I had earned next to nothing. However, the honor of being a teaching assistant and deciding on grades greatly flattered me. Besides that, Elihu, who became a friend of sorts, had all kinds of grandiose plans in which he intended to assign important roles to me. Indeed, a few of these plans came to fruition, such as the establishment of the Israeli Television. He had decided I was to be the director of the research department (sic, no more, no less!), a post I never held. Actually, another one of Katz's students was chosen for that job, but that department has never been established. Nevertheless, following the conversation with Dov, I was set financially and in fact, until this day, I have never earned so much money relative to my expenses, since I was still single and living at the dorms, a situation that was to change soon.

During the first meeting of the two research teams on modernization, Eisenstadt gave us an abstract lecture, as was his way. Most of his speech was already well known to me from his classes. After he spoke, Dov and Chaim tried to translate the abstract theory into more concrete and, most importantly, more comparative models, each in his own field. If I remember correctly, Moshe Lissak was the coordinator of the two groups. Pnina, Lydia, Miriam, and I were on the "agricultural team," where each of us had to deal with a different part of the world. Pnina won Latin America; Lydia, as far as I remember, got Asia; Miriam, Greece; and I got Africa, or to be precise, Ghana, Uganda, and the Ivory Coast. Moshe was my immediate supervisor and, within a few months, went to Africa to collect empirical data. He returned with a lot of government propaganda brochures and with reports written by researchers doing field work. Meanwhile, I went to the library and read everything I could find about "my" countries and about agricultural development. The subject even started to interest me to a certain extent, yet my dominant feeling was still the unpleasant one of participating in academic prostitution. Since I did not master French as was required, I received both the permission and the funding to employ Sarah as a research assistant to a research assistant. An additional benefit promised to us was that the result of our research would be considered as the thesis for our second degree. It seems to me that I was the only one to take advantage of this privilege and within two years, I completed my second degree and even managed to publish an article in an important international journal. In addition, I published my thesis as a booklet in an American series that was then considered prestigious. For years, my friend Naomi Hazan, whose academic career ran parallel to mine—except that she was in African studies and had really mastered the subject—lost her temper whenever she attended some international conference of Africanists and when asked where she was from, would get the response "Oh, you are from the same place as Baruch Kimmerling..."

Eisenstadt soon noticed, with a mixture of suspicion and appreciation, my developed imagination, which my defenders called "creativity." I was informed that Eisenstadt had nicknamed me a "juggler of ideas," meaning the circus performer who throws colorful balls upwards and amuses himself with them: in other words, brilliant but superficial. It was not a compliment, but I agreed with him wholeheartedly since I had no choice regarding subjects I was tempted to deal with other than to blow up colorful balloons and let them fly. According to our supervisors, the agricultural team progressed well while the educational team stalled on take-off. I was called on to help them out. Thus I wrote an article on the educational system in Ghana and I sent it to a respected journal. Even then, I had begun to internalize the academia's strict rule that you have to "publish or perish." The article was rejected this time and one of the experts who read it wrote, "Not all the memories of a graduate of the Ghanaian school system are worthy of publication." I, who had never set foot in Ghana, considered this an enormous compliment. In addition, the secondary study that dealt with the interviews of Israeli relief officials sent to developing countries, of which Eric Cohen was in charge, and, in my view, had the most potential to develop into a material worth serious research, did not progress and I was called in to perform a rescue mission there too. After investing a few months of very hard work, I managed, in my opinion, to produce an interesting and critical research report about the methods used in relief work. This report was never published, and it was not even handed in to the sponsors as a report. I have no idea why, but I had the impression that Eric had reservations about it and its author and also did not have enough time or motivation to invest more into that subject. It must be said on his behalf that he was very busy at that time with a survey he was conducting in Palestinian refugee camps and did not devote his attention to a subject that he considered marginal.

Even though not all the senior students—such as Gadi Yatziv, Yael Atzmon, or Yoram Carmeli, who were a number of years ahead of me—took part in the modernization research, my participation in those studies placed me in a position almost equal to them, especially since I was able to complete my second degree before most of them mainly because they had difficulties with writing. There may have been additional reasons that I shall write more about later.

The only student from my class that had been accepted into this "elite group" was Miriam Corellaro who worked exclusively and directly with Eisenstadt and was considered a genius. I appreciated Miriam greatly and thought that most of her strength derived from her perseverance and dedication together with her willingness to sacrifice her personal life.

Since I finished my second degree quickly and with honors, it was only natural for me to continue for the doctorate, even though when I entered the university, I assumed that completing the first degree would be an achievement. Afterwards, I thought the same about my second degree. But when I finished it, Dov Weintraub and I agreed that that my doctorate would be a continuation of my master's thesis on Uganda. This arrangement was also approved by

Eisenstadt. At that time the division of roles between them was unclear—a situation Eisenstadt always relished. The dissertation was expected to be a comparative study of two societies, the Ivory Coast and Ghana. In practice, I had already gathered most of the material for the paper while conducting the research on modernization and I estimated that within a year, I would be able to submit my doctorate and be comparable in the rapidity of my achievements to my venerable teacher, Shmuel Noah Eisnstadt. But things turned out differently and I was largely to blame for that.

It seems to me that I can accurately date the turning point of my career and perhaps also of my worldview. It was on March 6, 1969. I was going downstairs from my office on the third floor of the Kaplan Building to the cafeteria, as my usual routine at midday was to have a cup of coffee, eat some cake, look at girls, and just talk with friends. Suddenly, the building was shaken by a powerful explosion. I approached the large windows overlooking the National Library. At first I saw only smoke rising up from the large cafeteria windows. Then broken glass and lots of blood became visible. I froze in place. People were running from every direction towards the cafeteria, and I saw people covered with blood being taken out. It was not clear whether some of them were hurt or dead. We could already hear the sirens of ambulances and squad cars. Sabotage in our cafeteria? My cafeteria? Unbelievable, but this was the reality. Since I do not like crowds, I did not go down there but I continued to watch for a while from the window. Then I returned to my room without drinking my daily instant coffee. I locked the door behind me and sank into thoughts.

Within a week, the beautiful, open campus of Givat Ram had changed its appearance completely. An ugly fence surrounded it and armed guards thoroughly checked the people and their belongings before they entered. This new aspect of campus life induced great sadness in me. We, who lived in the dormitories at the far end of the campus, knew very well that the fence and the additional security were only superficial measures and that whoever wished to enter the campus could do so easily—and a lot of black humor circulated about this subject. I myself entered the libraries and decided to plow through them. There was very little material on the Jewish–Arab conflict, and what did exist was in the fields of international relations or history; most of it was apologetic to such an extent that it bordered on propaganda. I decided two things: first, to study Arabic (a decision I never carried out, to my regret, both because of my lack of talent in languages and because its implementation was always postponed to a period in which "I would have more time"); and second, to investigate the Jewish–Arab conflict and its impact on Israeli society. Surely, I told myself, it is not possible that an ongoing and violent conflict such as this would not have an effect on Israeli society. Much later, I also turned the question around and asked how the structure and culture of Israeli society influence the development of the conflict and maybe even its very creation. For years, I had been preoccupied with the conflict and I considered it from different perspectives, but it never stood at the center of my work and eventually I pushed it to the edges of my awareness. It was also clear to me that my work at the department, despite the fine salary earned, did not particularly interest me and that I was even at odds and unhappy with it.

I went to talk with Eisenstadt and I told him I wanted to change the subject of my doctorate and I asked that he continue to be my tutor. After all, he was the expert on Israeli society. I gave him a general outline of the subject that concerned me, and I expected that he would say to me, as his habit, "Submit a written proposal and I will think about it." But Shmuel asked to be excused for a moment to go to the bathroom. When he came back he ruled, "The subject is not sociological but political." I am almost sure that, later on, if he still remembered this conversation, he would have rescinded his ruling. I was already sufficiently aware of the fact that the determination of what is and isn't a sociological topic depends on the ideology of the person making the decision and the power he has to determine it. I tried to argue with him, but he hinted to me that the meeting was over.

In contrast, Dov Weintraub was far more practical, as was his habit. "Look," he said to me, "within a year, you will finish your doctorate, and then you can do whatever you want." This was wise and pragmatic but inaccurate advice. No one at the department did anything that Eisenstadt opposed. Besides that, there is an unwritten rule, valid to this day, that even the greatest genius of his era cannot earn a doctorate if for some reason he doesn't have, or can't find, a tutor. The universities continue to have, for better or for worse, a residual medieval guild structure, and at the end of the 1960s, it was much more rigid than today. There were magicians and there were magicians' apprentices, and if you weren't an apprentice, you didn't exist. But I was stubborn and from then on, I gained a reputation as a troublemaker.

At that time, the Psychology department offered a class based on Yehoshafat Harkaby's doctoral dissertation about the Arab view on the conflict. The theoretical background of his research was the "cognitive equilibrium" approach advanced by the American psychologist Leon Festinger. To the best of my recollection, the argument was that since the reality of Arab inferiority is not compatible with their image of power, they resolve this cognitive dissonance by adopting an anti-Semitic attitude toward Israel and the Jews. Harkaby, who was probably only just beginning to be accepted into academia, taught the class together with Ozer Shield, who later became an activist on the radical right. This was, I think, the first course in Israeli academia on the Jewish–Arab conflict and I rushed to attend it. I couldn't handle the massive amounts of material provided by Harkaby, who had been the head of the Intelligence Branch until he was discharged by Ben-Gurion following "The Night of the Ducks," an innocent public exercise for mobilizing the reserves which brought Israel to the brink of war. The Arab press, on which that material was based, overflowed with anti-Jewish and anti-Israel poison and it was full of anti-Semitic imagery which could have been taken straight from *Der Stürmer*. However, the theoretical background of the study and the class itself—which disguised a profusion of stereotypical images and hatred against the Arabs as science—did not convince me either and I tried to present explanations for the

Arabs' viewpoints on the conflict that differed from those offered by the two lecturers. I asked them if, perhaps, there existed reasons for the hostile Arab attitude toward Israel that were based more on reality than on mere anti-Semitism, imported Nazi racism, and the achievement of a "cognitive equilibrium." Both the lecturers and the students greeted my arguments with contempt and hostility, a response which was to repeat itself many times afterwards. One thing I certainly gained was the hostility of Ozer Shield, who at the time was considered a central figure in the department.

During that period, a new person came to the department, Michael (Mike) Inbar. An Israeli of French origin, he completed his doctorate at Johns Hopkins University on the way in which game theory could be used to simulate nuclear attacks on the United States. Mike was considered a star and the use of game theory was at the time the last word in social sciences. I thought he would be interested in tutoring me and we met for a number of long talks. I must say that I immediately liked two things about him: his sense of humor and his overwhelming and powerful energy. He spoke about any subject which interested him with immense enthusiasm. We "clicked" and Mike was looking for people to work with. The Jewish–Arab conflict did not interest him either at the time, but he suggested that I participate as an equal partner in a new study that his restless mind had planned. We were both single then (as far as I know, Mike has remained single to this day) and he would sometimes call me in the middle of the night to announce that a new idea had popped into his mind which might be worth a try. Fifteen minutes later he would show up at my place in his pajamas to spend the rest of the night discussing and arguing. The central idea was to examine altruism and egoism empirically by using substitution theory, which was then the latest thing in sociology and was expected to replace or correct the functionalist approach that had dominated American and Israeli sociology until then.

And indeed, we both poured all of our energy into building a quite ingenious research paradigm. A lot of what I know to this day about empirical-social research—beginning with the definition of the research question or the preparation of a questionnaire containing as few biases as possible—I learned while working jointly with Mike. At the end, even though we had planned from the start to write a book together and we invested a lot of time, effort, and money in this study, nothing was ever published as a result of our research. Mike abruptly lost interest while I was neither mature enough nor experienced enough at that stage to conduct such a large project alone. Anyway, my participation in it determined the course of my life to a large extent, as will be explained later. In the meantime, I continued the search for a tutor for my doctorate on the subject of the Jewish–Arab conflict.

Another person joined the department at the same time, and that was Dan Horowitz, known to everyone as Dindush. One day, the department held a party for the staff and the graduate students. I stood in a corner holding a glass of white wine (which I have always loved) and was engaged in the anthropological observation of the guests, most of whom I knew only superficially. Out of the blue, a person I had never seen in my life approached me. He too had a glass of wine in his hand and was somewhat clumsy and carelessly dressed, but not on purpose. It was not clear whether he stuttered a little because he was drunk or for some other reason. "How are you, Baruch?" he asked. He was surprised and offended by the fact that it was clear from my response that I did not know who he was. He knew everything about me and this was immediately evident from the conversation we plunged into, the content of which I am not able to reconstruct.

In any case, Dindush was well-informed about "everybody," politicians and statesmen and those who are now called cultural icons both in this country and among the Jewish population abroad. He was incurably nosy and a gossip, but he elevated these traits into an art and produced sociology from it, as he was also thoroughly up to date with social theory. The man was not only constantly in the throes of doubt about existential dilemmas, like a true intellectual, and a walking "who's who" (and with whom), but he also had enormous personal charm and drive. Those he loved, he loved with his whole heart, while he was capable of a fiery hatred for those whom he detested.

His knowledge was not acquired by chance. Apart from an insatiable curiosity, he was also the only son of the legendary David (Dolek) Horowitz, a man of the third *aliyah*, one of the most prominent figures of the labor corps and the left wing of the labor movement, an intellectual, writer, and economist and later on, the director of the Bank of Israel. Dan was almost as much of a non-conformist as his father. As a child, he sat in the laps of Meir Yaari, Ben-Aharon, Tabenkin, Menachem Elkind (who returned to the Soviet Union when he grew disappointed with Zionism) and, at a later stage, David and Paula Ben-Gurion and all the other giants. He describes part of the conversations he heard in an autobiography that he never managed to finish, *Azure and Dust: The 1948 Generation—A Self-Portrait*. In the 1948 war, he was in Gush Etzion during the siege and was taken prisoner by the Legion. When he was released, he was disappointed by the country he found, a disillusionment he described in a book he wrote as a young adult. He covered the Knesset for *Davar* and was also a soccer commentator. He moved to Jerusalem and studied law, but he was soon captivated by the secret magic of sociology, married Tamar, and traveled with her to London for his doctorate. There, Dindush wrote a thesis on the British conservatives' attitude towards the de-colonization processes. He did not believe that a doctorate on the effects of the Jewish–Arab conflict on Israeli society was not a legitimate subject for sociological research. On the contrary, he thought that it was probably the most important and urgent subject for sociological research. Despite the fact that his minor position at the time did not allow him to formally tutor me, when I was actually preparing my thesis, he became, in practice, my instructor and was, in contrast to my formal tutor, professionally as well as emotionally involved.

I do not know what made Dan interested in me; perhaps it was his discovery that an immigrant was able to delineate, with razor-sharp precision, processes occurring in the Israeli society and knew secrets that were supposed to be known only by a small elite belonging to the 1948 generation and their parents. In any event, a close and quite intimate friendship developed between us. We conducted endless but never vicious or personal debates and he was a friend, a mentor, and a sponsor to me until his death in October 1991.

For Dindush, even a short ride by car was an intellectual-strategic challenge. He knew every traffic light in Jerusalem, how much time he had to wait for the light to turn green, and when traffic was heavy during the day. He would calculate every route as if preparing himself for battle. Our talks, first in the staff room of the Kaplan Building and then mostly in my office on Mount Scopus, lasted for long hours. A series of those talks produced a joint article about the Israeli military reserve system, an article which even today is quoted by almost everyone who deals with the Israeli army.

An interview with me that was published in the university newspaper testifies to what extent I was influenced at that time by Dan Horowitz and by functionalism. Indeed, I did correctly define the goal of my research when I said "What will be carried out is an attempt to explore which institutions and positions were created within the State in order to deal with the conflict [the Jewish–Arab one] and where those were located in the social and economic system of the State." Then I reported my initial findings that army officers occupied the second most prestigious position (after that of scientists) in Israel and I came to the conclusion that the "officer had replaced the kibbutznik." I also claimed that "the great importance attributed in Israel to security roles adds an additional dimension to the components of the class structure in the State of Israel." Up to this point, everything sounds good and I would repeat the same things, even from the perspective of more than thirty years. However, when I was asked if, as a result of that, militarism exists in Israel, my words were summarized by the reporter as follows: "The researcher assumes that the reserves contribute, among other things, to the protection of the State of Israel from the danger of militarism. In different countries throughout the world, security matters are entrusted exclusively to a small group of people who can claim that they possess unique knowledge about the subject. At the same time, in Israel most men are involved in military affairs, each within the framework of his own unit, until an advanced age." The prevalence of military knowledge was supposed to constitute a protection from militarism. This was indeed a Foucault-style thesis, whose existence we didn't yet know about; however, the conclusion was too hasty. About a decade and a half had to elapse for me to understand this, and then I initiated a controversy, which has not ended to this day, about the essence of the militaristic culture in Israel.

Moshe Lissak, who was Dindush's friend from youth, was almost his opposite. He was an introverted and vulnerable person. It took me years to understand his inner motivations and to this day I'm not sure that I fully succeeded. Lissak always looked respectable and spoke in a moderate and measured way. I realized only years later that this was only the outward appearance of a driven man who zealously guards his status and his image. But Moshe Lissak was important to me because immediately after he was promoted to senior lecturer, I approached him and asked him to be my tutor, a proposal which, to my surprise, he accepted straightaway. He didn't even investigate or inquire too much about what I wanted to do my work on and how. If I'm not mistaken, I was his first doctoral candidate. Within a short time, a young Belgian, Eliezer Ben-Raphael, joined me in this status and afterwards had an impressive career at Tel-Aviv University. The next step was that I submitted a research proposal in his name on the subject of the doctorate and subsequently received quite a large budget which allowed me to employ research assistants, including Arabic speakers. The material I gathered in two years of this research was so voluminous that it could be used for a number of doctorates. I even used a portion of this material twenty years later when, together with my friend Joel Migdal, I wrote the first ever comprehensive social history of the Palestinian people.

The research project I had formulated on the effects of the conflict was pretentious and of such an extent that it was, in effect, impossible to carry out. If a doctoral candidate submitted such a proposal to me today, I would send him home to cut it down to size and focus on one specific subject, and I would expect him to explain his methodology to me. In praise of Lissak, I must say that he didn't do that; in fact, he didn't interfere at all and was almost uninterested in what I did. From my point of view, he was an ideal instructor, especially because when I was troubled by any problem, I would turn to Dan Horowitz. I have no idea what they said to each other about me, but I always had the impression that they did talk about me and my work and it is possible that this method of mentoring via messenger was more comfortable for Moshe too. However, this is all just my own conjecture. Maybe I should have asked Dindush about it at some point but I didn't.

Meanwhile, Lissak and Horowitz were awarded a large research grant to study the social structure and the development of the Jewish community in what was then called "Mandatory Palestine." They invited me to Lissak's home, laid out the research ideas and the outline of the book they were about to write, and proposed that I help them gather the relevant material—that is, to function as their part-time research assistant. The subject interested me, of course, and I was willing to be a partner in the project. I told them that, emphasizing the word "partner." When they didn't get the hint, I told them that my condition was to be listed as the third author of the book. This was clearly an audacious request, but it was not without merit. When Moshe explained the nature of the job to me, he also emphasized that they were also interested in my ideas. By then I was already convinced that work could be purchased with money, but that ideas must be paid for in a different currency. In addition to this, I was aware of a precedent. An important book was published that year entitled *Moshava, Kibbutz, and Moshav*, authored by Dov Weintraub, Moshe Lissak, and Yael Atzmon. Yael, who was two years ahead of me, served as Moshe and Dov's research assistant. I did not think that my capabilities were inferior to those of Yael. Maybe it is worthwhile to add that a few years earlier S.N. Eisenstadt had published his great book, considered a classic in sociology to this day, on the growth of bureaucratic empires in the ancient world. This was a project on which the whole department—doctoral and master students—was recruited to work, but only Eisenstadt received the credit. I felt, however, that Moshe owed me something, as my master's final paper, which was entirely the result of my own work, was published as a monograph under both our names. Out of politeness, I had suggested including Moshe as an author too; to my surprise, he agreed and with great pleasure.

The moment I expressed my conditions, a sudden silence fell on the room. At first I saw them turn pale and then become red with anger. Finally, Moshe took upon himself the task of explaining to me that this was out of the question, the book would be exclusively theirs, and that they had already invested many years of thought into it. Dindush, contrary to his habit, was silent. I got up and left Lissak's house in the Rehavia neighborhood.

## Notes

1. The national religious wear skullcaps that are knitted or crocheted while the traditional religious usually wear cloth skullcaps.
2. Professor Yeshayahu Leibowitz suggested transforming the area in front of the Western Wall into the country's biggest disco and calling it the "Divine Presence Discotheque" to make both the secular and religious communities happy.

# 12

## THE DEPARTMENT

From the end of the 1960s onward, the Department of Sociology, later known as the Department of Sociology and Anthropology, became my second home. My spouse even used to complain sometimes that it was my primary home. And it is in fact difficult for a young lecturer to have an academic career if research and teaching do not become his whole world and eventually, at least for some of us, a kind of "second nature."

I still love coming to the department because I love being among so many young, attractive people who are full of energy and hope and, sometimes, even a thirst for knowledge. I get a surge of adrenalin whenever I talk with them or teach them. The encounters with most of my colleagues are different since each of them is primarily concerned with self-aggrandizement and self-promotion, usually while demeaning the achievements of his or her colleagues. This too is part of the distortion existing in the profession, although it is not necessarily supposed to be that way.

Actually, it is very difficult to define what the "Department" is. It might be that today it is a group of men and women assembled together within a bureaucratic framework which provides services and support to promote teaching and research and nothing more. As a social network, the "department" sometimes throws parties for the beginning or the end of the academic year, for the celebration of a newly published book, or for the promotion of whomever the Head of Department favors or whoever pushed hard enough to get it. During the last few years, all kinds of personal congratulations and administrative announcements have been transmitted through the internet. As department head, Michael Shalev transformed the performance of administrative functions via the internet into an art, and Amalya Oliver continued with this approach, albeit in a gentler, more reserved, and more pleasant way. The use of the internet became essential, especially as more and more staff members have either never lived in Jerusalem or have moved to metropolitan Tel Aviv. At first, the university tried to address the phenomenon of Jerusalem's desertion, but most of the public cannot, or does not want to, deal with the issue. Thus today "the department" is actually active or exists only for three days a week, when most of the "Tel Avivians" come to teach, participate in one meeting or another, and sometimes attend a departmental seminar. I am not an ardent supporter of the department when it functions as a club for members.

Such a club might distort (for better and for worse) judgments regarding junior members (as indeed has already happened). At the same time, most of the talks, the stormy debates, and the professional-intellectual exchange of ideas at the department have declined or were silenced almost completely. The conversation in the corridors has decreased. The arguments over the image of the department and sociology that erupted when Eisenstadt—Israeli sociology's main figure and "legacy"—retired have now ceased. There are a few who collaborate with each other by working on joint research projects, but such cooperation rarely involves the whole department, and usually the other members are unaware of it.

Once I shared some of these thoughts with Amalya, whose loyalty to the department and appreciation for most of its people go above and beyond the call of duty. She was offended and "accused" me of missing the "old" centralized department in which, apparently, we all worked together under the guidance of the "professor" and felt some kind of personal and collective mission to help the Zionist revolution. Aside from the fact that I came to the department after its original structure had mostly changed, Amalya was right in that we were indeed quite an integrated group in which Eisenstadt was still dominant. However, he also presented us with professional and intellectual challenges, the burden of which I still carry with me—for better or worse—to this day. His method of teaching the masters degree students was through dialogue. In this system, we were required to read an enormous amount of material every week and then, during the lectures, answer the questions he asked based on our critical reading. This method has almost vanished from the world, mostly because students don't read and also because most teachers don't have Eisenstadt's intellectual ability.

\*   \*   \*

Mike Inbar went into the office of the department head, Rivka Bar-Yosef, and I waited for him outside in the long corridor on the third floor of the Kaplan Building in Givat Ram. The corridor was empty at that time of day. I don't know how long I waited until Mike came out of Rivka's room but at the time, it seemed like forever. I also did not know what to wish for since I had mixed feelings regarding all the possible outcomes. On one hand, teaching at the department was a dream I scarcely dared to contemplate, despite my tendency to fantasize. On the other hand, to stand in front of a class—with my barely understandable speech, occasional stuttering, and "unaesthetic" appearance—seemed impossible to me. "I'm a realistic person," I had told Mike a few days before, when he started trying to persuade me to teach one of his courses since he suddenly had to leave for the United States. "A realist," he replied with a winning answer, "is one who tries, and if he succeeds, he succeeds and if not, he goes back to his usual routine." In this way, Mike strengthened the challenge he presented me, and I was left only with the hope or the confidence that Rivka would refuse. "Everything is O.K.," said Mike coming out of Rivka's room.

"You are teaching the course." And I didn't know yet whether to run wild in jubilation or to withdraw into my anxiety.

I assume that no teacher, especially one in my condition, forgets the first time he enters a class. That was an elective course, so the students could leave the class *en masse* or not return at all for the next session. "Shopping" for classes and teachers is an appropriate and welcome activity. The class I entered as a teacher was quite large for those days. About thirty students sat around tables arranged in a square. I entered the class exactly when the bell rang (in those days, bells still marked the beginning of the class), but not before I had visited the bathroom a number of times. I approached the slightly raised teacher's podium. I made an effort to smile. I took off my jacket slowly and arranged it meticulously on the back of my chair to stall for time.

Complete silence prevailed in the classroom. "Shalom, my name is Baruch," I said. "To our regret, Dr. Inbar will not be able to teach the course this year because of an urgent trip abroad and he asked me to substitute for him. So, the main subject we will be discussing this year…"

After the first sentence, it was as if I had turned into another person. Adrenalin flowed through my whole being. I felt self-confident, something I usually experienced only after good sex. I was very focused on what I had to teach but at the same time I was also attentive to the facial expressions and body language of the students. I did not stutter, not even once, throughout that hour and a half. When I made a joke during the lecture and the whole class burst into thunderous laughter, I knew that they were "mine," they were following me and being attentive, and that the subject held them. And then, slowly, slowly, hands were raised and questions were asked. I knew the material thoroughly since this was the second year I had worked as Mike's partner researching that very topic. I didn't need any notes, not even a written outline. I asked questions (as I had planned in advance) so that the lecture would also be, in part, a kind of dialogue between me and the students and they were happy to respond, participate, and debate with me. Most students don't like the lecture format. As a strategic decision, I treated every answer as though it were correct and praised it, but I gave it my own interpretation when it was incorrect or irrelevant. In general, the class was quiet, but when someone talked to another student, I would interrupt the lecture for a few seconds, do my best to fix a "penetrating stare" on the speaker, and silence would be restored.

A week later, despite my fears, the entire class showed up again and there were actually no dropouts for the remainder of the term. The next year, I appeared in the course catalogue with my own class. It seems to me that if we exclude the psychologically-oriented class of Harkabi and Shield, it was the first lecture given at the university about the sociology of the Jewish–Arab conflict, which was the focus of my still unfinished doctorate. This was one of the courses I taught up until the time of my retirement, although I was constantly developing and updating it. Thus after two more years, I became a full teacher (at the level of instructor) at the Hebrew University and my academic career began, changing the entire course of my life. I must admit, however, that even after almost forty years of teaching, walking into each new class at the beginning of the academic year still caused me to be apprehensive about the unknown and there were some classes, though not many, that I never managed to "conquer." And when the lack of confidence would, for some reason, take control of me and the stuttering would also return, a vicious cycle was created, making communication difficult. Once, I clashed with some of the students in my class. This happened many years later, when I taught a section in sociological theory. The students thought I had assigned too much reading (I tried to be a bit "Eisenstadt-ish"), but since it was a graduate class, I refused to reduce the workload. As a result, I heard that some of them went to the department head and complained that they didn't understand my speech.

This is perhaps the place to acknowledge the openness and the courage shown by Rivka Bar-Yosef and most of the people in the department and the entire university when they accepted a severely disabled person as an equal among equals into their community in accordance with the stated standards of the institution—the person's ability and qualifications. There was no "affirmative action" involved since the concept and the approach itself were unknown in Israel then and are barely accepted today. I do not think that any public or even private institution was prepared then, and perhaps not even today, to employ a person in my condition (I did not forget my failed attempt at radio). There is, however, no need to get carried away by idealization and generalizations: from the beginning I also felt hostility, or at least ambivalence, towards me even on the part of department members, not to mention the university staff in general. One of them even took the trouble to explain to me a number of times that I had no chance at all for a university career and advised me to look for other employment. I can only admire his frankness, even though it seems to me that he never forgave me for proving him wrong. In one respect at least he was right: I was never entirely accepted by the whole aggressive university system. It seems to me that I am among the few professors with both a high profile within their institutions and an international reputation who were never appointed or elected to a major and genuinely powerful post there (except for being the head of the editorial staff responsible for a series of books in social sciences published by Magnes). The excuse usually was: "We do not understand his speech." I always smiled when I heard this argument. Many generations of students understood my "speech" well, but my colleagues, the professors, did not understand me, perhaps because they did not really want to understand. However, I also benefited considerably from this lack of acceptance since it saved me a lot of time and spared me the burden of dealing with the university bureaucracy and the resulting problems and stress.

Suggestions that I should look for another occupation only increased my motivation to succeed. What's more, academic teaching, research, and the publication of articles and books are addictive activities, especially for those who are able to endure the demands and the ongoing tension involved in meeting them. However, for a portion of people in academia, it is a constant nightmare. More than once, I have wondered why so many insist upon it while enduring great hardship, although in the past at least the title "professor" was a desirable one in Israeli culture—almost like that of a Brigadier General in the army. Still, there is something in the race to advance through the academic ranks that destroys at least some people for reasons unrelated to their intelligence. I estimate that at least one-third of the faculty in the second and third tiers of the department, after having been promoted to a certain level, become "dead wood" and either stop being productive or repeat themselves *ad nauseam*. There are those who have accepted their situation and even admit that they do not deserve a promotion, but most of them become embittered, generating tension and anger in the department and sometimes ostracism.

Later in my career when I encountered problems with my promotions, those were mainly because I was controversial and had professionally criticized the approaches used in Israeli sociology (which, to my regret, have more than once turned into serious personal conflicts). However, to the best of my understanding, the underlying factor was not my disability, but I may be wrong. Most of my criticism was directed against those researchers and writers of Israeli historiography and sociography who recruited themselves, whether intentionally or not, to defend Zionist ideology and actions while ignoring and twisting facts and inventing paradigms accordingly. From this standpoint, those who, over the years, labeled me a post-Zionist were right to attack me for that since science must be devoid of ideology.

"Zionist sociology," or sociology which is mobilized and apologetic on behalf of Zionism, is ideology and not science. Even though every nationalism, especially from a comparative point of view, is an extremely important and fascinating research subject, it must be conducted outside the ideology itself and not from within it.

# 13

## ON ZIONISM

After the outbreak of the 1973 war, the university gave serious thought to whether or not to begin the academic year while most of the students were mobilized and the war had not yet ended. It was finally decided that "the show must go on" and the year would begin, but that the docents would send detailed outlines of their lectures to every soldier requesting them (a decision that, to the best of my knowledge, was never implemented). I was left with a "research seminar" in which about twenty young women participated, and we were all depressed and frustrated. During the first session, it was decided unanimously that we would research the situation, namely the behavior of the home front during mobilization and wartime. It seems to me that I never had a class as enthusiastic and motivated to work as this one. I was also fortunate to have a brilliant, tireless, and energetic research assistant, Irit Becker. Having dealt with the sociology of war, I was partially familiar with the work of Richard Titmuss who, in a classic volume, reviewed British social problems and policy during World War II, a familiarity that helped me quickly formulate some of the relevant research questions.

The hierarchical division within Israeli society between the men who left the [civilian] system and the women who remained behind the lines or (to use the interesting British term) "on the home front" was immediately evident. Rivka Bar-Yosef and Dorit Padan-Eisenstark wrote a preliminary and pioneering article about the issue. However, the research developed by us covered almost the entire range of phenomena stemming from what I called "the interrupted system." The assumption was that despite the fact that in the Israeli society, most of the vital roles in all fields and at all levels were (then, in 1973) occupied by men, the existing social system still needed to be "maintained," at least to a minimal extent when they left it and this job was mainly carried out by women who shifted to "male roles." We decided that if this hypothesis is correct, we should examine how it works, especially in critical sectors.

Therefore, I assigned the students to research those bottlenecks that would make it difficult for normal life to continue for more than a few days. For example, we examined traffic and transportation because most of the drivers, trucks, and buses had been mobilized at the beginning of the war, sharply reducing civilian mobility and the delivery of essential goods. We studied banks because a shortage of available cash might have occurred and at the time, credit cards were unknown, and joint accounts held by husbands and wives were rare. We also researched mail delivery, kindergartens, and schools, as well as the activities of municipalities, *Melach* (which is responsible for the economy during emergencies) and *Pesach* (which removed corpses) and more. While research institutes operating at the time, like the Gutman Institute, interviewed people about their "mood" in order to measure "public morale," our team monitored the levels of institutional activity and how individuals and groups coped with various shortages.

In that period, practices interested me more than ideology, which can always be given different, and sometimes even opposite, interpretations. In my doctoral dissertation too, the emphasis was placed on Zionist tactics for appropriating the land and not on the ideology behind them. Therefore, at that stage, my research did not attract any special attention and was not perceived as "subversive," especially since all the discussions held in those days about Zionism were only within and between tiny political groups like Matzpen and Etgar which were, in any case, outside the mainstream. The research about the home front during wartime was comprehensive and original and was later summarized in a book in English bearing the title *The Interrupted System*. Its background was a comparison between the reactions of communities to natural disasters (hurricanes, fires, earthquakes), about which there existed an extensive literature encompassing both theory and research, and the responses of the home front to general mobilizations during wartime, a subject on which there had been almost no professional research. My intention was also to contribute to the general sociological theory about "special situations" in which routine social order either collapses or is about to collapse. However, except for the "Israeli issues," the book did not attract the attention of those who should have been interested in it. Nonetheless, as a result of this book, I received suitable compensation—the rank of senior lecturer with tenure, which even then was difficult to attain.

In addition to my promotion, the most significant fact connected to the research on the home front was that after repeatedly reviewing the accumulated research material, I first raised the possibility that Israel is indeed a militaristic society. I even mentioned this briefly in my book, although without drawing any final conclusion at that stage.

*    *    *

In the preface of the present book, I presented as an example of one of the changes I was able to introduce in the research and perception of the Israeli society, my understanding that it is militaristic, while drawing attention to the existence of different forms of militarism.

Actually, almost as soon as I started my second degree, I felt that the sciences in general and sociology in particular deserve both an internal and an external sociological examination and analysis. I soon discovered the analysis of Thomas

Kuhn who explained, brilliantly in my opinion, what science is as a unique activity and as a social institution. What interested him (and me too) was how revolutionary changes take place in different scientific fields. Kuhn principally had the natural sciences in mind, but I found many analogies to the social sciences in his work. In order to explain passages in this book, and what I did professionally for a number of decades, I will briefly explain Kuhn's approach.

Scientific interest begins when, after being carefully trained, especially at universities, scientists carry out observations on physical events or on human nature in specific fields (physics, sociology, etc.). The scientists' subsequent task is to interpret what is common to all those discrete phenomena and to formulate a generalization by which it is possible with the help of a causal interpretation to explain and predict the greatest number of additional phenomena in the field. This generalization is usually called a "theory." And the test of a theory lies in its ability to predict and explain also other observable facts or processes that haven't been investigated yet. Up to this point, nothing new had been introduced into the consensus that already existed regarding the nature of science ("normal science" as he called it). However, Kuhn went several significant steps beyond what was agreed upon in his explanation of the nature of science. The theory or theories in a specific domain are part of a paradigm. The paradigm is a research activity based on past layers of knowledge and it includes a series of questions or puzzles that have been already formulated and which the scientific community must research in order to find answers within the framework of an existing theory since in every field, enigmas always remain. What's more important though, in my opinion, is that the paradigm includes a closed community of scientists, researchers, and students, and it has its own language, terminology, and textbooks which determine what is the confirmed body of information in the domain and what is "correct" in every field, as well as which are the legitimate methods for the accumulation of knowledge and its limits vis-à-vis different and sometimes competing disciplines. The paradigm and the community included in it have also an almost exclusive control over the allocation of budgets, without which it is nearly impossible to carry out any serious research. It is interesting to point out that the concept of "discipline" has a double meaning: it indicates a branch of knowledge and also the training of mind and character to produce self-control and obedience. And indeed, one of the dominant functions of every paradigm is to discipline the members of the community not to deviate from what is accepted and to continue to teach, research, and produce knowledge as their teachers have taught them for generations. Otherwise their work would not be published in journals, which are also part of the paradigm, and they would either be excluded from this hierarchical system or fail to be promoted within it. In this way, a system that allegedly reveres innovation draws its boundaries beforehand and is fundamentally conservative, even though, in principle, it is possible to build different paradigms on the basis of the same observations and data and give them an alternative yet equally valid explanation; however, in general, this happens only rarely because of intra-scientific "politics."

But over time, observations, discoveries, and phenomena which cannot be categorized and explained by the ruling paradigm (and which are then called "anomalies") accumulate, a situation that Kuhn defined as a crisis. At first, their mere existence is ignored and those, mostly younger, scientists who acknowledge them may find themselves banished from the community. After all, no professor who has achieved a lifelong career, status, and reputation is interested in seeing all, or most, of his activities and publications come to be considered outdated or even incorrect. There are those who try, and sometimes even succeed, in expanding the boundaries of an existing paradigm in order to include the "insubordinate" phenomena within it. Others try to develop alternative theories to the ones existing within the framework of the paradigm. When this attempt is brought about by more established scientists, those theories cannot be ignored any longer and an "inter-paradigmatic war" breaks out. Today, in the internet age, it is easier for "crazy" scientists, or even amateurs, to forward articles to others in order to convince them or for the purpose of publishing them virtually, and the community has lost a lot of its ability to supervise and discipline. There is also a big disadvantage since huge portions of the material published online are partially or completely fraudulent. Therefore, "serious" scientists still prefer to publish in journals whose publishers make sure that the manuscript is evaluated and revised by expert-colleagues usually at the price of perpetuating the conservatism in the field.

And yet, in spite of this built-in conservatism, science changes and renews itself in leaps, and when a number of authorities in the field can no longer deny the accumulation of anomalies, only then are the basic assumptions, questions, textbooks, and sometimes even the research methods of the field partly or entirely changed. Kuhn also emphasized that a scientific revolution is influenced by changes in the social worldview in addition to having an effect on it, although these correlations are usually concealed and even denied by the claim that the "scientific establishment" is independent of the entire society and the state.

\*   \*   \*

In retrospect, the change for the worse in my status was rather to be expected. As I had mentioned previously, a big conference was held at the beginning of the 1990s when Eisenstadt retired. Prominent sociologists from all over the world came to pay him homage and give lectures in his honor. One of the sessions was dedicated to the study of Israeli society and I too participated in it. My lecture indeed included some justified tributes to the founding father of Israeli sociology, but it was principally a severe criticism of the basic assumptions which guided these studies and especially of the distorted positions occupied by Arab Israelis and Oriental Jews in this society. My lecture aroused considerable indignation among most of the faculty's senior staff; however, it seems to me that this would never have resulted in more than temporary anger. On the contrary, my arguments stimulated healthy professional discussions in the hallways. What was inexcusable was that I turned this lecture into a well-documented article in English and submitted it for publication in the world's most prestigious journal—*The American Sociological Review*—a periodical which every sociologist at least skims through and which accepts approximately one article for every forty submitted to it. To my utter surprise, the article was accepted for publication. This was already too much: not only did I air dirty laundry in public, but I did it in a journal which evokes the envy of every professional in the field. No combination is tougher than anger mixed with envy.

Actually, I already had become aware of this fact a few years earlier. Since I had at my disposal lots of data and material which had been gathered for my doctoral research and had not yet been used, I decided to write an additional study which was later published in a book entitled *Zionism and Economics*.

The well-known American historian Frederick Jackson Turner claimed that the existence of a frontier is the source of American individualism and of the aspiration for a weak and decentralized federal government (at least in the first century of the republic). In other words, contrary to the situation in the old world where land was a scarce resource and most of the political, economic, and social class relationships stemmed directly or indirectly from the control over the land, this commodity was available in the new continent in such great abundance that it had almost no financial value. The immigrant and his family could always move west, stake a claim, and fence any plot of land, declaring ownership over it and protecting it with his gun because he and not a central government represented law and order there. In this way, they also avoided the price—such as tax payments—exacted by the country for providing its citizens or subjects with defense and other services. I came along and reversed the research question and asked what happens in a society of immigrant-settlers when the most expensive economic resource is the land and most of the immigrants depend on different kinds of private or public institutions (which, like the Jewish National Fund, belong almost completely to the state) in order to meet the basic need for land to settle on. In this need, I have identified one of the sources of Israeli collectivism and of its social regime.

The economists felt that I had invaded their territory and started to spread the rumor throughout the faculty that I had published a terrible essay without understanding a thing about economics. Actually, for a long period of time, the sociological examination of economic systems had traditionally been a part of a comprehensive study which included religion, family, education, social status, army, law, etc. It should be pointed out that the majority of the founding fathers of sociology began their careers by studying capitalism as part of the development of the modern world. Talcott Parsons, who formulated the structural-functionalist paradigm which ruled sociology for three decades, was a professional economist. My book, too, dealt with the sociology of economics, a fact the economists did not understand. One of them took the trouble to publish aggressive and destructive critical essays about the book in a number of journals; however, in spite of all of the energy he invested, he managed indeed to find within the text itself one mistake in economic theory and a second error in the index, which I did not even prepare. What is typical and interesting was the fact that the economists were either unwilling or unable to deal with the central thesis of the book. The real damage to me was that the book, of which I am proud to this day, delayed my promotion and tenure for a year, even though no one was able to attack its main thesis. Economists have more power and prestige in the faculty than sociologists.

*   *   *

Besides *Zionism and Economics*, I consider two additional books to be my main contribution to Israeli sociology. When I first began to deal with Israeli society, I became convinced that there is no real possibility of understanding it without knowing and understanding the one which stands opposite to it, namely the Palestinian society and the interrelationships between the two. However, for nearly twenty years during which I have dealt with this conflict, almost nothing new had been established by the research on this society. The decisive majority of those engaged in this field, especially the Orientalists, took an ideological, moral, or apologetic stance on one side or the other. Therefore I was happy when my friend, Joel Migdal, offered me a position at Washington University in Seattle during my sabbatical. Joel wrote one of the first balanced and systematic books about the Palestinians in which he focused on the *fellahin* (farmers) since his area of expertise was peasant uprisings and, later, interactions between state and society. He also carried out research on stateless societies. I suggested to him that we write the social history of the Palestinians together, a proposal he accepted enthusiastically. In spite of the fact that I still had at my disposal huge amounts of unused material, gathered for my doctorate and covering substantial areas of the Arab issue, which mirrored parallel ones in Jewish society, we worked for about two more years to complete and update it. The actual conceptualization and the writing itself took nearly one more year. Joel had two advantages over me: first, his English is beautiful and all of his writings sound like poetry, and secondly, he was able to moderate my aggressive writing and smooth its rough edges. Even though we saw eye to eye on most things and we had a very good relationship, arguments between us over content and formulation were not unknown. For example, the biggest discussion we had was about whether to use the term "ethnic cleansing" regarding the results of the 1948 war, when 750,000 Palestinian Arabs were uprooted from their homes and their land. Joel claimed, and he was probably right, that there is a limit to what readers are ready to accept. Eventually we found alternative expressions to describe those events and that was actually the biggest concession I made in this partnership. The book came out in a respectable commercial edition and its success was so considerable that the conservative Harvard University Press purchased the publication rights, published its own edition, and after a few years asked us to update it. The extensive rewriting of the updated version justified changing the title and regarding it as a new book.

This became a textbook on Palestinian social history at prestigious universities all over the world and gave both Joel and me an international reputation. The Palestinians themselves responded to the book with mixed feelings: on the one hand, they could not claim that it lacked objectivity and empathy; on the other hand, it was, after all, written by two Jews who did not hide being Zionists. One of my Palestinian colleagues wrote to me, maybe in jest, maybe seriously, "You first seized our lands, expelled us from our country, and now you are writing our history from the position of victors."

The problem was that the book came out just as Benny Morris' invention of the "new historians" had unleashed a new round of polemics in the country. Morris formulated a number of correct assertions, especially in regard to the official historiography of the 1948 war and the issue of the creation of the refugee problem. However, the "school" he invented was, maybe deliberately, almost devoid of real professionals (excluding perhaps Avi Shlaim and Ilan Pappe), and was dichotomous—since the partition between the "good" (primarily Morris himself) and the "bad" (all the rest) lacked nuance. This does not diminish the importance of either his book on the refugee problem or the controversy itself, which also extended to other historical and socio-political issues and perhaps it even included an attempt to change the paradigm. Yet in addition to the lack of agreement with Morris concerning the pre-planning of the expulsion, some of his explanations, which stemmed from a lack of minimal knowledge of the Palestinian society, were strident. This lack of knowledge was even more obvious in his pretentious book on the history of the conflict (published in Hebrew under the title *Righteous Victims*). In this book, although buried in almost unbearable detail, there already existed an almost total acceptance of the canonical historiography that he so heavily attacked.

Even before I was aware of it, our book was immediately categorized by both opponents and supporters as a revisionist book belonging to the new school of historiography, which was perceived as anti-Zionist. This was quite ironic since Morris himself always swore by the Zionist Moloch, and whoever read his book carefully could discover that, as in *Zionism and Territory*, there was no condemnation or moral qualms in it. He actually determined unequivocally that the expulsion was not planned and he clung to the quasi-official version that it took place as a consequence of both the course of war and the dynamics of battle. Two alternative explanations are possible: either that, as a professional historian, it is not his role to judge events but only to document and explain them—an approach with which I strongly agree—or that Morris actually justified the expulsions as *realpolitik*. With the publication of the new, enlarged edition of his book, it became clear that the second explanation was more accurate and that my perception was correct: the thesis was indeed that the Jews committed atrocities and massacres (including Tantura),[1] raped and even slaughtered here and there—it's not fair, but that's the nature of war and especially of one for survival. Moreover, the mass expulsion was justified; without it, a Jewish state could not have been established, and it is a pity that it wasn't complete. If the expulsion had been complete, the wars between the

Arab countries and Israel would have ceased—it is not clear how and, most of all, why. In this way, Morris encourages us to complete the act of ethnically cleansing the Arabs from the country if, in the future, a constellation of events develops which would make that possible. I must point out that even before Benny came out of the closet, he offered me a chance to be included in the anthology he planned. My intuition, once again, did not disappoint me and I refused politely. When *Righteous Victims* appeared, I wrote an unflattering but impartial critique of it. Morris felt offended and as a "reprisal" wrote a very harsh criticism of the updated *Palestinians* in the conservative American journal *New Republic*. I smiled. This is how it is in this profession—you knock and get knocked about. His criticism increased the sales of our book significantly.

As mentioned before, when the book about the Palestinians was published, I was not yet aware that I had fallen into hot water. I brought a copy of the book with a warm inscription to my instructor, Moshe Lissak, who was supposed to help promote my career, and told him that in my opinion, this book, along with my other publications, justified starting the process for my promotion to the level of associate professor. Lissak smiled sourly and said nothing. Within a short time, I learned that he convinced most of the senior faculty to block my advancement. However, when the delay started to look odd, the faculty dean, Gershon Ben-Shachar, began forming a committee that, after being approved by the rector who, at the time, was Yehoshua Ben-Arie, should have made a decision about my promotion. Ben-Shachar submitted the names for such a professional committee after conducting the usual international survey among researchers in the field regarding the quality of my work and whether they would have promoted me to the same position in their own institutions. However, the rector refused to approve the dean's list of names. After his third refusal, the dean understood that no committee, regardless of its composition, would be approved. He invited me to lunch and suggested that we wait two years until the rector left office. Did I have a choice? And indeed, the procedure, which in itself lasted a year, began only after Ben-Arie and Lissak retired. During that same time, wild personal attacks against me started to be spread by key figures in Israeli culture like Aharon Meged, Amnon Rubinstein, Dan Margalit, and others. From the content of the attacks, it was quite clear that several of them had not read the book, but had been "briefed" about it.

After the book had been published, Shabtai Teveth,[2] who led an ongoing, contentious public debate with the "new historians," called me and asked: "Where have you been until now?" We held fruitful discussions about various historical subjects until shortly before his death. He and his wife Ora even visited us at our home in Mevasseret.

\* \* \*

All my books were my children, but among them, some are, in my opinion, less important while others are more so. One of the most important is undoubtedly *Immigrants, Settlers, Natives*, on which I worked intermittently for about seven years. This was an ambitious attempt to narrate Israeli history in a new and comprehensive way according to my approach, which is based on the viewpoint that Israel is a state of immigrants and settlers. This book includes both the separate history of all its component groups and their past and present inter-relationships since its foundation. In the summary chapter, I wrote that the Israeli immigrant-settler state was formed by waves of immigrants who arrived in this territory and formed superimposed layers which could be compared to geological strata. The bottom layer, chronologically, is composed of the remnants of the Arab population that did not flee after the 1948 war and that partially succeeded in returning to normal life as time went by. The void left by the Arab population was filled by waves of Jewish immigrants. The most recent layers are the thick Russian and the very thin Ethiopian ones. Every new wave of immigration significantly changed the entire whole and had an impact on the status and character of the other layers. Every wave caused a social earthquake and a series of aftershocks which have not yet ceased to affect us to varying degrees.

The cultural and political earthquakes caused by the waves of immigration were actually subsumed in those resulting from periodic wars and the various armed conflicts in which the Israeli state was involved. These are the two outstanding characteristics of Israel as an immigrant-settler state which continues to be in conflict with the original population, the Palestinians, found both inside and outside the country. It is not surprising, therefore, that from its founding to the present day, Israel has been involved in more wars than all the other states that arose since World War II. In that respect, the uncertainties which make life in Israel comparable to life at the mouth of a volcano, its characteristics as a country always on military alert and under siege, the sensation of physical-existential danger, and the material, social, and human costs involved in it, were even more salient than the uncertainties caused by the waves of immigration. On top of all this, we have to add the problematic character of the legitimization of the existence itself of an immigrant-settler society whose establishment was made possible by uprooting 750,000 Arabs, destroying their society, and demolishing them as a political and social entity. Even though on a cultural and cognitive level, the state developed various mechanisms to create its own legitimacy (including a systematic denial of the events of the 1948 war), the question of "the right of this society to exist"—an internal as well as an external challenge—could probably only be resolved with the end of the Israeli–Arab conflict in general and the Jewish–Palestinian one in particular.

An additional, multi-purpose mechanism for the direct management of the conflict and the simultaneous manipulation of the "right to exist" issue was the creation of the cultural code: "to think army." That meant adapting the state from the institutional and ontological perspectives to be constantly prepared to go to war, a readiness which has been achieved more than once, and allocating a substantial portion of its material, human, and emotional resources for this objective—even more so when the events it had been prepared for become a reality. In spite of the disappearance of the hegemony and the advent of such vastly different cultures and anti-cultures, the code of conflict (the permanent war of "the few against the many" forced on the collective) unites and unifies to this day all the Jewish citizens of the state. This is also the common basis for the development of a collective identity and of a new Jewish nationality which can be labeled "Jewishness" and which (contrary to "Israeliness") is actually defined by the group that is not included in it: the Arab citizens of Israel. The significance of this Jewishness can be based on sheer secular ethno-nationality, on Judaism as a religion in all of its variations, or on combinations of these when different weights are given to those components. Therefore, the conflict, the wars resulting from it, and the waves of immigration were among the factors that shaped the national identity in this place. However, the national identity and the waves of immigration also had (and continue to have) an impact on the conflict itself, sustaining it and determining to a large extent its manifestations. This fluid national identity, which is invented and reinvented again with each wave of immigration, the conflict, the wars, and their repercussions shape to a large extent the political, economic and legal arrangements within the country also.

**Country without borders:** The 1967 war and its consequences had even more far-reaching repercussions than all the other wars (the 1948 war excluded). This war not only brought the national-religious social movement to the center of the political map, indirectly caused the disintegration of the Labor movement's ruling hegemony, reopened the geographical and social borders of the Israeli state, and turned it into a colonizing society, but has even transformed the country into a state which pursues one central aim at the expense of all other goals and issues usually found on the agendas of open societies. This single mission is to continue to dominate and settle part of the territories which were conquered during the 1967 war in order to expand the country's borders. Vast national resources have been allocated in order to realize this goal while all the other common objectives (education, health, welfare, economic development, social equality, etc.) have become relatively marginal. In addition, not only most of the public and ideological discourse was limited to one subject, which is the fate of the occupied territories and the act of settling in them, but also the debate about their religious, symbolic, and ethical significance as well as their importance to national security became the most controversial subject in the Israeli public arena. There even developed a tendency to link this issue to all the other ones. Yet beneath this major issue lies another hidden one: the problem of the relationship between religion and state and the place of religion in the nation.

However, the above consequences are not exclusively within the ambit of responsibility of the religious-nationalistic revolution created by Gush Emunim and the settlers in the occupied territories. If the country had not extended its military protection to the settlers, invested huge amounts of money in constructing settlements and financing their infrastructure, and if it had not subsidized almost every facet of their existence, this "settlement enterprise" could not have been established. Hence the Israeli government and society responded to ancient codes which were latent in them and in the culture of the irredentist society of immigrant-settlers. In this way, the state played a role in the genesis of the disagreements, instability, and additional earthquakes caused by the settler society which has risen up against its creator.

**The centrifugal and centripetal trends:** The book *Immigrants, Settlers, Natives* has presented and analyzed two main trends—as well as their historical background—which developed in the Israeli state throughout the more than fifty years of its existence. One trend is the development of an increasing level of cultural diversity and variety. This diversity has transformed the country into a fascinating mosaic of cultures, to the point that it is now difficult to consider "Israeli society" as one society, and it is necessary to regard the state as it actually is today—a shared framework of cultures and anti-cultures which have different degrees of autonomy and separate institutional development. The hierarchical yet unstable character of this structure (which partially coincides with a multi-dimensional class structure) has turned the Israeli state into an arena where series of inter-cultural and political struggles take place simultaneously in different fields and with varied and changing intensities. It is important to notice that even though these conflicts revolve around various subjects, they overtly or covertly intersect and flow into the complex relationships existing between religion and nationality and between religion and state. As mentioned before, this last issue arose with greater intensity after the borders with the occupied territories had been opened and the debate about the legitimacy of settling there had begun. Nonetheless, all sectors of the population, including the Arab citizens, have a common interest that overrides those of every group and culture (although not the marginal organizations within them or individuals) presented in the book in confining these conflicts, severe as they may be, within the aegis of agreed-upon rules and continuing to maintain the shared framework of the state.

When the processes occurring in Israel are examined over time, it is possible to identify many various contradictory and conflicting, though at times complementary, trends and dialectical outcomes stemming from the confluence of the different orientations. These contradictions often create unexpected syntheses, such as the one between ultra-Orthodox nationalism and the Russian one. In the same way, the Arab population too attained a relatively substantial empowerment and an increasing involvement in the reciprocal inter-cultural struggles in spite of the ongoing exclusion from the national symbols and the civil discrimination they experience. This empowerment is mostly a result of two factors. First, it is easier to integrate into a structure that is no longer homogeneous and in which multiple cultures exist and compete among themselves. The status of the Arabs in the cultural hierarchy is indeed low; however, today they are included in it whereas in the past they were completely outside any framework whatsoever. Secondly, the fact that Arabs constitute twenty per cent of the country's overall population has turned them into a critical mass which, as long as Israel has free elections, can no longer be ignored. Yet the overt and covert calls for the political and even physical removal of the Arabs from within the Israeli collective are intensifying. The events of October 2000 pushed the ethnocentric orientations of both sides to their extremes, precisely because of the empowerment that the Arab citizens attained during the previous decade. On the Jewish side, the above mentioned trend toward "Jewishness" gathered strength, as did the lack of tolerance even towards those voices among the Jewish populations themselves which deviated from this consensus. In the Arab society, the inclination toward separatism and the tendency to return to religion became stronger. Also the propensity to go back to a kind of neo-pan-Arabism, but not necessarily to Palestinianism as it was represented by the Palestinian National Authority, the Fatah movement, and its leader, Yasser Arafat, gained strength. The solidarity of the Arab citizens is no longer mediated by the Palestinian leadership which failed, in their opinion, to build an open and liberal regime, but is passed directly to the people who are doubly oppressed, directly and indirectly, by the Israeli occupation and by the Palestinian Authority's authoritarian regime.

Another population, which is found within all the cultures presented and analyzed in this book, is that of women, whose status has become a central issue in the public arena. This population has attained a differential increase in power according to the women's position in the class hierarchy, which partially overlaps the cultural one.

In the past decade, these populations and their own status in Israeli society have brought the problem of civil equality and the related question of the democratic character of the Israeli state to the surface. The problem of women's status and rights stems not only from the position that religion has in the state and from the macho culture resulting from the conflict and militarism, but also from the given structural inequality that raises an additional significant and almost insurmountable barrier to change.

**Between civil war and multi-cultural arrangements:** Every society is supposed to have institutional mechanisms that are acceptable to the majority of its citizens, if not for the purpose of solving internal conflicts, then at least for reaching a consensual, if at times indefinite, deferral of the resolution of disagreements, like those described in this book, about ideology or the allocation of resources. Common mechanisms of this kind are: elections, about which there is a consensus regarding their democratic character, and the existence of referenda, of a legislative body which passes laws, and of courts of law, especially the High Court of Justice which issues legal interpretations and rulings. However, as mentioned before, the indispensable condition is that all those are accepted by a decisive majority of the collective's members and should not represent only a portion of them—a situation that for now does not correspond to the Israeli reality. Within the given context, the term "status quo," which is used in regard to the relationship between religion and state, as much as it is or was (intentionally) vague, also functioned like a mechanism of this kind. Even the police and the various "security forces" might, under certain circumstances, serve as mechanisms for the mitigation and control of cultural, class, and political conflicts, provided that the state uses them wisely and sensibly.

The struggle between cultures, if it is not accompanied by physical violence and if it does not blatantly violate the rules of the game and the basic conventional norms, is a sort of mechanism for mitigating conflicts, like a safety valve which facilitates not only "letting off steam" but also the formation and consolidation of internal norms both within each group and between different ones. However, in the case of social situations in which it is not possible to solve, mitigate, or postpone conflicts, or when mechanisms serving those purposes are not available, cultural struggles might then descend into civil war or even into coups and revolutions. Many societies have been incapable of ending cultural-political conflicts or of reaching a modus vivendi among their own different cultures without finding it necessary to resort to some level of force and violence.

The Israeli state, as mentioned before, is currently in the midst of a multidimensional cultural war which might assume various forms, including different levels of civil war in which the use of force and violence would cease to be prerogatives of the state. But a state or society does not necessarily disintegrate "from within" with the weakening or even the complete disappearance of the hegemony, although it is possible that this kind of change might be accompanied among the ruling classes by apocalyptic feelings that it is the "end of the world." This would especially be the case if that process occurs quickly or relatively suddenly and it is associated with regime change, as it happened in 1977. However, the decline or the end of hegemony is usually not felt or recognized until after it has already weakened considerably. It seems that in Israel it is possible to regard the results of the 1977 elections (also known as "the turning point") as a shift which indicates, symbolically if not de facto, the beginning of the change in the socio-political order.

As we have seen, in a situation without hegemony, cultures and subcultures of different socio-political groups will exist on a cultural-ideological level within the system. Those cultures will compete among themselves in a kind of political and ideological "free market" model. However, even in a situation devoid of hegemony like this one, a dominant culture can and must nevertheless exist, although no longer as a single, legitimate, exclusive, and obvious culture or ideology. This will usually be, by definition, a prestigious and elite culture, which will indeed represent part of the power of a dominant group or stratum; yet under these circumstances, a considerable degree of bureaucratic and aggressive coercion will be required to maintain social order in the state.

An additional alternative can be the consocional one, which means an arrangement agreed upon at the elite level by all the sectors of the population about the differential allocation of material resources and symbols of prestige, the part played by the various groups and strata in the country, and even about the provision of an autonomous cultural status for each of them, not by virtue of their rights as citizens of the state, but as members of ethnic, national, or religious groups. This is principally an instrumental-allocational arrangement which ensures the protection of the minimal interests of the strong ethnic, religious, and class groups in the country without necessarily assuming the existence of a shared culture and identity. If the elites do not succeed in reaching a consocional arrangement or compromise when hegemony is disrupted, the system might easily slide into violent conflicts between the different political-cultural sectors. Multiple cultures, in the absence of multi-culturalism, increase fluidity and social uncertainty. Multi-culturalism is a socio-political situation in which not only do cultural dissimilarity and variety exist but, in addition, institutional autonomy and legitimacy are granted to the different cultures, as every culture and the state itself recognize their uniqueness, their right to be unique, and the particular requirements of all the other cultures. In this way, values and myths are also created which acknowledge cultural variation as well as its legitimacy and its power as a social ethos of the country itself, while the hierarchical relationships between the various cultures are reduced.

This is a kind of reversal of the melting pot ethos which played its role for better or for worse and vanished a while ago. Only recently, however, have the Israeli society and state started to notice its disappearance. Multi-culturalism by itself, at its various levels, is not a positive or negative value, but an additional political mechanism and a means of social regularization by which the state manages itself.

In spite of the institutionalization of social and cultural diversity, Israel is a strong and powerful country which is now exploring effective ways in which to complete the two remaining central tasks that lie ahead of it. The first is gaining acceptance in the region in order to bring about the end of the conflict—a conflict which, until recently, was inevitable given Israel's position as an immigrant-settler state established against the will of the local population. The second task is the genuine normalization and democratization of the country's internal social order. An essential condition for a normalization of this kind is, inter alia, to constitutionally protect two basic civil rights—freedom of religion and the right to be free of religion—and to institutionally and legally modify the state so that the realization of these rights becomes possible. An additional challenge would be to impart full and complete civil rights to the individual and to the various groups existing in the state, while fully recognizing their right to be different as part of civil equality.

**The transition from an immigrant to a native-born society:** One of the main conclusions drawn from the book *Immigrants, Settlers, Natives* is that the pool of Jewish immigrants—and with it the possibility of potential waves of immigration—is being drained. Even if new Jews like "the Sons of Menashe" are invented in various remote corners of the world, still only fifteen per cent of Jews currently live outside the two centers of Israel and North America. Marginal bi-directional immigration shifts between those two centers will indeed continue to take place; however, additional waves of Jewish (according to a religious, ethnic, or national definition) immigration to Israel are no longer expected. This means that, with the absorption of the last waves of immigration from the Commonwealth of Independent States, Israel will cease to be a country which absorbs massive numbers of immigrants and within a generation it will become essentially a nation of the native-born.

One less obvious consequence inherent in this new situation is the fact that the importation of highly skilled people whose education was financed in part by other countries will cease. Moreover, a self-evident outcome will be that in the future, the country will achieve increasing social, political, and economic stability since it will no longer be tossed about between waves of immigrants and will be not forced to endure the burden of their cultural, social, political, and economic absorption.

It is possible that closing the social borders (but not hermetically sealing them) will exacerbate inter-cultural conflicts in the short term; but, in the long term, it can be expected that the relations among cultures will be stabilized and institutionalized, regardless of whether the hierarchy between them will be preserved or if more equal relationships will be created.

Another process indirectly stemming from the transformation of the Israeli population into a largely indigenous one is the change among the different cultures and populations in the relative demographic strength and consequently also in the political balance of power between them. In spite of the slow decrease in its birth rate, the Arab–Palestinian population will approximately constitute, within about two decades, at least twenty-five per cent of the country's citizens. Indubitably, a people constituting such a large percentage of the population cannot be classified as marginal and certainly cannot be easily discriminated against. We have to assume that, in order to deal successfully with this situation without risking a real civil war, the state will have to change some of the conventions and basic assumptions on which it is built.

Furthermore, the European and Oriental ultra-Orthodox and national religious populations will experience a slightly increased rate of demographic and political representation in spite of the steady loss of members from the margins of their communities. Consequently, the political system will be increasingly compelled to take their demands into account. However, since they are not capable of providing a comprehensive alternative to the socio-political arrangements that are acceptable in the modern world, it is highly unlikely that they will be able to impose on Israel the regulations and the identity of a state ruled by the Torah (unless they adopt far-reaching interpretations of Jewish religious laws similar in spirit to those found in the American Reform movement).

In principle, we can assume that the Israeli state will reduce its ethnic and religious profile and will gradually separate religion and state, while within groups belonging to the civil society, the importance of religion and ethnicity will increase. The state will be forced to become increasingly indifferent to individual identities; however, it will continue to fulfill, perhaps to an even greater extent, its instrumental functions (ensuring security, maintaining law and order, providing for the welfare and the social rights of the individual). As for all the remaining pan-social tasks, the state will share their implementation with the various components of the pluralistic civil society which is developing in Israel. All this can happen on the condition that within the foreseeable future, the Jewish–Palestinian conflict will end. However, even if the end of the conflict is not so close, those processes will probably continue to take place, although their institutional and political results will be postponed to the more distant future.

**The possibility of ending the conflict, and its results:** The Israeli state faces a difficult dilemma between two contradictory major objectives structured in it and as long as the choice continues to depend on the state itself, it will not be able to decide between them. On the one hand, there is the objective of building the nation by settling the land next to the borders and constantly expanding the boundaries of its control (while incorporating the smallest possible portion of the local Arab population). On the other hand, there is the objective according to which the warrant for Israel's ultimate victory and for the consolidation of the state lies in its acceptance as a legitimate and integral part of the region by its residents, peoples, and states. From this point of view, Ze'ev Jabotinsky was right when he discerned as a necessary condition for achieving this objective the creation of an "iron wall" (namely military, economic and social power), which would convince the region's inhabitants that the Israeli immigrant-settler state constitutes an accomplished fact and cannot be destroyed.

And indeed, after the bloody 1973 war, and more precisely from 1977, a slow and incomplete process of peacemaking began to develop between the peoples in the region, their states, and the State of Israel. At first, a peace treaty with Egypt was signed; afterwards, a declaration of principles was achieved in the framework of which the mainstream of the Palestinian national movement recognized the right of Israel to exist and Israel acknowledged the right of the Palestinians to political self-determination. All the conflicts which occurred and are yet to follow after this agreement have been and will be the manifestation of the attempts on both sides to maximize their own interests as they perceive them. The processes which motivated both sides to try to bring an end to the conflict that has already lasted for several generations are complex and probably the conditions needed to achieve an agreement are not yet, even today, fully ripened. Nevertheless, in spite of the crises accompanying this process, which may yet include a war of some size, there is a high probability that the borders of the Israeli state are about to be delineated and sealed,[3] more or less according the basic lines of the 1949 ceasefire, and in this way the anomaly of a country without borders will end. Thus Israel will not only cease to be a nation of immigrants but also of frontiers and settlers.

All these processes and changes will require adjustments both at the level of the national-collective consciousness and at the level of social and political arrangements. To bring these about, the intellectuals in the Israeli state, their Jewish colleagues outside its borders as well as the Arab intellectuals, wherever they are, will play a crucial role as creators of thoughts and ideas. It is to be expected that those changes will still be accompanied by serious struggles and cultural wars since they concern not only the external status of the state but also the position of all the opposing cultures existing in it.

*   *   *

Actually, a kind of "preview" of the central ideas of the book *Immigrants, Settlers, Natives* had already appeared in the first part of the little book *The End of Hegemony of the Ahusalim* (an acronym formed from the Hebrew words for Ashkenazi [Jew from Central or Eastern Europe], secular, long-time Israeli citizens, socialist and national—an attempt to create an equivalent in meaning to the American WASP]. This was a kind of humanistic manifesto which belongs to my public, political writing and was published as part of a series of "subversive" books commissioned and edited by Gideon Samet. Even though the book was a bestseller, the concept itself did not catch on and I consider this to be a failure. An additional public-political book was *Politicide*, which was also written at the request of a publisher (British this time) and was published in seven languages, but not in Hebrew, and about which I've already written. The concept of politicide refers to a combined military, political, economic, diplomatic and cultural process aimed at preventing an ethno-national entity from having the possibility of and the option for self-determination. The fundamental means used to achieve this aim are the destruction of its institutional infrastructure, the elimination of its leaders and activists, and the de-legitimization of its request for self-determination and the establishment of a state. The book was written during "Operation Defensive Shield" and I used Ariel Sharon's political biography both as a metaphor and as a way of personifying the "Israeli situation" since 1948. I read everything possible about him; however, except for a number of episodes from his childhood, I did not delve into his personal life. That is not my style. I must also confess that with all my repulsion for the man and his abhorrent actions, I was deeply impressed by his formidable abilities and by his talent for taking advantage of situations and turning every failure into victory.

As mentioned, I worked on *Immigrants, Settlers and Natives* for about seven years and it was published by Am Oved Publishers with the unfailing support of my editor Nitza Drori Perman (better known as the editor of the periodical *Two Thousand*). Actually, this book was also a cause for disappointment since, in spite of having reasonably good sales for a textbook, it attracted very little public attention. The only review that was published about it appeared in the *Haaretz* book supplement and it was evident that the reviewer, although sympathetic, hadn't really read the book.

# Notes

1. A graduate student at the University of Haifa, Theodore Katz, wrote a master's thesis in which he claimed that a massacre had occurred in 1948 in the Arab fishing village of Tantura. This thesis elicited great controversy, with many claiming that the massacre did not in fact occur.
2. Shabtai Teveth was an Israeli journalist and writer who often wrote about Israeli history as well as the history of the Jewish community in Palestine.
3. By this I mean that the borders would have to be recognized and fixed so that people would have to follow standard procedures in order to cross them.

# 14

## BETWEEN BOSTON AND TORONTO

After the completion of my doctorate, my marriage, and the birth of two babies, employment and career issues became once again more pressing. Although I usually felt that most of the members of the department appreciated my work, my position there was far from secure and the road to tenure seemed longer than ever. Doing a post-doctorate at one of the best universities in the world was considered indispensable, especially for a person like me who had obtained all of his degrees at the same institution which, with all its pretensions, was and remains to a large extent parochial. The university always encourages the young and the not-so-young faculty members to leave for post-doctoral work and sabbaticals and is even willing to support them financially. The choice of where to go is very important since every excellent location has its own areas of expertise or its own internationally famous "stars" in one field or another. It is most effective to go to a place where you can both update your knowledge in your own field or fields and add other interesting ones for your own development and for that of the department on your return. Usually those who go abroad also teach a few classes at the host institution, thus supplementing the income provided by the university. I was not prepared to teach because of my disability and also because I did not feel confident enough of my English. It is actually very difficult to find a place in a good university since the best researchers from all over the world try, obviously, to find positions there and become intoxicated by the inebriating aroma.

I therefore consulted Eisenstadt with the intention of asking for his aid since at the time he was regarded as part of the family at Harvard University, which was and remains to this day one of the world's most prestigious academic institutions. Eisenstadt immediately agreed to help me get to Harvard, but a brief inquiry unearthed the fact that it required payment for the services it provides for visiting scholars wishing to live on campus, while the money the university had budgeted for me was barely enough for subsistence and a modest rent. Eisenstadt, knowing all the tricks, suggested a way to bypass Harvard. The Massachusetts Institute of Technology, itself a very prestigious university, had developed over the years departments and institutes of social science (political science, some fields of philosophy, psychology, linguistics, and especially economics and business administration) in addition to its departments of engineering and "hard" sciences. It had also established an Institute for

International Studies. In the U.S., every social, political, or economic subject which does not deal with the United States is defined as "international." This institute sponsored a joint discussion and research team with the Harvard people that was headed by a bright and rising star—Samuel P. Huntington. Within three weeks, I received a polite invitation from MIT.

Amy was the administrative manager who directed the Institute for International Studies. As a matter of fact, I got to see the academic administrator (whose name I don't remember) only twice: the first time when he entered my office in a whirlwind and welcomed me on my arrival, and the second when I had arranged a meeting with him right before my departure. Amy, a big woman with a rare sense of humor, was always in her office and managed the institute with great efficiency. A spacious office and an electric typewriter were allotted to me. In 1978, personal computers did not yet exist, not even at MIT. On the other hand, however, at about the time I arrived there, the latest technological wonder was acquired by the institute—the word processor and printer which occupied an entire room and was operated by a person whose sole function was entering the texts to be processed. Every staff member or guest at the institute was entitled to have his or her articles and books processed and a long waiting line formed immediately. To my Israeli eyes, the huge abundance of resources which were at the disposal of the institute and the whole university was astounding. According to my head count, for every two researchers at least one secretary, clerk, or some kind of assistant was available and most of them were more than polite and ready to assist the academic staff.

The people at the institute were extremely diverse. Among them, a group of senior military officers on sabbatical stood out. These men, with the rank of colonel or higher, studied intensely and diligently or wrote articles. One of them, Jack, with whom I formed an immediate friendship, wrote in such a critical fashion about the American army's machismo that it surprised me. Another colonel from the strategic [air] command even took me once for a day-long visit to his base in Maine and proudly showed me the command bombers (the well-known "flying fortress" B-52s), which took off while loaded with nuclear bombs for their routine stay in the air. It must be remembered that we were then in the middle of the Cold War.

One African-American female officer gave me a detailed lecture about the American nuclear deterrence strategy, the meaning of "second strike" and the doctrine of mutual assured destruction. The truth is that I already knew all the theory (I had read Thomas Shelling, David Rapoport, and Robert McNamara's books while still in Israel). When I asked her if she was not afraid that I could be an Israeli, Soviet, or Romanian spy, she burst into laughter and explained to me that whatever was said and seen at the base was available as public information to everyone. On the way back, my friend the colonel (who, by the way, was born as a German in Germany, emigrated to the United States of America with his parents when he was a baby, and was very proud that as a bomber pilot he managed to bomb Berlin) told me that publicity was part of America's deterrence strategy.

During that period, like most Israelis, I still felt deep appreciation for military men and was drawn to the values of Israeli militarism in a way that was unconnected to my reservations regarding Israeli policy in the occupied territories. It seems to me that to this day at least a portion of the Israeli public—even among those that are called "leftists"—do separate this feeling of appreciation, if not admiration, for the army as an institution, with all its various security services, from their attitude toward the occupied territories. This distinction is made as if the army (together with the reverence for the security idol inculcated in us by the military culture) is not the main instrument by which the anomalous situation of a prolonged occupation became possible.

But all of this was actually marginal with regard to my encounter with Boston, which was then and remains to a large extent even today the intellectual capital of the United States and therefore also of the whole world. In and around the Cambridge area (the academic suburb of greater Boston) there is a very high concentration of universities (I'll mention only two additional ones here—Boston University and Brandeis University which, when Jews could not be accepted into Harvard, was almost exclusively Jewish). All the people whose books and articles I had read walked through the corridors or had their names displayed on office doors. And even those who weren't employed at Harvard or MIT dropped by every now and then from all over the U.S. and the world for a lecture, workshop, or seminar. The atmosphere at this highest summit of "Science" made my head spin. I ran from lecture to lecture about almost every subject of which I merely had a bit of understanding and I did not feel satiated.

The Institute for International Studies itself was a kind of Noah's Ark full of more or less fascinating individuals: a Pakistani nuclear physicist (with a doctorate from MIT), a Soviet ethnographer, a Taiwanese geographer, a Saudi prince who never spoke to anyone, a Swede studying communications, and more young researchers, some of whom I will write about later, in addition to the large coterie of generals and colonels. The Pakistani physicist told me that he was determined to go back to his country and build the Pakistani bomb (and he may well have succeeded). Totally alarmed, I was dragged into endless discussions with him when I argued against scattering nuclear weapons all over the world. "Tell that to the Indians," he would say. "And why is Israel allowed and we're not?" he asked. "Because we (the Israelis) are in danger of extermination," I would reply ("a few against too many") and I added the worn-out rationale about the Holocaust which must never happen again. "You have managed well without it up until now," he smiled. "Because we used it as a deterrent," I answered and he smiled dismissively. The only claim that made him lose his temper, and rightly so, was that irrational countries shouldn't have nuclear weapons. "Who told you that we are less rational than the Americans, British, and French and especially the Israelis? That is a racist remark, if you didn't notice," he retorted. Despite our differences of opinion and out of mutual curiosity to know more about each other's country and culture, we had a cordial lunch at a restaurant near the institute. At MIT, the lunch hour between twelve and one o'clock was sacrosanct—no classes or lectures took place and everyone ate lunch while simultaneously holding professional or friendly conversations with each other.

The day I arrived at the institute, I encountered there someone from my faculty, Michael Hendel, who belonged to the Department of International Relations. In Jerusalem, we didn't know each other at all, but in Boston we became good friends almost immediately. Michael was an intelligent, original, and brilliant man who, nonetheless, was lacking in self-confidence. He completed his doctorate at Harvard and was the first to write a comprehensive essay about Israeli military doctrine and was accepted in Jerusalem with open arms. He had a red sports car and would sometimes invite me for a drive outside the city (we traveled as far as New Jersey) to wonder together at the amazing colors of New England's autumn foliage or the springtime's budding greenery. Being single, he courted a beautiful woman named Jane but after she responded favorably, he started hesitating. A number of times I met the young woman, who was willing to convert for him, and I found her warm and intelligent. They got married and when we returned to Jerusalem, we continued to be friends and even Diana, who does not socialize easily, liked Jane and Michael.

However, the woman who grew up in Vermont did not feel comfortable in Israeli society, she did not learn Hebrew, and they eventually returned to America. Michael taught at the United States Military Academy and our contacts became sporadic. My Google search revealed that Michael died a few years ago. It is my feeling that his decision to leave Israel was not only related to his wife, who bore him four children, one right after the other. From the beginning of our relationship, Michael expressed doubts about Israel's chances for long-term survival.

At the institute, when I first began conversing in Hebrew, apparently quite loudly, with Michael Hendel, I heard a call from the other end of the corridor, also in Hebrew (with a bit of American accent) "What, you too?!" The question was directed at me by Ian Lustick (he later claimed that the origin of the name Ian, is "ayin" the Hebrew word for eye). Ian had just completed his doctorate at the University of California, Berkeley and was looking for a permanent job. It might be interesting to mention that the prestigious Ivy League American universities do not usually offer positions to their graduates. They send them out to establish careers at other universities and if they succeed, they are invited back but by then, most of them do not want to return. This situation prevails because there exists an open academic market with mobility among thousands of private and public institutions and the academic "star," whose prestige is measured by his salary, research budgets, and fringe benefits, may negotiate the financial compensation.

Ian wrote a doctoral dissertation about the mechanisms of oppression and expropriation used against the Arabs in Israel and in spite of what I already knew about the subject, I refused to accept his approach and he was angry with me; consequently at that stage, we did not find common ground. After a short while, he disappeared from the institute since he found a position in a small but famous university. From there he made his way to a chair at the illustrious

University of Pennsylvania and became one of the most outstanding political scientists in the United States. Over time, I discovered that his theoretical approach towards the Arab problem in Israel was correct and that his doctorate, which was published later on as a book (and even translated into Hebrew), was considered a breakthrough in the field. As time went by, our relationship improved greatly and we co-operated here and there. However, we never really became friends, perhaps also because of his somewhat introverted character.

The highlight of the Boston experience was undoubtedly the Harvard–MIT joint seminar. The universities took turns hosting the meetings and it was quite obvious that there was a subtle competition since each tried to outdo the other. The seminars were divided into four parts. Initially, one of the university stars—including young ones who had just completed their doctorates—gave a lecture. I remember especially, to this day, lectures by Teda Scotchpaul on social revolutions and the state, by Suzan Berger on multi-national corporations, and by George Dominguez who, less than a year before it happened, spoke about the Iranian Islamic revolution in front of a completely skeptical audience. That was actually the first time I heard about Khomeini. At the head of the table, Huntington functioned as a priest (I am using this term intentionally), to whom everyone else served as an acolyte.

After the lecture, a dinner with at least five courses accompanied by fine wines was served with exemplary ceremony by waiters. "Would sir prefer caviar or maybe chopped liver?" was an example of the crucial questions we had to decide on at this stage. After the rich meal, we had approximately half an hour to rest and digest with the help of strong drinks. However, the main purpose of this respite was to make private conversations possible and fix dates for "business meetings." On some of these occasions, I managed to approach the grand priest, especially when he was already quite drunk. He told me that he had heard about me from Shmuel, who regarded me highly, and that he would be happy if I came to his office for a talk. I was the happiest person on earth at that moment. I was already dreaming about a position at Harvard…

After the digestion phase came the last part which was usually the most interesting. During this period, the participants asked questions or argued with the lecturer. In most of the cases they did not spare the rod: their critique was lethal and in general also sophisticated and relevant. It was a kind of competition as to who could catch the lecturer making mistakes in fundamental assumptions or methodology and contradict his thesis. This was the name of the game and the seminar would then turn into a kind of arena for intellectual gladiators who destroyed each other lustily, although with extreme politeness, the way that lawyers frequently do in court. I must admit that I didn't understand everything because of my poor English and because I was not familiar with the nuances of many of the fields which were not related to mine; however, I understood the spirit of what was said there very well.

It is worthwhile to explain briefly why it was essential for me to go to Boston, apart from the necessity of supplementing and updating my knowledge which, in the pre-virtual age, could not be accomplished in Israel.

As I mentioned earlier, there is a need to be "connected"; it is vital to create a professional network of acquaintances in order to make your work known, read, and quoted, and to elicit responses to it. Whoever is not cited does not exist, and the more one is quoted and widely known, the better the chances are of his articles and books being published. It is a kind of vicious and merciless cycle which every young researcher must break; otherwise he has no chance of survival.

I came to Boston with a translated draft of my doctorate and additional raw material, mainly about the economic relationships between Jews and Arabs, intending to write at least a monograph on the subject. But hundreds walked around Boston with similar goals while the great ones learned how to protect themselves and their time from nuisances like us. Furthermore those divine beings have incredibly inflated egos and WASPS are by nature polite, yet cold, and keep their distance. In short, I did not succeed in gaining the interest of that generation's distinguished personages in me and my work and at the time I did not consider the less influential ones who were at the same level as me. Consequently, I was very happy when I received Huntington's invitation to his office. By the end of the next day, I had arranged an appointment with his secretary for a meeting.

His office was located in a modern, multi-story building that was unlike most others at Harvard and MIT which, although periodically renovated, were one or two hundred years old. One whole floor of the giant edifice carried his name and the office looked in every respect like a spacious apartment. Besides a conference room, huge book shelves, and filing cabinets, the floor included other rooms, but since I never went into them, I don't know what they were. Later on, I learned that such luminaries are entitled to private bathrooms, showers, gyms, and places to rest. There is no doubt that the big universities know how to reward their stars. Of course, those are private universities and they are not a burden to the public although they do benefit indirectly from large federal budgets that finance research on subjects which interest the government. (Many years later, I found out that during the 1960s, Huntington himself worked for the Central Intelligence Agency and many of the books which made him famous were based on those studies.)

A very elderly secretary looked at her calendar and both inquired and determined: "Dr. Kimmerling, I assume? The professor is waiting for you." I entered a relatively small room which was very tidy compared to the chaos I had passed through on the way in. In contrast to the friendly encounter during which Huntington invited me and spoke highly of me, he was cold and distant. "How can I help you?" he asked. I naively wanted to give him my manuscript to read in case he would be willing to recommend it to some publisher and perhaps even to the Harvard University Press. But he refused politely and didn't even show any interest in the subject of the book. Later on, I learned that he had never been interested in Israel (even though it could apparently be included within his areas of expertise). "Turn to Joel Migdal. He might be able to assist you," he said and hinted that the meeting was over.

I left his office totally crushed. I knew vaguely who Migdal was since he had also participated in the seminar and I knew that he was considered one of Huntington's outstanding students and that he even spoke Hebrew. He had published a study about peasant uprisings and also a book on Palestinian politics, a subject which at the time was not yet linked to my work. During the next seminar, I approached him and we set a date for lunch at the Harvard and MIT joint faculty club.

Indeed, Joel did show great interest in my work and also saw himself as a pupil of Eisenstadt who would periodically give classes at Harvard. A Zionist and a graduate of the Labor Party youth movement in New York, he completed his doctorate in 1970, accepted the position offered by Tel-Aviv University, and taught at the Department of Political Science, where he was expected to have an outstanding career. But when the 1973 war broke out, his wife decided that "This is not the place for us" and the Migdal family went back to Boston, where Joel had no problem being accepted again at Harvard. However, apart from attention, sympathy, and interesting conversations, Joel also could not really help me at the time. A number of years later, Joel received an offer he could not refuse: to establish an institute for international studies at the University of Washington in Seattle. Consequently, the Migdal family moved from the East Coast to the Northwest Coast of the continent. The friendship and closeness between us continue to this day and led us to cooperate and write a joint book which became a classic and appeared in many editions, some of which were published by the Harvard University Press.

While I was having mixed feelings about our stay in Boston, Diana's feelings were unequivocal. This sabbatical was very hard and frustrating for her. She had to take care of a baby, a toddler, and of everything else in addition to driving me wherever I needed to go. She had no company at all and the neighbors were not friendly to us. In addition, the money we had at our disposal was extremely limited, a fact that worsened our situation still further. Indeed the Friedman family, Menachem, Tamar, and the children too, were on sabbatical in Boston that year and sometimes invited us for Saturday meals, but there was a tone of arrogance in their attitude and Diana was very sensitive to it. She even prepared a chart and counted off the days that were left until we returned to Israel.

For the second sabbatical we went to Seattle. In between, Na'ama, my wonderful youngest, was born and I became a senior lecturer with tenure at the university. Every promotion to a higher level within the university is important, but the position of senior lecturer is, as mentioned before, the most important since it ensures that the staff member cannot be fired under any circumstance unless a criminal act is committed. The only sanction the university can implement against someone who breaches the trust stemming from this position (for example, by failing either to publish or to publish at a suitable level) is to block additional promotions (to the next levels—associate professor and "full" professor or "finished professor," in Agnon's provocative terminology).

In Seattle I enjoyed excellent sabbatical conditions, which this time also included a generous stipend that, in addition to the university salary, considerably improved our quality of life. That year, the weather was excellent and not rainy. The Pacific Northwest, including the northern Seattle area and Vancouver, is situated in a warm bubble and amazed us with its water, lakes, fish, and greenery. Diana fell in love with the place and felt great, as did the children. My academic productivity benefited from the whole situation. In the meantime, the Intifada broke out. I felt awful when watching the atrocities on the news but later found out that the Israeli public had not been exposed to most of them. The pictures of Israeli soldiers breaking young Palestinians' limbs will be engraved in my memory forever. Later on, I will write about the archaic dimensions of this conflict.

During that sabbatical, I finished editing a book of articles about Israeli society. Meanwhile, Migdal and I began consolidating an extensive research project on the social history of the Palestinian people. We completed it after three years with the writing of a comprehensive book during an additional half-year sabbatical in Seattle. It may be interesting to mention that substantial parts of the book were written via the internet. When I had finished writing a draft of a chapter, I would send it as a file to Joel. He would return it to me with his corrections and remarks and I would return it to him again. That way we played a kind of intellectual ping-pong and we even fought from time to time…

\*   \*   \*

Diana and I are sitting on the sidewalk of a downtown café in Toronto, drinking coffee and trying to eat an inedible cake. The baked goods in Toronto are terrible, including the bread. Maybe in Montreal the French know how to bake. We are watching throngs of people passing by and simply enjoying the experience. First of all, the people are of different colors and speak a variety of languages—a real Tower of Babel. They do not look embarrassed to converse and sometimes even to shout publicly in the languages they have brought with them from all over the world. Secondly, and most importantly, they possess a kind of basic serenity and peace of mind which Israelis would envy. Some of them smile at me. It is not that they know me or care about me, but the North Americans like to smile at each other for no reason. In spite of this, what bothers me and desperately increases my longing for my crazy country is that of all the tens of thousands of people passing by us, I don't know anyone and no one knows me. In Jerusalem I cannot walk five meters without being stopped by an acquaintance or a friend. This anonymity makes Diana feel good.

In the mid-1960s, Canada decided to change her flag from the British Union Jack, which also symbolized the governing white Anglo-Saxon class, to a neutral flag—red with a white square containing a maple leaf at its center. The maple is the most common and impressive Canadian tree and the country's national symbol. The Canadian Federation's Coat of Arms remained highly "royal" and still symbolized the origins of the English, Scottish, Irish and French founders of this enormous country, the world's second largest, yet having a population density of less than four inhabitants per square kilometer.

In this emblem there is not even a symbolic place for the original inhabitants—who are now called the "first people"—most of whom had been cruelly annihilated. A student of mine, whose family had lived in Canada for generations, told me that if I want to send shivers down a Canadian patriot's spine, I have only to suggest the possibility that one day the surviving members of the "first people" will appeal to the High Court of Justice or some international forum and demand the return of their lands.

In 1971, Canada declared itself to be a multi-cultural nation—which means that it provides every ethnic and national group with equal status and the right to cultivate its own heritage with the help of the state—a kind of state belonging to all its citizens. Canada also opened its gates to immigration from all countries of the world but limited it to the needs of the country, giving preference to physically and mentally healthy young people and to those whose professions and skills were required. As of now, close to twenty per cent of Canadian citizens are immigrants from countries where neither English nor French are spoken. Toronto itself is mostly inhabited by "non-original" Canadians. Citizenship is acquired through a rather long process which involves tests on the knowledge of the history, laws, and one of the official languages of the state (English or French). In the end, a naturalization ceremony, which includes swearing loyalty to the flag and the federal laws, is held. A couple of American friends from California who had been through the swearing-in ceremony when we were there spoke about it with excitement. So far, the method works remarkably well and thanks to it—and also to its wealth and boundless resources—Canada is prospering in spite of the uncomfortable climatic conditions. People coming from different countries tend indeed to live in separate neighborhoods, but a common economic life flourishes and there is almost no tension or violence between communities and between races.

\*   \*   \*

The departure for Toronto was too hasty. For many years, I did not go on sabbatical because long flights harmed me physically. Sitting for long periods of time in airplane seats was devastating for my already deteriorating spine. However, with the beginning of "Operation Defensive Shield," the atmosphere in Israel became unbearable and my son, who had just finished a difficult mandatory military service in the territories, did not want to return there under any circumstances. The whole family decided to leave the country for a while. In addition, I had accumulated two years of sabbatical pay from the university. At that same time, by coincidence, I was invited to become a member of a promotion committee for a staff member seeking a full professorship at the University of Toronto. While talking with the head of the department there, I asked him if he would accept me for a sabbatical at his department. Within a week I had a position as a guest professor at the University of Toronto in addition to a quite suitable research grant. We left the country hastily, almost as though we were running for our lives, partly because the Canadian academic year was about to start.

Professionally and intellectually, there was an important reason to choose Canada as a destination for advanced studies and learning. For many years, I had been engaged not only in academic pursuits but also in what today is called "public sociology," which involves making public statements—political ones if you like—while trying to establish myself in this area, not only on the basis of ethical values but also by using portions of the professional knowledge I had acquired. As mentioned above, Canada had moved to a kind of multi-cultural system which I strongly hoped would be adopted by Israel, albeit with modifications, and which I had recommended in my public book *The End of Ashkenazi Hegemony*.

At the department in Toronto, I had been received reasonably well; however, because of their own difficulties, they didn't have office space for me. Although I was allowed to share a colleague's office, I did not take advantage of it, and I learned instead to work at home in a spacious office I had set up. Most of the staff members worked at home too and came in just to teach or for meetings. Only the head of the department and the administrative staff were usually present (almost like Jerusalem and completely unlike MIT and Seattle). The majority of the people at the department showed very little interest in my work. The fact is that today, sociology is not divided into professional and intellectual schools of thought but rather into "quantitative" sociologists who use hard data which can be measured by sophisticated statistical methods, and "qualitative" sociologists who deal with softer materials such as historical records, content analysis, observations, and ethnography. Today, the quantitative sociologists "rule" over the profession, and the results of their studies (usually, but not always) are considered trivial and boring by their "qualitative" colleagues, including me. On the other hand, the "quantitative" sociologists do not regard their "qualitative" colleagues as real people of science; nevertheless, they use their ideas extensively. Since the "quantitative" sociologists ruled in Toronto, we had very little to offer to each other.

Two additional factors influenced my relative disconnection from the department. When I asked them before my arrival if I would have easy access to the department with my scooter, their answer was affirmative. But I subsequently discovered that it was cumbersome and very difficult. Socially, Canada is one of the most progressive welfare states but this awareness had not yet reached the University of Toronto, especially if an expenditure of money is involved. Another factor we did not take into account was the great distances existing within a city of about six million citizens. In North America it is extremely difficult to find a house without steps and when we found one, we were relieved. The neighborhood was very beautiful, but it was located half an hour away from the center of town where the university is, even when using the excellent subway system. As long as my son Eli' could take me and the heavy scooter downtown by car and then bring me back, I could sometimes go to the university and other places. However, when his classes started, he was no longer available and Diana found the task too difficult to bear, especially during the long winters when the temperature would drop to thirty or forty degrees below zero and the snow was one meter deep. Therefore I stayed at home most of the time and kept in touch with the world through the internet. The benefit I derived from this situation was in the amounts of material I could read, write, and think about.

It must be said that no academic institution is able to compete with Harvard's libraries—even in subjects like Judaism, Israel, and the Middle East. However, the Seattle and Toronto libraries had amazingly rich collections on those subjects too and I found books there—even in Hebrew—that I would not have dreamed of finding even at our National Library.

# PART FOUR

## ENTERING THE PUBLIC ARENA

# 15

## On One Hand and on the Other Hand

My entrance into the public arena was gradual, and I became aware of its full significance only with hindsight. As mentioned earlier, I wrote articles in *Maariv for Youth* and *In the Gadna Camp* and, later on, also radio plays. For me, writing was easy and it flowed smoothly. I love to see my ideas take shape into words, sentences, and ultimately into a self-contained text incorporating some kind of statement with a beginning and an end. Writing for the general public is addictive and when time passes without my name appearing in print, I begin to feel a certain discomfort and my sense of self diminishes.

Gradually, not only did I develop an awareness of a kind of mission, but my writings and their publication—as well as the responses to my articles—facilitated the consolidation of my own theoretical and political views. From the beginning, most of my writings and energy were oriented toward subjects dealing with the Israeli–Arab conflict and the occupation, which I considered to be the Gordian knot that must be cut before the rest of the problems in Israeli society can begin to be addressed. I have not changed this fundamental stance since the late 1960s even though I have not been consistent in the details of my approach and many modifications have taken place over the years. There are also those who claim that my opinions have undergone an unbearable process of radicalization, but I consider the continuous worsening in the political, security, socio-economic and ethical condition of Israel to be the reason for this radicalization. Moreover, my voice was not among the first to insist on the dangers stemming from the institutionalization of the occupation and who called for a withdrawal from the occupied territories and a search for ways to make peace with the surrounding Arab region. I was preceded by people like Yeshayahu Leibowitz, Loba Eliav, Matti Peled and Shulamit Aloni. Yet those who adopted these approaches, perhaps with the exception of Uri Avnery and Arie Loba Eliav (who themselves were not consistent), lacked a well-organized theoretical approach and relied instead on slogan-like statements devoid of ideological and strategic depth. Among them, the most outstanding for both his good intentions and the shallowness of his thought was Abie Nathan. Aside from them, there were also people who were classified as "marginal" such as the Communists and the various factions of Matzpen, but they were virtually unrepresented in the public arena and their views were not regarded as legitimate.

Using a method of trial and error—which I have practically continued to apply to this day—I tried to form a kind of coherent theoretical system in the field of Jewish–Arab relations which is separate from but at the same time also supported by my research. Actually, throughout approximately thirty-five years, if not more, during which I searched for an approach, my basic assumption has never changed: namely, that Israel has absolutely no chance of long-term survival in the Middle East without its right to exist being acknowledged by the inhabitants of the region. In addition, I reached the conclusion that it is highly improbable that Israel will become a reasonably enlightened, ethical, civilized, and egalitarian nation as long as the conflict in its two forms—versus both the Palestinians and the Arab nations—is not resolved.

The fact is that during the decade between 1967 and 1977, a state of absolute bewilderment regarding the possible ways of approaching the conflict prevailed in Israel. On the one hand, by August 1967, the Movement of the People for a Greater Israel had published the well-known manifesto demanding the immediate annexation of all of the "Land of Israel" which included even the Sinai Peninsula and the Golan Heights. At the same time, they also called for the granting of full human and civil rights to all the residents of the territories. Most members of this movement came from among the core supporters of the Labor Party, although it also included a number of fanatical rightists. Those who were even more extreme, like Geulah Cohen and Rabbi Tzvi Yehuda Kook, refused to sign the manifesto since, in their opinion, it relinquished the real greater Israel, which was supposed to incorporate the Jordan's East Bank as well. I was impressed by the intellectual caliber of the manifesto's signatories, which included names such as S.Y. Agnon, Nathan Alterman, Moshe Shamir, Yehudah Burla, and Haim Guri. Yigal Alon, who for some reason was considered a "dove," came out with various versions of a plan to annex a wide strip of the Jordan Valley and of the southern West Bank in order to add "strategic depth" and to settle them with Nahal groups. Moshe Dayan wanted to establish urban centers in the West Bank to be inhabited by career soldiers, service providers for the camps, and their families while he "waited for a call" from [King] Hussein (who was supposed to assume responsibility for the Arab population of the West Bank and perhaps also for that of the Strip, whose residents would have to be transferred to the West Bank). Dayan also wanted to annex the territory running from the northern Sinai to Sharm-el-Sheikh, which had to remain under Israeli rule for security reasons. Dayan decided on the "Open Bridges" policy with Jordan and intended to create some sort of Palestinian self-government ("indirect rule," in the colonial mindset) and everyone—with the exception of the Palestinians themselves—agreed that the occupation is indeed "enlightened."

The Palestinians responded with guerilla warfare, initially from within the territories and later from across the Jordan River ("the pursuits' phase"). After their cruel eviction from Jordan ("Black September," 1970), they operated from an autonomous area along Israel's northern border that they had established in southern Lebanon. This area was called Fatahland by the Israeli media, even though it was not yet entirely clear whether Palestinians (who at that time were simply called Arabs) existed at all. For the Jews in Israel, it was difficult to understand why the Palestinians responded with violence and ingratitude in light of the humane and enlightened Israeli policy. Even for me, it took time to grasp the reasons behind their reaction.

Despite what was perceived as an unprecedented military victory, in actual fact the warfare did not end and even after it did, the number of victims continued to grow. The Egyptians launched a war of attrition along the canal while the Palestinians continued their harassment with highly inefficient, small-scale military actions from both inside and outside the occupied territories. Even as early as March 21, 1968, about twenty-five Israeli soldiers were killed in the Battle of Karameh, which was an attempt to gain control over the Palestinian guerilla headquarters on the East Bank of the Jordan. Thus, despite the unprecedented "strategic depth" and the "safe borders" attained by Israel after its so-called "brilliant" military victory, the land did not rest. It took me some time also to understand what lay hidden behind those pseudo-strategic concepts.

Yisrael Galili, who was the secret advisor to Levi Eshkol and Golda Meir and an expert at making vague statements, formulated the "Oral Law" of the Ma'arach (the electoral alliance between the Labor Party and Mapam [United Workers' Party]) and the government, which more or less included both the Alon and Dayan Plans. Pinchas Sapir, the mythological finance minister who was supposed to be not only a "pure dove" but also the strongest man in the government, was either almost silent or neutral when directives were given regarding the establishment of facts on the ground. Golda Meir, who succeeded Eshkol, claimed that she herself was a "Palestinian," and that aside from her, no other Palestinian existed. Years later, it became known that she had even rejected a political accord proposed by President Sadat and that this rejection was one of the direct causes of the 1973 war. She probably refused to accept the same agreement that was eventually signed by Menachem Begin under conditions which maybe were even less favorable for Israel. Raanan Weitz, Chairman of the Jewish Agency's Settlement Department (who was considered a well-intentioned dove), came out with a plan for settling refugees from the Gaza Strip in the northern Sinai and the West Bank and for annexing the latter to Israel. His suggestion led to a cacophony of voices and ideas accompanied by the ravages of interpersonal and inter-factional struggles. These were intertwined to the point that even a curious and skeptical person like me, in spite of being compulsively attentive to the media and a participant in campus debates, lost his bearings and found it difficult to put together a clear picture of the situation since there was probably none to be found. I read the *Combatants' Talk* and, like everyone, was proud of Israel's soldiers. And I also read *Exposed in the Turret* in the same vein. Because of my physical aversion to crowds I did not participate in the protest movement which arose after what was called "mehdal".[1] I did not want to vote for "Dash"[2] in the 1977 elections as most of my friends did (even though I do not remember exactly how I voted), and I did not hold the celebrities heading it in very high esteem since I had already heard a lot about Yadin's questionable personality on campus. Later on, I understood that the wars of 1967 and 1973 were in effect different stages of the same war.

There was more than talk. Action was taken and facts were hastily established on the ground, some of which became public without delay while others became known only much later. East Jerusalem was immediately joined to Israel, a fact that was interpreted as a sign, by those who were looking for one, that Israel was not interested in annexing additional territories. Construction of the city's surrounding neighborhoods (Neve Ya'akov, which had been a Jewish settlement until 1948, Ramat Eshkol, the French Hill, East Talpiot, and Armon HaNatziv) began apace. Additionally, construction started on settlements lying just outside Jerusalem such as Giv'on and Ma'aleh Adumim. Mayor Teddy Kollek opposed this construction since he feared that suburbanization would weaken the core of the city, which in any case included more Arabs and ultra-Orthodox than he thought desirable. It was also decided to reestablish the Jewish settlement in Gush Etzion which had been captured during the 1948 war.

In a burst of nostalgia and patriotism, and with the encouragement of the government, the senate of the Hebrew University deliberated and decided to return to Mt. Scopus. This hasty resolution, which was to provoke internal controversy in the future, called for the construction of a new campus by integrating additional buildings with the old ones. This campus was destined to become, in a short while, my second home.

After the kibbutzim succeeded in pressuring [the government] to conquer the Golan Heights, they pushed to settle parts of them and in this way established the nuclei of the first settlements there. One of them soon became Marom HaGolan, which was founded at the initiative of United Kibbutz and Tabenkin on the ruins of the village of Alika. In a statement reminiscent of Alon, those settlers were defined as a "group of volunteers who collected stray cattle."

During the Passover of 1968, Rabbi Moshe Levinger's group first took up residence in the Park Hotel and then settled on the ruins of Sebastia in Hebron with the intention of reviving the Jewish settlement in the "Ancestral City," whose community was annihilated in the 1929 massacre. As a "compromise," the group was transferred to the nearby military camp, and ultimately it was allowed to settle within the city and also to build "Upper Hebron" (Kiryat Arba). This was a decade of alternating euphoria and despondency, joy and mourning, a new kind of social protest ("the Black Panthers"), big plans and tough quandaries, only part of which my political and social "antennae" were able to sense as they were happening.

At the beginning of June 1968, I sent a critical essay on "modern" and "elevated" culture to Binyamin Tammuz, editor of the "Culture and Literature" section of *Haaretz*. The article was crammed into half a page of the newspaper on June 21, without cuts or any other editorial changes. I didn't know it at the time, but in retrospect this marked my entrance into the heart of public life. In this essay, I tried to address the assertion that in "contemporary society" pressures are applied to create (or more accurately, to produce in order to market) artistic and literary works which are mediocre at best. In the first part of the article, I rejected the materialistic claim that since the market determines what is produced and since it is intended for consumers who are below average, only creations of this sort would be advertised and marketed, and we wouldn't know about the existence of good works of art even if these were created somewhere because they would not reach the market. This line of argument was refuted by the objection that high and elitist culture had always been created for a selective and narrow audience, and that this limited body of consumers has improved in quality and quantity over the last centuries due to the invention of the printing press and the spread of education and literacy.

In the second half of the essay, I attacked the problem, not in terms of consumerism but rather in terms of creativity. I argued that in order to have the ability to create valuable products in a specific field, a person must have as necessary—although not sufficient—conditions both high intelligence and a very solid sense of self as a creator. Later in the article, I claimed that the distribution of intelligence (represented by the bell-shaped curve) throughout the population is unvarying and that those who possess high intelligence are a very small minority. At the same time, in modern society, where specialization is required, fields demanding intelligence and creativity (such as science and technology) have increased. These are, materially as well as in terms of prestige and social status, more rewarding than the classic fields of the creative arts, a fact that not only reinforces the regression towards the mean but also decreases the level of creativity in these fields. In the next part of the essay, I also expressed concern about the specific content of the products of modern culture, especially literature. It is not surprising that under the present circumstances it is more difficult for creative artists working in conventional artistic fields to consolidate their identities as authors especially because, perhaps more than ever, marginal people are attracted to these fields. In this way, marginality—in the quality of their work and in the promotion of their image—becomes a saleable commodity. All this becomes the source of an unexpected difficulty in the development of the artist's identity in our society. The adoption of Freudian theory and its promulgation, especially in its popular forms, led to extensive changes in the content of cultural products, in their role and in the values embodied in them. However, it also changed the way of thinking about the origins of the creative impulse. According to Freudianism, the story, the picture, or the melody is only a refined way of releasing urges which have not found a more natural expression or sublimation. And when creativity is brought down from the Olympus of the muses to the deep pit of the "dark" urges, it becomes difficult for the artist to adopt the identity of a creator.

In retrospect, I probably wouldn't put my name on an essay of this kind today, not only because of the additional knowledge I have gained throughout more than thirty-four years, but mainly due to my current skepticism regarding the concept of "intelligence" and, even more, the distinction between "high art" and "art for the masses" that I made then, apparently because my role as a teaching assistant had stuffed me with [theories about] functionalism, communication, and modernization. And yet it seems to me that had this comprehensive article (which must be read in full for anyone to have a chance of agreeing with me) been published in French (in *Le Monde*, for example), and had I persisted in this line of thought, it could perhaps have made me, even then, famous and widely quoted. This assumption is based on an amusing and ironic article I read a number of years ago entitled "How to Become an Esteemed French Philosopher in Five Lessons," allegedly by Michele Lamont.

My friend Nachman Ben-Yehudah claims that part of the problem with Israeli science is our location in the geographical periphery, certainly in relation to the United States, but also to Europe. I am not sure that I agree with him. However, although this article was written in Hebrew, it apparently made the appropriate impression, and even the gates of the *Haaretz* op-ed pages opened for me. I did not understand then the far-reaching implications that this fact would have in the future.

\* \* \*

After the publication of the essay in "Culture and Literature," I mustered the courage to begin sending articles to the editorial page. During this period, I made an effort to write in a rational but authoritative tone, and I often used professional jargon and foreign words which, at that time, probably did not bother the editor of *Haaretz*, Gershon Shocken, and the assistant editors who supervised the editorial page. Shocken, whom I never met, had edited the paper with an iron fist since 1939 (the year of my birth) until he became ill and died in 1990. It seems that he liked my writing and usually gave me a place of honor in the editorial page. I got along less well over time with the young editor Hanoch Marmari, who was considered a star of Israeli journalism (after he edited a successful local paper), and even less well with his deputy Yoel Esteron. As for my relationship with Tamar Litani—who was friendly to me as long as she edited the inside pages of the weekend paper—it became slightly strained, which was partly my own fault, when she was appointed assistant editor. One day I sent her an article over the internet and about two days later, two articles appeared which contained ideas more or less overlapping with those expressed in mine. Anger consumed me and I protested. Litani responded with a cynicism until then unknown to me, which led me to believe that the article would not be published. I submitted it to Ynet without informing her. The next morning, the same opinion piece appeared both in *Haaretz* and on Ynet, the occurrence of which is incompatible with accepted journalistic norms. Litani was furious, and rightly so, and called the act "a breach of faith." Now I was at odds with both communications media which were my main public platforms. However, that happened when I was already sixty-six years old and had begun view my writing with a certain irony.

From the outset, as mentioned earlier, my public writing focused mainly on the analysis of the results of the 1967 war, the Jewish–Arab conflict, its roots and all kinds of proposed solutions—some of which seem to me today, from the perspective of so many years, to be fanciful and naïve. In the following pages, I will present a survey of a small portion of my first articles, not necessarily in the chronological order of their publication but in the order of their importance in my eyes today, as milestones in the formation of my worldview, and perhaps, in part, also of the dovish ideologies in Israeli political culture. These views and their transformations are also drawn from the academic knowledge I acquired, accumulated, and partly also developed.

I experienced both benefits and costs from my entrance into the public sphere and from its connection to the academic fields I dealt with. The gains were the personal satisfaction of being known and praised and the illusion of having a certain influence. The losses were my colleagues' envy and the derogatory label of "journalist" which was bestowed on me with extreme glee by some people in academia. In most cases, academics did not read my professional articles but mainly my public works, which were inherently sharp, extreme, and, some say, provocative. Indeed, it is not possible to write editorial pieces and begin sentences with "it can be assumed that…" or "perhaps," "it is possible that…" and "on the other hand…". A 600–700 word article must deliver an unequivocal message, without uncertainty and probabilistic approaches. Very few of my academic colleagues understood this and my opponents and all those who for various and strange reasons did not want to have me in their professional and social circles used this fact in an attempt to hinder my academic advancement when they were no longer able to get rid of me. Much later, as a result of my publications, I also became the target of hate-filled attacks both from within the country and from abroad. Letters of incitement and threats amused me but not my family members. An even less entertaining aspect of this activity of mine was the appeal by colleagues and friends for my help in getting their articles published in *Haaretz*. They could not believe that I had no influence at all on the editors of the newspaper.

Approximately a year and two months after the end of the 1967 war (starting on August 27, 1968), I published a series of three articles in *Haaretz* entitled "People and the [Israeli-] held Territories." In this series, I partially laid the foundations which would serve me in the analysis of the conflict to this very day. First of all, I asserted the futility of expecting something good to come out of separating the people living in the Israeli-held territories from the territories themselves. It seems that I understood even then that the inability to separate the "liberated" territory from the conquered population induced a kind of national schizophrenia in Israelis that has led them to swing between the poles of a nationalistic lust for territory and the pursuit of peace to this day. In the absence of a satisfactory plan or a vision regarding the nature of the possession of the territories, the political system went into gridlock since neither the right nor the left wanted the integration of millions of Arabs into the "Jewish State." Moreover, the Arab population is not interested in being included in the framework of such a state. Later, when the debate over the demographic issue became widespread, I understood in addition that the "national camp" and, in practice, the whole country and its policy are booby-trapped between two contradictory "patriotic imperatives"—the aspiration to control the maximum amount of territory and that of having a state with an exclusively Jewish (or at least non-Arab) population. In this same way, the "demographic left" sprouted and, either in good faith or as a tactic to counter the aspirations to annex territories, aroused the specter of the "demographic demon" from which wafted the foul odor of racism. I must say that from time to time I too used this argument since I found it most effective in the debate over the future fate of the "territories."

At that time, my awareness that the 1967 war constituted more of a defeat than a victory also came to fruition since beyond the purely military aspect, the great paradox of the Israeli victory in that war is that one of the central demands of the Arab countries, namely that Israel should take back into its territory a large portion of the inhabitants who fled or were forced to flee in the 1948 war, was fulfilled. From this point of view and in light of the present reality, the possibility of Israel attaining additional territories is of only minor importance. In the article, I subsequently explained why Israel lost the war in which it allegedly gained a decisive victory, the reason being that Israel was transformed de facto into a bi-national system with its own dynamics.

It should be pointed out that despite the correct diagnosis and prognosis of the conversion of the Israeli ruling system into a bi-national one, at this stage I still accepted most of the basic hegemonic assumptions (for example, that the situation was "forced upon us") and the official semantics which used the expressions "held territories" and "the land of Israel" to designate the entire area controlled by the British until 1948. In hindsight, I am also surprised while reading these articles by the fact that I ignored the Arab civilians and accepted the axiom that Israel has to remain an exclusively Jewish nation. Moreover, the Palestinian problem was in my eyes still a "refugee" problem," even though I attributed the utmost importance to its solution and considered this a necessary condition and even a prerequisite for a regional accord (October 4, 1968).

In addition, my partial acceptance of the positions on which there was then a consensus within the Israeli hegemony was mixed in this article with a lack of comprehensive knowledge about, for example, the fact that not all refugees, but rather less than half, were at that time under Israeli control. I also overlooked the issues of internal refugees who were Israeli citizens. Yet at the same time, there can be found in this article a departure from accepted positions, the proposal of alternatives, and the introduction of question marks. Since I expected that the existing "temporary" situation would become a permanent "temporary" one, I proposed in the following section that we should take advantage of it to solve the refugee problem so that when the time for peace negotiations with the Arab countries came, this problem would not constitute a primary obstacle to the achievement of an accord. Israel, I wrote, "considering itself to a certain extent responsible for their fate," is obligated to solve this problem, both for reasons of self-interest and of ethics. In that article, I also suggested the accelerated industrialization of the occupied territories by international, Israeli, and local Palestinian entrepreneurs who could utilize the existing cheap work force. Industrialization would have resulted in an increased standard of living and a greater provision of local services and would have brought about the rehabilitation of the refugees in their places of residence. Furthermore, the article foresees no alternative to the integration of both economies, which would also have resulted in accelerated development and the building of infrastructure in the occupied territories and in Israel itself. In 1968, the Jewish colonization of those territories was not yet on the agenda, at least not in the circles I moved in, which definitely were not close to the Merkaz HaRav Yeshiva or Tabenkin's people.

While reading anew the third article of the series (October 6), I was surprised even more by its first part since it absolutely contradicted my later research, writing, and thought. Referring to the book entitled *The Arabs in Israel* by Sabri Jiryis, a young Arab–Israeli lawyer, I rejected his approach, which described the permanent and continuous struggle between the state and its Arab citizens, mainly over land, which was considered to be the major focus of conflict between the two peoples in Israel. I was not yet able to admit that "my" country continued, even after its foundation, to systematically evict the Arabs from their lands and deprive them of a whole variety of civil and human rights. I therefore argued, as opposed to Jiryis' approach, that it is not surprising that the most powerful slogan for preserving Palestinian political identity was the one calling for the return to the village in the homeland. This call, I specified, was anchored in pre-modern worldviews held where the land was the national resource and the main basis for personal status and where almost no compromise could be found between the victor and the vanquished.

Since I could not contradict the content of Jiryis's book by using facts, I invented some kind of questionable pseudo-sociological theory to use against him which did not take into account the fact that modern nationalism is territorial too. I maintained here that the Arabs' demand to regain their lands stemmed from the fact that they were not modern enough. It seems to me that this is the most dilettantish and demagogic passage I ever wrote in my entire life. In addition, I didn't know that, at that exact time, Jiryis was being held in administrative detention in order to prevent the publication of his book in foreign languages and that most copies of the book had been either confiscated or collected by a mysterious hand from the stores. After a number of years and with great difficulty, I located one of them through Yisas'har, the campus's eternal student and a collector of rare books, and paid for it quite dearly. Since the book had also disappeared from the department library, I would lend students my private copy. Two years later, I began focusing my doctoral work on the territorial dimensions of the Jewish–Palestinian conflict and realized that even Jiryis himself was not aware of their full extent and depth, perhaps because he was not familiar with the historical and documentary material from the Jewish perspective and knew only the actual results rather than what lay behind them.

In any case, later in the article, I adopted a superior tone and advised the Palestinian Arabs, wherever they are, to abandon the conflict from the "conceptual" and general point of view. I suggested that any individual or family having a claim to a specific house or field should submit it and expressed confidence that just solutions would be found for every claim of this kind. My appeal anticipated a later Israeli formulation which recognized the rights of Arab citizens in the state as individuals but not as an ethnic or national collective. The second part of the article slightly contradicts the first (and is even separated from it by an asterisk). It deals with the Palestinian "entity" and identity and contains the unequivocal assertion that the latter exists independently and even in opposition to the other Arab identities, a statement which in that period was definitely contrary to what was accepted by the great majority of the Jewish public, and it was advanced as a response to Golda Meir's declaration that "There is no such a thing as Palestinians."

The most conspicuous error in this article was the determination that the Jordanians had preserved the Palestinian identity when in fact its disappearance was actually a common Israeli–Jordanian interest. I am also astounded today by how, despite the fact that, albeit with some confusion and reservations, I acknowledged the existence of a Palestinian identity and even of a Palestinian people, I was far from drawing the appropriate conclusions, or perhaps I did not yet dare write about the ones that were taboo. In addition, I am amazed by how I totally adopted the "religion of modernization" whose source undoubtedly lay in my sociological studies and the beginning of my work in this field at the department. Only after more than a decade did I apparently begin to understand the "Palestinian problem" better and it was then, during my first stay in Seattle when the first Intifada broke out, that I suggested to Joel Migdal that we work together on a comprehensive study on the subject. At that time I also grasped that the conflict could not be fully understood by studying only one side—in this case the Jewish one—because a conflict is a complete system of interrelationships between all parties, whether they are involved directly or indirectly.

Almost three years had passed since this series of articles and, being more involved with my university studies and work, I did not continue publishing, except occasionally in *Haaretz*. Meanwhile, the atmosphere in Israel began to change too and euphoria made room for a kind of routine acceptance of a depressing conflict between the communities which claimed victims on an almost daily basis. At the time that I was writing those articles, Gush Emunim had not yet appeared in public; however, within the National Religious Party— the eternal partner of Mapai (within the Ma'arach)—the "young generation" (Zevulun Hammer, Hanan Porat and Yehuda Ben-Meir) had already begun to assume control and to become prominent. They brought with them a messianic eastern wind which began to hover over the entire country, a contagious plague just starting to spread while still remaining unnoticed. The public was mostly preoccupied with the War of the Diadochi,[3] referring to the fights between Alon and Dayan over succession, while each of them tried to promote political alternatives which were not genuine but rather based on the status quo that had already been determined three years earlier.

## Notes

1. "Mehdal" means both "omission" and "failure" and designates the terrible mistakes that were responsible for the disastrous course and results of the 1973 war.
2. A Hebrew acroym for "Democratic Movement for Change."
3. *Diadochi* is a word meaning "successors" and refers to the leaders who, after the death of Alexander the Great, fought a series of wars to determine whether his empire should splinter into smaller states or remain intact, and who should rule.

# 16

## ANCESTORS' SEPULCHERS AND SONS' GRAVES

I remember being outraged by the buffoonery of those who claimed a historical right and the cult that developed around them. It was then that I wrote a series of three quite sharp and ironic articles entitled "Ancestors' Sepulchers in Exchange for Sons' Graves." However, my articles were difficult to swallow, even for a liberal newspaper like *Haaretz*, and for the first time they were rejected by an assistant editor. I sent the articles to *Davar* which, to my surprise, published them. But this too was not that easy, as I was told later. The paper's editor, Chana Zemer, phoned Nisan Oren, a pleasant lecturer of international relations, and asked "Who is this Kimmerling?" The identity of the writer was more important to her than the content of the articles. Oren told her that he had only a superficial acquaintance with me but advised her to contact Dan Horowitz, who was supposed to know me well. Zemer immediately called Dindush, who of course vouched for me from a political standpoint, saying something akin to "He's one of ours."

The third article in the series, which was published on May 2, 1971, dealt mainly with current events of that time; however, it did contain some indications of the more solid and comprehensive system of thought I developed later about the subjects pertaining to the Jewish–Arab conflict. The beginning of the article was clumsy and full of mistakes (and was probably printed without being edited), but its message was clear and pointed: the Israeli government must retain all of the "seized" territories as bargaining chips but must stipulate that they can be relinquished "in exchange for everything." The existence of the settlements did not occur to me at all at that time, even though a small number of communities had already been established by then in Gush Etzion and the East Jerusalem neighborhoods. I probably perceived the imposition of Israeli law on East Jerusalem as an impediment to the achievement of an overall agreement or to "the uprooting of the conflict," an expression I used in this series of articles. In fact, to this day, I am of the opinion that only in exchange for a withdrawal from all the territories (up to the 1967 border) can a comprehensive settlement and the end of the conflict be attained. I consider all of this to be a series of formal institutional arrangements that could be implemented immediately. I deliberately avoided using the concept of "peace," which seemed to me at the time, as it still does today, to be a prolonged sociological and cultural process that would develop gradually on all sides for generations, if indeed the conflict and its causes could be brought to an end. The distinction between "genuine peace" (and not just a state of non-belligerency) and the existence of an agreement was shown in the models provided by our relations with Egypt and Jordan.

From these fundamental positions, the article proceeded to analyze the internal situation between the coalition government and the opposition in order to examine to what extent the Ma'arach (the [ruling] political block formed by the Labor and Mapam parties) was indeed able to keep the territories in an "unfrozen condition" while awaiting the achievement of a comprehensive settlement with the Arab countries. I reached the conclusion that Golda Meir, Yigal Alon, and Moshe Dayan were already committed to specific regions in the territories to which their names were connected (for example Alon to the Jordan Valley and Dayan to the northern Sinai and Sharm el-Sheikh). The National Religious Party, which had the ability to tip the balance of political power in favor of either Ma'arach or Gachal (the Heirut-Liberal block that was the precursor to the Likud), was already prepared to abandon its "historical alliance" with Ma'arach and had set its sights on its old rival. Moreover, Gachal had already calculated by then that a situation might develop for the first time in which it could gain enough public support to be able to compete against its traditional opponent for the leadership of the country.

Subsequently, I wrote about what was to become one of the central topics for me and others in the critique of the Israeli political culture: "Tribal worship of patriarchal and matriarchal sepulchers and myths about them were either revived or created out of nothing. It cannot be said that these are not genuine and sincere feelings, and their role in solidifying a collective identity cannot be disregarded either. We may even recognize that a predisposition to feel nostalgia for the original borders of Palestine [within the boundaries of the British colonial state] existed among a large portion of the population. However we are a pragmatic society, capable of evaluating the costs of nostalgia and myths, and when given the option of paying for (highly improbable) ancestors' sepulchers with the fresh graves of sons, it is almost certain how we would decide." The extent to which I was wrong in regard to the pragmatism of Israeli society and its ability to deal with the manipulation of myths and symbols can be inferred from the approximately thirty-five years that have elapsed since I wrote these articles. Nevertheless, I was not completely naïve and identified one of the main obstacles standing in the way of a possible settlement: "Most serious of all is the fact that the requests for a complete (or even partial) withdrawal from the territories in exchange for peace are associated with marginal, socially stigmatized groups like Ha Olam Hazeh, Rakach, Siach, or Matzpen. This conditioning is so strong that many of those who reached conclusions which might be suspected of being close to those made by these groups prefer to keep them to themselves in order to avoid being marginalized."

It seems to me that this phenomenon is even much more widespread and dangerous today. Anxiety about the possibility of being expelled from whatever consensus is now dictated by the nationalist factions of Israeli society paralyzes entire parties and social movements that do deviate from it and risk being labeled traitors, anti-Zionists, or radical leftists. This rhetoric hinders almost all criticism or opposition despite the far-reaching changes which have occurred since then in the collective Israeli consciousness, such as the recognition of the existence of a Palestinian people and of the right they have to their own state alongside that of Israel.

In the next part of the article, I outlined a number of additional difficulties which could constitute obstacles to ending the conflict once and for all and then asked whether there are opposing forces in Israeli society that might encourage decision-makers to move in a desirable direction. I reached the following conclusion: "Those who make decisions are exposed to attacks and are very sensitive to political initiatives coming from circles which are not considered 'political,' and whose claims are based on core values of Israeli society. It seems that the famous 'Letter of the Twelfth-Graders'[1] did more to temper Israeli positions than did organized political factions. An additional example is the appearance of the Black Panthers, young people who, in the name of widely accepted social values, made requests that led immediately to the allocation of quite substantial material resources to social problems. Responses of this kind might vary and not necessarily towards flexibility; however, if one takes into account the fact that the problem of 'peace' also lies in the domain of emotions, every stimulus from the politically unorganized periphery which deals with missed opportunities to reach an agreement might indeed elicit such a response."

In retrospect, it is possible to reach a number of conclusions concerning the assertions I made in May 1971, and to examine how accurate they proved to be over time. Those who made political decisions apparently continued, after the 1977 change of government, to be sensitive to "core values" even though they manipulated them. This manipulation actually led to quite deep changes in the values themselves, however not to the extent of making real differences in policies or lack of policies. The biggest success in this sphere was surely achieved by a political group that operated outside the conventional party frameworks—Gush Emunim,[2] which undertook its activity "on the ground" only about three years after the publication of this article. However, the developments—for example on the matter of finding arrangements to solve the conflict—were not unidirectional and linear and definitely did not stem from public initiatives that were unconnected to the decision-makers.

The "Letter of the Twelfth Graders" was engraved in the collective memory as a first attempt to undermine the aggressive-militaristic approach as the exclusive means of managing the conflict; still, it is difficult to estimate its real long-term effect. Almost every year, similar groups emerged and with time their protest evolved into refusal to serve in Lebanon (a war that was defined by Prime Minister Menachem Begin himself as a "war of choice") and, much later to serve in the army for reasons of conscience and politics during the period in which it attempted to suppress the Second Intifada. But as these lines are written, the refusal did not develop into the "critical mass" needed to exert an influence over government policies. However, a "non-political" group such as "The Four Mothers" did indeed have a considerable effect on the ultimate decision to withdraw from Lebanon (although it may turn out that the disaster of the collision of the two helicopters had a greater impact).

The same considerations apply to the example of the Black Panthers. While they actually shook up the political system at the time, they did not bring about real changes either in social policy or in the allotment of social resources unless we consider the phenomenon as part of a continuum of events, the cumulative effect of which is not linear and which splits into a number of opposite directions, with Shas at one end and the Mizrahi Democratic Rainbow at the other. The political system, regardless of whether the so-called right or left rules, does a good job of managing this kind of Jewish protest, either by isolating, ostracizing, and pushing activists out of the consensus, by co-opting them, or providing social palliatives such as projects to restore poor neighborhoods.

And indeed, government officials, provided that they present confident, unequivocal messages and avoid the expression of conflicting opinions, are usually able to shape political realities (mainly by creating threatening emergency situations), in ways that are favorable to them while both the general public and the opposition lack the means to deal with such constructions of reality. This conclusion was correct at the time and remains so today, as in the case of Ariel Sharon's success in evacuating settlers from the Gaza Strip. From this point of view, when introducing political and ideological alternatives, anyone in the government who knows how to use his position has a great advantage over those located outside the centers of power. Today, I would add an additional condition, namely that the government must be efficient in achieving its goals and has to achieve them at a reasonable cost, as was not the case in the Second Lebanon War. Indeed the "reasonableness" of this cost can also be constructed, but only to a certain extent. Approximately two-and-a-half years after the publication of this article, the protest movements in the wake of the 1973 war proved what would happen to a government perceived as inefficient in managing an essential function of the state such as security, especially in light of the costs involved in what is believed to be its failure. This government remained in office until 1977 but despite its efforts to present the war as a great victory, it already had, as early as 1973, made a lasting impression of being unsuccessful.

The end of the article dealt with the international sphere, which was still bi-polar, and no one at the time could guess what would happen. I wrote, probably referring to the initiative of the Secretary of State William P. Rogers: "Israeli maneuverability and freedom of action can only go as far as the United States allows and no farther. The U.S. government, too, is in fact restricted by certain rules of the game and, perhaps more than any other regime, it is motivated by abstract ideals; however, first and foremost, it concerns itself with the global interests of the United States and, in its opinion, what is good for the U.S. is also good for Israel. [But] if this powerful country reaches the conclusion that Israeli withdrawal from the territories will give it a renewed foothold in Arab countries, pulling back will be only a question of time. And if the withdrawal will be a mere function of American pressure, our gain [from it] will be extremely minor."

Since the publication of this article, a lot of water has flowed in the Potomac and the Volga, and much less in the Jordan River. The world has become unipolar, and it seems as if the entire world system has changed. At times, one also gets the impression that the Israeli lobby, with the support of the Bible Belt, directs American policy to such an extent that the U.S. sometimes seems as if it were an Israeli satellite. In any case, American neo-conservatism has definitely found common ground with different factions of the Israeli right, and vice-versa. This phenomenon has become apparent primarily since the catastrophe of September 11, but it had already began to take root long before, and it conspicuously manifested itself during the Israeli invasion of Lebanon. It became undeniable during the Camp David talks, in whose framework even a president as familiar with details and as involved in the issue as Bill Clinton was distinctly inclined to express extreme pro-Zionist, Protestant sentiments which made the Palestinian delegation lose its temper and which were to a certain extent responsible for the failure of the talks.

And indeed, it sometimes seems that the tail is wagging the dog. Those actions that America permits Israel to carry out (while backing it in the face of worldwide opposition by exercising its veto in the Security Council) are not only perceived in this country as allowable but even as ethical. And it is exactly for this reason that one must take into account the fact that, in the long run, the American government, its political culture, and both its foreign and domestic policies, are capable of being constantly altered; therefore what I wrote on this topic in 1971 appears to me even today basically valid and enduring.

## Notes

1.  This was a letter sent in 1970 to Prime Minister Golda Meir by draft-age young men who expressed their reservations about the occupation, the war of attrition, and the fact that the government failed to take actions that could have ended the warfare.
2.  Gush Emumim is a religious and ultra-nationalist movement founded in 1974 whose main objectives are to establish settlements in the occupied territories while expanding its influence into the Israeli army and the political culture.

# 17

## About the Nuclear Issue

Two additional niches in which I could express my opinions and ideas were the "Culture and Literature" section (where, as mentioned, I first began writing) and later the "Books" supplement. My writing for the literature section ended at some point, and I do not know exactly why. Beni Tzifer, the editor, broke off contact with me. I very much like reviewing theoretical books, mainly because struggling with the ideas of whoever thought about them and took the trouble to write a book or a monograph constitutes a challenge in itself. Every writer should be treated with respect, even if disagreements exist. Everyone who, like me, also writes books and considers almost each one of them to be the height not only of his efforts but also of his achievements (until the next one), must be committed to this approach. In addition, the critic is allowed to express his position in most reviews because otherwise, in my opinion, the result is anemic. A good critique must be a kind of dialogue between the critic and the author being criticized. In addition, the critic is obligated to actually read the book. More than once I have become extremely angry while reading a critique of one of my books—even a favorable and laudatory one—since it was clear to me that the critic did not read it but only leafed through it.

One subject of the utmost importance to which I have dedicated several articles is the nuclear issue. There were many reasons for my call to close down our reactor, even though I thoroughly understood the motives for its establishment: to grant Israel, when it still was considered weak and vulnerable, a kind of insurance policy against threats to its existence. Those threats were genuinely felt during the 1950s and the beginning of the 1960s. On the other hand, it was completely clear that Israel's possession of the nuclear option would sooner or later lead to the nuclearization of the Middle East, a situation which could endanger not only the state and the region, but the entire world.

Regarding the existence itself of the nuclear option, I was not completely convinced that the benefits balanced the costs although I also understood that its very existence was irreversible. Even though I do not like fighting for what I know are lost causes, I was incapable of letting go of this subject. And I had many additional reasons for this. As I wrote, for example, in a review of two books about the Israeli nuclear issue (*Haaretz*, "Book Review," September 28, 2005), I assumed that in regard to this topic, there is a reason for the broad consensus in Israel, a reason which is not easy to mention and which is the only area of tacit agreement still existing between the purest doves and the most predatory hawks in Israeli society. The group known as the national camp views the existence of the nuclear weapons supposedly found in the basements of Israel[1] as a guarantee that no external or internal pressure (perhaps with the exception of the "demographic demon") would be able to force Israel into real territorial concessions. The dovish camp perceives the existence of the Israeli nuclear arsenal as their most substantial basis for assuming and claiming that Israel is so strong from the military standpoint that it can allow itself generous and even far-reaching territorial concessions in exchange for peace agreements, and that in the new and frightening nuclear world, territory is almost devoid of strategic significance. In this crucial controversy, both sides consider nuclear devices to be an ultimate, although hidden, kind of weapon in their domestic battle over public opinion.

However, my anxiety about the nuclear research plant in Dimona was rooted in other reasons and in one of my reviews, my critique of Avner Cohen's approach was worded as follows: "Avner Cohen dedicates much space [in his book] to the environmental safety problems of the Nes Tziona 'institute' — which, 'according to foreign sources,' is engaged in the development of chemical and biological weapons and their countermeasures—and warns of an environmental catastrophe that might be caused by human error or other disasters. He also expresses deep sympathy for a large group of cancer patients and their families or those who have already died from the disease that was probably caused, at least in some cases, by their exposure to radioactive and other kinds of materials while working at the nuclear research plant in Dimona. By the way, in spite of that, the state refuses to accept any responsibility for their condition and that of their families. Cohen also mentions a number of accidents of varying severity that have occurred over the years at the nuclear research plant. At the same time, Cohen is absolutely unwilling to discuss the predictable dangers posed to the very existence of Israel or to considerable portions of its population and to the other peoples living in the region by a reactor that is over forty years old, even if well-maintained, when other countries have already begun to seal off similar facilities. This is indeed a facility in which one accident—a strong earthquake, an act of terror, or damage to an active reactor caused by penetration bombs or missiles able to breach its defenses—is likely to bring about more deadly results than a large-scale Arab attack on the country. We have to take into account the fact that no accident-proof facility has yet been built and that the risk must be calculated by multiplying its severity by the probability of its occurrence, so that no [figures showing a] low risk (if it is at all possible to estimate it) can express the gravity of the potential damage. Moreover, it is necessary to ask where and how nuclear waste and other dangerous materials, which sometimes have a lifespan of thousands of years, could be stored when it is clear that their storage containers will disintegrate long before the materials will have ceased to be dangerous."

This was also the summary of the approach I had presented earlier in a number of articles in *Haaretz*. Avner Cohen's main arguments were against the policy of "nuclear vagueness" which Israel adopted, especially internally, and the ridiculous censorship of this subject which, in his view, endangered Israeli democracy. I saw no great fundamental difference between the existence and non-existence of this policy mainly since Cohen supports the continuing development of the nuclear option. What, then, was left to talk about in the public discussion he required?

## Note

1.   Israeli military secrets are often referred to as being hidden in special basements.

# 18

## THIS CONSTITUTION IS PROSTITUTION

I devoted several articles and numerous lectures to the constitution's structure and to the verdicts of the High Court, mainly regarding the status of Arab citizens in the state and that of the residents of the occupied territories. In one lecture (the date of which I do not recall) during a conference held at Bar-Ilan University in honor of Justice Aharon Barak, I claimed, *inter alia*, that the judicial activism shown when ruling on the rights of the Jewish population stands in sharp contrast to the extreme restraint exercised by the Court when intervening in matters regarding the rights of Israeli Arab citizens and those of Palestinians residing in the occupied territories. By the way, I would not have referred at all to issues pertaining to the occupied territories had it not been for a High Court of Justice decision, allegedly among its most enlightened but actually one of its most unfortunate. This was the decision to extend its jurisdiction over the actions of Israeli authorities operating inside those territories and to grant restricted legal standing and right of petition to its residents. In this way, the High Court of Justice actually bestowed legitimacy on the continuation of the occupation itself and on its appearance as an enlightened one without the possibility (or perhaps even the willingness) of offering any real relief to the residents. At the same time, it blatantly helped Israel violate international conventions that it had signed. From that point on, the High Court of Justice, both by its actions and its failures, became one of the key instruments for managing the Jewish–Arab (or Palestinian) conflict while it protected what is perceived as the ethno-national Jewish interest as it is understood and presented by the government, the regime, and Zionist ideology. By doing so, the Court filled a role no less central and crucial than that of the settlers, the IDF, the bureaucracy, and the rest of the state agencies referred to as "security forces," along with the legislators themselves, in solidifying and entrenching the occupation. The Court did so mainly by using a very simple, almost simplistic, yet amazingly effective technique: its method of interpreting and using the concept of security. First, as long as the state used the pretexts of "security requirements" and "on security grounds" in order to justify acts of commission or omission, the Court was predisposed to accept the argument in nearly all cases without any substantive examination. Secondly, the concept of security was almost never analyzed in the context of the case submitted and the Court, sweepingly and without objection or reservations, conferred the exclusive right of determining "security needs" on the state and its executive authority. This situation, I continued to argue, cries to heaven, mainly in view of the fact that the Court considers itself an expert with the authority to issue decrees in every sphere of both public and private life—economics and banking, the efficiency of the government, medicine, biology, religion, education, communication, etc.—except for those areas which the state claims are connected to its security. The Court can use independent expert witnesses in every field but whenever security matters are considered, almost the only expertise recognized is precisely that of those entities the Court was supposed to regard with suspicion in the first place: the state, the army, and the security forces.

Thirdly, in many cases, the Court agrees to the state's demands to have government experts give their testimony secretly, leading to a situation in which evidence and exhibits are withheld from the legal representative of the party challenging the state and its authorities. It must be assumed that even when the justices act in good faith, the principle granting the state exclusive control over information about security issues opens gates that are numerous and wide indeed and which allow for huge distortions of the law. This in turn broadens the gap between the "perception of natural justice" and the impression left by the trial itself.

Indeed, there have been two important rulings protecting the rights of Palestinian minorities which are thought to be progressive. One is the Katzir verdict, which ruled that no public body, including the state, may discriminate against an Arab citizen in the matter of residential land allocation. However, it should be pointed out that in this case, the defendants did not maintain that the discrimination was based on security reasons and, most importantly, although ten years had elapsed since the petition was submitted and five years since the verdict, as these lines are written, the decision has not yet been implemented. Thus the state's democratic character is preserved by the High Court of Justice while the state's Jewish character is preserved by ignoring its rulings. The second ruling, reached in 2002, revoked the recommendations of the Landau Commission, which allowed the General Security Services to use torture (described by the code words "moderate physical pressure") while investigating suspects; however, de facto, it left the GSS with the option of using methods of torture which were not specifically prohibited by that same commission, such as solitary confinement.

The attempts, from 2001 on, by the Israeli Institute for Democracy (and later, by other groups) to legislate what it called a "consensual constitution" seemed to me to be a very dangerous undertaking. I wrote several articles about this too, and I'll present here the summary of the one I published in the periodical of Adalah (August 2005), the organization for the protection of Arab citizens' rights, and earlier in *Haaretz*. I argued in those articles that, contrary to what is generally accepted, I am not of the opinion that a country needs a constitution at all or that this can solve real and fundamental problems latent in the regime or political culture. The U.S.S.R., for example, had a magnificent constitution—and a regime of terror to go along with it. The classic constitutional nation, the U.S., proves that it is precisely in times of crisis that a constitution cannot grant relief and protect basic rights, such as when the regime becomes heavy-handed toward minorities or other groups perceived as constituting a "danger to the state." To this day, the American constitution has not really succeeded in granting fully equal rights to African-Americans, women, and people with sexual tendencies which differ from "accepted" ones. Despite the fact that this constitution's first amendment establishes the separation between religion and state, this separation is apparent rather than real. The American constitution did not provide protection for American citizens of Japanese origin who were transferred to concentration camps for "security reasons" during World War II. Neither did it protect those who were persecuted by McCarthy, or the victims of the "Patriot Act," which was enacted in the wake of 9/11. In contrast, the British democracy, which is not based in principle on a constitution, does not function badly (with a few exceptions), and constitutes one of the world's most enlightened regimes, at least as far as its own citizens are concerned.

Moreover, in a constitutional system, there are more than a few potential harmful effects and dangers, especially when constitutions are meant to cover for governments whose political practices and cultures are fundamentally distorted. A constitution grants the appearance of normalcy and enlightenment to the regime and increases its legitimacy, even when in fact it denies universal human and civil rights. At the same time, a constitution can be advantageous as a final, ultimate, and concluding step in the democratization processes of the state but not as an instrument for carrying out reforms in its regime or political culture.

The concept itself of a "consensual constitution," as it was presented by its proponents, constitutes a smokescreen for the tendency to legislate a constitution out of compromises between enlightened-universalistic approaches and the religious, nationalistic ones. In the best case, such a constitution may reproduce and stabilize the existing status quo. However, it appears that the draft proposal of the constitution, as it was formulated, also violates the existing status quo in an ethnocentric direction even more than the present juridical situation does. Indeed, in the draft dated November 24, 2004, it was determined that "All are equal before the law: there shall be no discrimination between individuals for reasons of race, religion, nationality, gender, ethnicity, country of origin, or any other reason, provided that there is no relevant reason for the discrimination." However, many discriminatory clauses included in the draft contradict the previous one. Thus, for example, under the heading "Return" it is written: "Every Jew is entitled to immigrate to Israel. A law regulating this right will be established, as long as restrictions designed to protect the public health and well-being or the security of the state will be imposed only by law." In other words, there is no mention of the right of non-Jews to immigrate and a restriction on the extent of eligibility allowed by the Law of Return is also alluded to, so that the above mentioned clause has an even more exclusionary character than the one existing today. And in order to remove any doubt, the "citizenship" clause states that "Israeli citizenship is to be conferred on anyone born to a father or a mother who was an Israeli citizen or resident and to whoever immigrated under the provisions of the Law of Return." This practically prohibits the future conferral of citizenship to anyone who is not Jewish. It is also hard to seriously regard as liberal a constitution that, on the one hand, hermetically seals ethno-national borders and, on the other hand, is unable to define national geo-political ones. From this it is possible to reach an additional generalization: as long as the country's geographical borders—which will actually determine its ethno-national composition—cannot be decided, there is absolutely no possibility of legislating a constitution and determining the supposedly definitive "rules of the game."

For example, according to the legal situation existing today, the Arabs have a unique collective right, which is the equality, at least in theory, between the Arabic language and the Hebrew one. In the proposed constitution, Hebrew is the only official language of the state, while "the Arabic language has a special and recognized status in Israel," a vague wording, devoid of commitment, that in any case nibbles into Arabic's equal status, and encloses it in a linguistic ghetto. Since Israel was indeed established as a Jewish state (despite the fact that there is no agreement even among Jews on the interpretation of this "Jewishness"), I do not think that this identity should be taken from it, just as in principle Italy is an Italian state. But in a country whose population is more than twenty per cent non-Jewish, this obvious self-definition does not contradict the fact that it can be also the state of all the rest of its citizens. Even more puzzling is the coupling of the concepts "Jewish" and "democratic," a pairing created so that one balances and limits the other.

I tried in vain to argue convincingly that Israel can be both Jewish and democratic yet without linking these two concepts together into "Jewish democracy"; these concepts belong to different content areas and shading democracy with the hue and unique content of "Jewishness" is reminiscent of such concepts as "people's democracy" and "Islamic democracy." At this point, it is possible to include in the constitution a declarative clause that Israel is a Jewish state and the state of all its citizens and, in an additional clause, that Israel is a democratic state. I proposed adding operative clauses which explain what kind of democracy Israel is (parliamentary, for instance); how it is actually put into practice (by elections); and what mechanisms for checks and balances need to be implemented in it.

Additional massive disadvantages in the proposed constitution are the lack of separation between religion and state and the fact that the judicial proceedings concerning personal status issues are left exclusively in the hands of the religious authorities, the principles of whose laws differ from those of the modern civil state and contradict its egalitarian principles. In light of Israel's special situation, it is notable that the proposed constitution lacks articles mandating separation between the military and the political system (requiring, for example, the complete subordination of the entire defense establishment to the civil authorities and calling for an extended waiting period before senior officers can move to major political roles and so forth). On the other hand, the proposed constitution emphasizes property rights, as is appropriated to this era, yet lacks guarantees of a great many of the social rights that are taken for granted in a sound welfare state. The reaction of the Arab minority to the attempt to legislate such a constitution came without delay: in December 2006, a counter "vision" was submitted under the cover of the Follow up Committee, which constitutes a kind of general and weak leadership of Palestinian Arabs in Israel. This expression of their deepest longing contained a demand for [mainly cultural] autonomy for the Arab minority in the state which, in effect, constituted a retreat from the formula of a "state of all its citizens." This document provoked strong antagonism from most of the nation's Jews, even among the elite that had previously struggled for civil equality in the country.

# 19

## THE MOUSE THAT ROARED

In the wake of the 1967 war, an additional phenomenon in the form of an ethno-national revival and protest by Soviet Jews emerged and attracted public attention both in Israel and abroad. Groups of Jews sent open letters to the Israeli government and to humanitarian organizations worldwide declaring that they regard Israel as their historic homeland and demanded that action be taken to secure their permission to emigrate from the Soviet Union to Israel.

Meanwhile, the Soviets did allow the departure of a limited number (about 100,000 between 1968 and 1973) of Jews. They became the foundation on which Russian culture established itself in Israel and constituted an infrastructure for the million that arrived later on when the empire disintegrated. The drama reached its peak at the end of 1970 when a number of Jews tried to hijack a plane on a domestic route. It is not clear whether they actually intended to fly it to Israel or to make a dramatic move that would shock the world. The hijackers were caught, stood trial, and received severe punishments that were eventually mitigated.

In Israel itself, a debate broke out over whether to continue the policy of quiet diplomacy in order to enable those defendants and all the other Jews to leave or to come out with an open, frontal offensive against the "Iron Curtain" policy. I commented on this phenomenon in a comprehensive, five-column article which took up nearly an entire page in *Haaretz* (January 3, 1971) and was entitled "The Genuineness of The Mouse's Threat." The article assumed that the U.S.S.R. was stable externally and extremely vulnerable internally because communism had not succeeded in overcoming two ideological currents lying below the surface of the federation: on the one hand, there were nationalist movements such as the Russian one represented by Alexander Solzhenitsyn and, in particular, those of other nationalities that desired to secede from Mother Russia and whose separate identities were only strengthened by brutal Russification attempts; on the other hand, there was the movement represented by Andrei Sakharov which demanded democratization and liberalization.

Under the oppressive Soviet regime, there was no connection between those two movements, and their separation more or less safeguarded the regime's stability. The demands of Jewish nationalists, as exemplified by Natan Scharansky, were not motivated by universal values either. At the same time, within the Jewish national movement, there existed elements which had the potential of creating a link between those two segregated movements, and therefore the Jewish rebellion could have constituted a stronger threat to the regime's existence than those two movements which, in any case, were based on conflicting principles.

The article compared the mass emigration of Jews from the USSR with a possible secession of the Ukraine, Georgia, and others from the federation. I also compared Romania's withdrawal [from it] and Czechoslovakia's attempted disengagement: the former was bearable due to its continuation of a Stalinist regime while the Czechs strove for a liberal democracy. The movement called "Prague Spring" ceased to exist in 1968 with the arrival of Soviet tanks in the streets of Prague.

Thus, justifiably or not, I also explained the central place occupied by anti-Zionism in the Soviet ideology. This article laid out the parameters of the dilemma created by the Jewish unrest. On the one hand, it could be partially suppressed; however, because Jewish dissent was partly identified with that of the intellectual classes, it was likely to become connected to requests for liberalization and actual regime change. On the other hand, mass emigration of Jews could accentuate the secessionist trends of the non-Russian nations from the union. I also described the Israeli response as a dilemma: whether, in order to help the Jews emigrate from the USSR, it would be more effective to continue using "quiet diplomacy" or to go on confronting and embarrassing the Soviet power by using the mouse's roar.

At midday after the article appeared in *Haaretz*, I received a telephone call from Benyamin Halevy, who was at that time a Knesset Member from the Herut Party,[1] and who played some sort of role either inside or outside the Knesset in the struggle of "Silent Jewry," as Soviet Jews had been called until then. Halevy was not a neutral public figure for me, since he served as a judge in several of the country's most important trials, at least two of which indirectly concerned me. In the Gruenwald trial, Halevy ruled that Rudolf Kasztner had sold his soul to the devil. In the trial of the Kafr Qasim murderers, Halevy decided that obviously illegal orders exist, that a black flag flies over them, and that the command to slaughter the villagers fell into this category; nevertheless, he sentenced the killers to ludicrously light penalties. In the Eichmann trial, Halevy pressed to be appointed to the bench but was very restrained throughout.

I was extremely curious to meet with him and when he arrived in my office, he told me that the article had aroused a stormy debate in the Knesset, yet the conclusions drawn in regard to the Israeli policy were not clear. The truth was that the "conclusions" were not clear to me either, and I tried to explain to him that I had only stated the advantages and disadvantages of each policy and that it was the role of the politicians to decide. The man who spent much of his life writing decisive verdicts was unable to understand or accept my approach, and I felt that he left my office disappointed and angry. It is possible, actually, that he was right: a newspaper article cannot be just an intellectual game.

After President Mikhail Gorbachev, following his decision to liberalize the country, opened the borders of the U.S.S.R., more than a million soviet Jews emigrated to Israel in the early 1990s. A decade later, with the help of my former student Alec Epstein, I conducted a study on Russian immigrants, whom I was very much interested in studying, and came to the conclusion that within a short time, they would change the face of Israeli society.

A completely opposite case to that of the aircraft hijacking affair was the Rosenwasser incident. At the beginning of 1971, a Palestinian organization kidnapped an elderly immigrant from Metulla who tried to earn a living by doing some kind of work. He was handed a rifle he did not know to use and given work as a guard. The Palestinians demanded that a large number of their prisoners be released in exchange for him. Prime Minister Golda Meir, followed by all the spokesmen, immediately began to proclaim the inflexible position that Israel would neither surrender to blackmail nor negotiate with terror organizations, since those acts would constitute their recognition.

This made me angry. Too many Israeli political "principles" regarding Palestinian guerilla warfare were being heaped on a helpless man who happened to be in an impossible and unfavorable situation. On January 28, 1971, I published an article in *Haaretz* entitled "The Cost of a Principle," wherein I scorned Meir's assertions.

I argued that further kidnappings of Israeli civilians would not derive from this or from another kind of Israeli "surrender," but rather would be the result of opportunities enabling the organizations to carry them out. By the way, this is still true today in regard to soldiers. As for the assertion that negotiations with terror organizations might signal their recognition by us, I pointed out that in the case of prisoner exchanges, the negotiations are in any case carried out by international groups such as the Red Cross, which fact does not constitute recognition of the legitimacy of the Palestinian organizations.

My main argument, however, was that the objective probability of an Israeli civilian becoming the victim of a terror plot was even lower than that of being the victim of a traffic accident, but studies whose results had not yet been published openly—I meant those conducted by Mike Inbar and myself—showed a tendency toward a very high subjective estimate (between twenty-five and fifty per cent) of the chances of being a terror victim. How could it ever be possible to live a normal life with such an assessment? Those same studies found a high willingness to live in danger for those who are ready to maintain symmetrical relations; i.e. people are ready to sacrifice (in this case, personal security) when it is certain that if a similar incident happened to them, they and their families would be taken care of.

Israeli culture itself, as well as the education received during army service, instilled in us the tradition of helping at any cost, making it one of the rules of the game in the psychological mindset of the Israelis. The handling of the Rosenwasser affair is exceptional and can be dangerous from this point of view. Even if the state had solid and enduring justifications for not negotiating, it seems that the damage to morale does not justify it.

Two weeks after the publication of the article, a deal for the exchange of prisoners was carried out. Obviously, I couldn't actually ascribe any influence on that outcome to my article; however, an event occurring a short time later did inflate my ego. I went with a friend to a play at Binyanei haUmah. I can't recall either the show or the friend now, yet there is one thing I shall never forget.

I noticed that all of the front rows in the center of the hall were empty and that we, who sat in something like the tenth row, were closest to the stage. The house lights went out and "gorillas" appeared in both entrances; marching energetically behind them was a figure we could not mistake—Golda. As soon as she was seated, the curtain rose and the show began. When the lights went on in the interval, Golda rose, turned around, and surveyed the auditorium. Our eyes met. She hurried into the aisle, took a few steps in my direction and blurted out, "So, Baruch Kimmerling, are you satisfied now?" She then turned sharply on her heels and left the auditorium. I was no less shocked than my companion and it took me several seconds to understand: Rosenwasser.

I disliked Golda Meir and the more I learned about her later, the greater my aversion to her grew in light of the disasters she brought on this country. Yet I do miss the days when a Prime Minister took a critical article published in a newspaper seriously. I don't know how Golda knew who I am, but I could have a good guess; above and beyond all, in my appearance, I am a man who is marked and "unforgettable."

## Note

1.  Herut was a right-wing political party led by Menachem Begin. In 1973, it joined with the Liberal Party to form the Likud.

# 20

## THE MINI-STATE OPTION

For a long time, I didn't publish any further articles in newspapers. I had already decided in any case that I would publish only when I felt I had something to say that no one else could. My next article, which appeared almost a year after the 1973 war, on August 1, 1974, bore the misleading headline given to it by some editor: "A Palestinian State Will Exacerbate the Conflict in the Middle East." It seems to me that this article presented a more detailed plan than any piece I have ever written, even though today it would not sound correct from a political point of view. I had dealt previously with many of the topics covered in it; nevertheless, it did contain a number of new elements. In this article, I referred to the 1967 war as the greatest change in direction that had occurred in the Middle East, not because of Israel's overwhelming victory but rather because the results of the war were a political setback for Israel, what I called "the return to the situation that preceded the founding of the state" and the reestablishment de facto of a bi-national entity. By this I meant that the populations of the three regions which composed the British colonial state (Israel, the West Bank, and the Gaza Strip) found themselves again under a common political umbrella. Between 1948 and 1967, a process of de-Palestinization of the Palestinians took place; carried out mainly by Jordan and Israel, it turned them into Jordanians and Israeli Arabs respectively. Israel's contribution to this development was reflected in its silent support for the persistence of the oligarchic rule of the Bedouins over the great majority of the Palestinian population in the Kingdom of Jordan. The reunification of a considerable portion of the Palestinian people under Jewish rule reawakened them as a political entity which, as even the U.S. recognized at the Madrid talks, requires its own country. Indeed the PLO had already been established in 1964; however, at the beginning, it seemed to be an ephemeral organization dependent upon the Arab states. The defeat of the Arab states in 1967 weakened them while at the same time strengthening the PLO and reducing its dependence on them.

In the new situation, an international request was made for the establishment of a Palestinian state, at the very least in the West Bank and Gaza. I argued that such a state, if realized, would inevitably be irredentist toward both Israel and Jordan. Inside the narrow and arid territory of Gaza and the West Bank, it is unlikely that a country would be sustainable and able to absorb returning refugees; it would, however, nurture the dream of the Greater Palestine that existed before the 1922 partition. I concluded, therefore, that the two big losers of the 1967 War from a political point of view were Israel and Jordan. As time went by, I understood that there was only one big loser: Israel. Jordan strengthened its internal stability when it got rid of the inhabitants of the West Bank and in 1988, it even renounced them formally. Hence I reached the conclusion that for the sake of its own long-term interest, Israel must cease to support Jordan and let the Palestinians gain control over it. Once a Palestinian state is established on what is now Jordan, the most demonic dimension of this inter-ethnic conflict would disappear and it would be possible to negotiate the conditions under which control over the West Bank and Gaza could be transferred to it. It is, after all, much easier to achieve an agreement between nations than between a country and an amorphous ethnic entity, especially when the overall territory is much larger.

Within a month, Ariel Sharon published a long article in *Haaretz* which included similar arguments, but reached the opposite conclusion: Jordan is the Palestinian state and Israel must help the Palestinians to adopt that identity while renouncing the West Bank and the Gaza Strip.

On August 1, 1982, with the beginning of the Israeli invasion of Lebanon, my eight-column article "The Most Important War (Since the War of Independence)" was published. In hindsight, I read this article with curiosity since it dealt with many more subjects in addition to the invasion or what had been openly defined as Israel's first "war of choice." My point of departure was that the novel and most important aspect of the 1982 war was the fact that it was the first Israeli-Palestinian war since 1948. My second determination was that Begin and Sharon read the international map correctly when they calculated that there wouldn't be any American or Soviet obstructions and constraints which could have prevented Israel from implementing an aggressive policy the way it wanted to. Even the peace agreement with Egypt, though put to a tough test, did not collapse.

I ascribed the attempt to destroy the PLO in Lebanon to an effort to annihilate the Palestinians as a political and social entity (which, in a book I wrote twenty-one years later, I called "politicide"). "In the eyes of the territories' residents, the occupation turned the PLO into both their legitimate and sole representative because, as the Palestinians justifiably state, agreements achieved with people or leaders living under occupation are not valid."

Nevertheless the dominant ideology of the PLO, I believed then, is the rigid and uncompromising traditional one of "everything or nothing," as it was expressed in the covenant. Under such conditions, I thought, those who claim that there is no one to talk with are right.

"Yet the 1982 war (I wrote) could have several consequences which were unintended by its Israeli planners. The destruction of the PLO infrastructure, particularly the Fatah, in southern Lebanon and west Beirut might bring about the tempering of the PLO positions (which even then contained echoes in this vein), and the decision to establish a Palestinian state in the West Bank and Gaza bordered by the Green Line."

It is interesting how deep my ignorance regarding the Palestinian issue was at that stage. Indeed, as early as July 1974, at the twelfth meeting of the Palestinian National Council, on Naif Hawatma's initiative, the decision to establish a "Palestinian national authority over all the territory liberated from Israeli control" was reached; pragmatically it meant exactly what was referred to in my article. Consequently to that decision, that September, George Habash, from the "Popular Front for the Liberation of Palestine," withdrew his support for the "mini-state" idea and founded the "Refusal Front," which accused the PLO of betraying Palestinian interests. The Refusal Front was a coalition of the pro-Iraqi guerilla organizations "Arab Liberation Front," "Popular Front – the General Headquarters" (under the leadership of Ahmed Jibril), and the "Front for the Popular Palestinian Struggle." Yet Fatah and most of the PLO did not reconsider and the rifts among Palestinian [factions] became overt, deep and acute, leading even to armed confrontations.

It's likely that my ignorance stemmed from the fact that Israel—under the influence of the military historian Yehoshafat Harkaby—hastily interpreted the decision in favor of a "mini-state option" as a mere tactical change in direction and called it "a plan by stages" (for the extermination of Israel). But whoever closely followed the internal struggles among the Palestinians could not fail to discern a great shift—brought about with a heavy heart—within the mainstream of their political thinking, regardless of what their secret aspirations might have been. In retrospect, it is likely that precisely this dramatic change was one of the causes for the 1982 war. In any case, the myth of the "stages doctrine" became an asset that was too valuable for the Israeli right, and even sections of the left, to relinquish. Yehoshafat Harkaby, who invented this interpretation—just as he was the responsible for the translation and promulgation of the Palestinian Covenant and for the excessive importance given to it—sorely regretted this in his old age ("I was a complete idiot," he told me in this context on one of our trips together).

An additional consequence of the "war of choice" into which Israel was dragged by Begin and Sharon in 1982—as I had predicted six weeks before the Sabra and Shatila massacre—was to be a decrease in willingness and motivation to serve in the Israeli army, since this consists mostly of civilians (reservists) who are not ready to serve in a military that is exploited for political purposes, especially if those are controversial. This prediction materialized, yet only to a small extent. In Israel, for the first time in its history, a movement of conscientious objectors emerged and a high-ranking officer, Reserve Brigadier General Eli Gheva, refused to obey an order and preferred to give up his military career. Nevertheless, despite these cracks, the militaristic ethos continues to prevail in Israel until this very day.

Once again and for long periods I didn't publish frequently. Then, on August 1, 1984, I violated every taboo and welcomed the election of Meir Kahane to the Israeli parliament. I did so for two main reasons. Firstly, if tens of thousands were ready to vote for him, it means that Kahanism has become a social, political, and ethical phenomenon which can no longer be ignored.

Secondly, Kahane constitutes the biggest challenge to the Israeli right that had annexed *de facto* the territories since his doctrine is the only extant logical answer to the internal contradiction which the right has fallen into: their will to hold and ultimately even to annex most of the occupied territories as if these are not inhabited by Arabs. If, as it declares, the right rejects the Kahane doctrine, then it is incumbent upon it to provide an alternative answer to the most serious challenges that this doctrine presents to the secular right's ideology and the state's actual practices.

Since, and if, mass eviction does not constitute—genuinely and seriously—a realistic and ethical option and if there is no intention of perpetuating the situation of a bi-national entity, how do they intend to manage the conflict and what is their vision of the future other than a regime with South African characteristics? And what constitutional, legal, economic, and military regulations will such a regime have? Not only the (bi?)-national camp owes itself and the country's citizens an answer to those questions. If Kahane's election compelled the state as well to respond to this conundrum, it would then turn out to be a great blessing.

I didn't think even for a moment that the "national camp" aspires to establish *de jure* a bi-national state, but I wanted to bring the argument and the rhetoric I have used for years to its logical extreme since I have noticed that the right has no real answer to this line of argument except Kahane's. Later on, there came, with a wink, Rachav-Am Zeevi's answer of "voluntary transfer" and afterwards that of Avigdor Lieberman and friends. As mentioned, I was aware of the fact that the demographic argument has clear racist implications, yet I couldn't give up such a powerful argument that struck directly at the heart of the Zionist theme of Israel's being a pure Jewish state. I tried to use it as a provocative expedient to push my political adversaries into the corner and it seems to me that I indeed succeeded (although not all by myself) in bringing the issue into public awareness and later on to the center of various politicians' agenda, including that of Ariel Sharon. This process—for which I feel an ethical aversion—placed me once again in a difficult dilemma: either to retain an impeccable intellectual and moral position or to offer politically pragmatic arguments that could advance an ethical cause.

As a person who considers himself close both ideologically and emotionally to the remnants of the Peace Covenant's approaches, I indeed felt attracted to the idea of a bi-national state (even before a small group of Palestinian intellectuals tried to revive the idea). In addition, I saw in it the opportunity for a possible correction of some of the injustices suffered by the Palestinian people, who had been uprooted from their homes, fields, and motherland as a result of the success of Zionism. However, I was also as aware of the utopian visions and risks concealed in this idea, at least during the present phase of history. Too many disparities and too much resentment had accumulated between the two peoples for it to be possible to attain a common and genuinely egalitarian country where mutual hostility wouldn't continue pulsing amidst the two ethno-national tribes. I was convinced that in the initial stage of a bi-national state, regardless of its constitutional and political structure, the Jewish economic, cultural, social, and political dominance would inevitably continue, ultimately causing it to explode and drown in a Balkan-style bloodbath.

Apart from this, there exist two additional arguments that make the idea of a bi-national state seem impractical to me. First, the vast majority of both Palestinians and Jews prefer to live within the framework of some sort of national state. Personally, I am not a zealous supporter of the concept of national identity, as it is liable at any moment to roll down a slippery slope into nationalism which, together with religious extremism, has inflicted massive disasters on the human race. Nevertheless, it is necessary to recognize that national identity is a dominant social and ideological element for both sides and the world. Secondly, we have no encouraging historical and sociological experience with bi- or multi-national entities, except for extremely rare instances where the circumstances are completely different from our own. Even the Czechs and the Slovaks, who have an advanced political culture, eventually decided to separate from each other.

# 21

## THE RIGHT TO RESIST THE OCCUPATION

Before I get into this painful and complicated issue, it's worth clarifying several points even though they look obvious at first sight: the project of colonizing the territories conquered in 1967 could not have been implemented at all without the approval and massive support of the state and all of its governments. If this had not been carried out under the aegis of the military (and the General Security Service) and if huge amounts of funds had not been invested in building infrastructure and subsidizing, directly and indirectly, both the public and private needs of every settlement, not a single settlement would exist today in these territories.

Those resources were derived, in part openly but mostly covertly, from every part of the government's budget, making it impossible to estimate their actual extent and the degree to which the income of the country's entire population was distorted as a result. Finances were transferred without going through the customary decision-making procedures every democratic government uses when public funds are to be reallocated between the different populations existing in the state. For example, the state allotted to citizens living beyond the Green Line on average several times what it apportioned to the rest of the population.

It wouldn't be right, of course, to ascribe all the corruption of the country's public sector during the past decades to the settlements. Yet whenever an additional "bank account" is created through which the state, its leaders, and its functionaries can channel payments without reports, supervision, and public debate, it becomes acceptable to spend public funds irresponsibly and siphon them off for the non-normative needs of the economic and political institutions and for private interests.

This "settlement enterprise" caused further massive damage since it deflected the army from its exclusive assignment, the protection of the country's borders and its citizens, toward the role of a police force that oppresses, restricts, and controls the Palestinian population while it protects the settlements and their access roads. The transformation of the army into a politically controversial entity even created a negative selection by affecting the willingness to serve in it, the propensity to volunteer for a military career, and the advancement of soldiers in the officer corps to the highest ranks. If the Israeli army had invested its efforts in devising combat strategies to meet the requirements of future military conflicts, including guerrilla warfare and terror, and not in methods of controlling a civilian population—which would have no reason to resist a nonexistent occupation—its quality could have been greatly improved. Additionally, as Moshe Lissak warned during the first intifada, the use of violence learned in the territories would creep into Israeli society and result in its brutalization.

It seems that the most provocative article I ever published, and this too after months of pondering, was "The Right to Resist the Occupation" (*Haaretz*, March 27, 2001), wherein I claimed that, as hard as it is for us Israelis to admit it, it is important for us to have a clear understanding of the present political, legal, and moral situation in its historical context.

Since 1967, millions of Palestinians have been living under the rule of a military occupation, lacking civil rights and in most cases also some fundamental human ones. This continuous state of occupation and oppression gives the Palestinians, according to every criterion—from the perspectives of natural law, international law, and ethics—the right to oppose the occupation by employing all the resources at their disposal, which even means rising up against it by using violent force. The problem is greatly aggravated on both sides in light of the physical proximity, the intertwining of one population with the other, and the combat methods forced on the two parties as a result of this closeness. The indiscriminate Palestinian (particularly the Islamic) terror which is carried out deep in the heart of Israel and harms civilians is immoral. It also boomerangs since it leads to increased anger and hatred among Israel's Jewish public and hinders its possibility of relating empathically and rationally to the legitimate requests of the Palestinian people. This terror is even consciously used as a cynical political tool by the right-wing Israeli political leadership and recently by some of the highest-ranking officers in the army in order to torpedo any possibility of furthering accords between Israel and the Palestinians which would bring about the end of the occupation and hasten the decolonization process. On the other side, the reactions and, too frequently, the initiatives of the Israeli army and settlers also result in indiscriminate and unreasonable killings among Palestinian civilians, which are themselves considered to be both war crimes and crimes against humanity.

At the time this article was published, the Palestinians had reported over six hundred killed—more than sixty of them children—and thousands injured since the outbreak of what is called the "Al-Aqsa Intifada." Furthermore, there is a continuous increase in Israel's use of collective punishments that are forbidden by international law and treaties, including the imposition of blockades, the demolition of houses and entire neighborhoods, the administrative detention of thousands of Palestinians, and the use of roadblocks to divide the territories and prevent freedom of movement within them. Israel also adopted the habit of carrying out acts of terror against any individual it classifies as being involved in hostile activity and even against the political leadership of Palestinian organizations. The right of the Palestinians to resist the occupation becomes even stronger in light of the fact that the Fourth

Geneva Convention prohibits creating irreversible facts on the ground in occupied territories and, in particular, transferring populations from the conquering country to the conquered territory in order to settle them there. This is valid despite the fact that Israel has conveniently avoided defining itself as a conqueror by using the questionable pretext that the territories it now controls have had no sovereignty of any kind since the British left Palestine, and the Palestinians rejected the 1947 partition plan which included the establishment of an Arab country alongside a Jewish one. Additionally, according to the verdicts of the Supreme Court, which is strongly conscious of the significance of the Fourth Geneva Convention, all of the settlements established beyond the Green Line were allegedly built for "security reasons," which is the legal loophole in the international conventions that Israel has exploited as a pretext for founding them.

The second "legal" loophole Israel has used to grant legitimacy to the settlements and "peace of mind" for anyone who might be worried about this issue, in particular the High Court justices themselves, was to allegedly refrain from expropriating private land and to build settlements on "state land" only. Since 1967, over sixty per cent of the West Bank's lands have been declared to be state property, which in reality constituted a selective, *de facto* annexation of the territories. This "legal" move was made possible because most of the West Bank's lands were neither regulated by law nor registered in Ottoman, British, or Jordanian land registries. (It must be pointed out, however, that all these authorities recognized the right of possession and the traditional land ownership of the West Bank's farmers and residents.) The questionable legality and ethics of all the Jewish settlements and outposts in the territories stem from these facts and even the Oslo agreement and those that followed—as well as their implementation on the ground—did not change this situation.

A number of phenomena blurred and dimmed the political and ethical senses of Israeli society. First, until the end of 1987, the Palestinian resistance to the occupation was minor and restrained. The entire Israeli society, including the Israeli Arab citizens, enjoyed the fruits of the "temporary-permanent" occupation without paying any significant or immediate price. In this context, it was easy for the combination of religious-messianic nationalism, secular chauvinism *à la* Likud, and securitism, which was forged by the Israel Labor Party and the Labor Unity Party, to dominate Israeli political culture. Therefore, I wrote the following:

"Even today [in 2001] most of the Israeli public is not yet aware of the fact that every separate act of aggression committed by Israel against the Palestinians—and all the more so when they are taken en bloc—borders on war crimes and cannot discern the black flag of obvious illegality waving above them. A country which considers itself part of the enlightened world cannot behave like a terror state even if it is itself forced to suffer terror. Israeli politicians, military personnel, and ordinary citizens themselves must notice this black flag before it is too late and the deepest darkness will cling to us all."

At this point it is right and proper to clarify a fundamental issue: every indiscriminate injury or killing of unarmed and non-combatant members of any civilian population is attempted murder or murder and sometimes massacre and is considered by every criterion to be a war crime. Indisputably included in this category are attacks on buses and all other civilian targets in Israel, which cannot be considered legitimate resistance to the occupation. However, the targeted killings by Israel, which are in effect executions without trial, cannot be considered legitimate either, especially when they result in the "unintentional" killing-murder of hundreds of innocent bystanders and the army and its leaders are very much aware of the likelihood of such an outcome in those circumstances. From this point of view, the right of Palestinians to resist is limited to actions within the territories and against unambiguous military targets in Israel. What is also worth mentioning and considering is the convenient way in which the terms "war" and "terror" are alternated according to the context. This method of criminalizing the enemy or adversary is not new, and usually it succeeds when implemented by the superior power. One of Israel's contentions is that in time of war, it is inevitable that civilians would be injured; at the same time, however, it does not regard Palestinians it holds as prisoners of war (although, in most cases, the Red Cross is allowed to visit and check their condition), but rather as criminal terrorists, some of whom have "blood on their hands," without applying the same criteria to its own actions and to those of its soldiers.

The article about the right to resist was indeed published; afterwards, however, the newspaper's vice editor (who was in charge of the editorial page and was considered to have quite radical "leftist" opinions) suddenly began to reject, one after the other, the publication of my subsequent articles. I do not and never did have any idea about what happens in *Haaretz*'s editorial office, but I guess that the newspaper had received many protests as a result of having published my article and therefore decided to cut back on the dreadful Kimmerling's shows or to stop publishing me altogether. In any case, they did not inform me of this, hoping that I would take the hint—or at least that was what I, maybe somewhat hastily, deduced. An exchange of furious faxes between the editors and me began. At a certain point, I even complained directly to Amos Schocken, the publisher of *Haaretz*, who replied that he [usually] doesn't interfere with the decisions of his editors. I grinned bitterly to myself. *Haaretz*, which had been my "public" home for many years, and where I was among the most senior writers for the op-ed page, apparently no longer required my services. Only two months later it was made public (not in *Haaretz* itself) that, probably following a drop in circulation, it had been decided, primarily under the influence of the editor-in-chief, to move the newspaper toward the "center" and to reduce the number of articles being published. One of the most prominent among the article writers told me that he had been allotted space to publish an article approximately once a month. I decided then to look for another "home" until the storm blew over and I found it at *Ynet*, the online version of *Yediot Aharonot*, where I had already published articles in the past.

One of those, a few years previously, had aroused such a fury on the part of the *Haaretz*'s vice editor that he sent me an angry fax demanding that I choose between *Yediot* and *Haaretz*'s op-ed page. I was flattered by this, yet I felt uncomfortable nevertheless and asked him whether I had become a feudal-style vassal of the newspaper. *Ynet*'s advantages are a much wider circulation than that of *Haaretz* and a nearly non-existent editorial policy; its big disadvantages are that its influence on decision-makers is probably much weaker than that of *Haaretz*, and its English edition is meaningless.

As a compulsive reader of the foreign press, I must remark that the Israeli one, and *Haaretz* in particular (even in its less bright days), is much more open and has more varied opinions and commentaries than the best liberal newspapers of the West and especially of the U.S. It's very rare for newspapers like the *New York Times* or the *Washington Post* to deviate from the positions held by the mainstream of the Democratic Party. More than once, I tried to publish articles in western newspapers but with very limited success. Some of my articles did appear in the *Boston Globe*, the *International Herald Tribune*, *The Nation*, and in the online *Salon*. I also published an article in the Higher Education Supplement of the Dutch *Time*, in which I attacked the academic boycott against Israeli institutions of higher education. Despite the fact that I understood very well the intentions of those who proposed it, I considered that boycott to be a mortal blow to the concepts of academia and academic freedom. In the same spirit, I published an article in the prestigious *Logos*.

# 22

## KULTURKAMPF

I have published many articles on the separation of religion and state as a necessary condition for the normalization of the Israeli government's domestic policies and the settlement of the conflict with the Palestinians. At the same time, I pointed out the difficulty stemming from the fact that, although Zionism originated as a secular national movement, the choice itself of Zion as the target destination that would solve the national problem and the use of religious symbols par excellence—which were meant to encourage mass immigration in order to colonize the territory and build the state—introduced into Zionism archetypal religious motifs whose effects were not obvious before the 1967 war. And indeed, in spite of the fact that laws pertaining to marriage, immigration, and naturalization bore, from the beginning, a clear religious, ethnocentric character, they had been accepted even by those who, while belonging to the country's Jewish society, considered themselves to be secular. This phenomenon stemmed partially from two different yet related anxieties which were—and still are—built into this society: the angst about the legitimacy of its existence in the region as an immigrant-settler society, and the concern about its ability to survive in such a place in the long run.

Israeli political culture handled the latter anxiety about Israel's ability to continue existing with considerable efficiency by developing an advanced army, establishing a "nuclear option," recounting stories of military power, and creating myths.

However, when it seemed that the defense establishment did not perform as expected (as in the 1973 war, the 2006 war in Lebanon, and what is perceived as the future Iranian threat), the social and political system went into a frenzy. The government responded with a mixture of reassurance, claiming that the army's "deterrence capability" had not been negatively affected, and manipulative rhetoric designed to frighten the public and channel its fury.

The other anxiety—about the legitimacy of the state's existence—was less explicit and more subtle, and therefore the cultural system had difficulty dealing with it at the same level of efficiency with which it coped with the existential one. One response was the manipulative and obsessive preoccupation with the Holocaust, from which the sole alleged inference was that only the establishment of a Jewish state could guarantee its people that the horror would not be repeated. This argument is somewhat questionable in light of the opposite contention that it is actually in Israel itself that a danger to the existence of the Jewish people as a collective is imminent. However, the Holocaust is not brought up only to justify the establishment of the state but also its policy, which too often lacks all restraint toward Gentiles in general and Arabs in particular. The Holocaust had formidable emotional power both over the country's Jews, including me, and Jews and non-Jews abroad. Therefore, the Holocaust was almost the only subject I didn't feel able to deal with, either emotionally, professionally, or publicly, in a neutral manner, although more than once I felt irritated by and angry about how it was being manipulated. By the way, when I speak about the "right to exist," I do not mean the legal, political, or even moral right, which no political or legal institution can grant or negate. Countries exist because they exist; there is no inherent justification for their existence or non-existence. This debate concerns social constructions, usually manipulative in one way or another, that are established within the political culture through a complex internal and external discourse. From a sociological point of view, when such a subject arises, it definitely indicates a society in distress.

At the Anthropological Association conference held during the summer of 1999 in Nazareth, which Edward Said[1] and I were given the honor of opening, I mustered the courage, as I occasionally do, and argued that it is impossible to compare the *Nakba*[2] with the Holocaust, except for the fact that each of the two peoples emerged wounded and with severe emotional trauma. Said was angry but responded in a gentlemanly fashion as was appropriate. However, our friendly relationship was negatively affected and became distant. It is hard to know if this was actually the reason because he was already suffering badly from the effects of cancer treatment, which are now about to shorten my own life. The second time I dealt with the subject of the Holocaust and the death cult in Israel was in an extensive survey of the books by Idit Zartal and Yosef Grodjanski in the American weekly *The Nation* (January 10, 2005).

An additional mechanism meant to deal with the legitimacy problem of the existence of an immigrant-settler state in the region was the reliance on religious symbols and myths as if it was linear history. The Bible, a moral and a religious book, was turned into a constitutive document linking the ancient Jewish kingdoms and tribes with "the Return to Zion" as if nothing had happened during the previous two thousand years to the world's Jews and as if the history of the region had been frozen in time. For this purpose, especially from 1967 on, both the cultural and the political systems in Israel underwent massive processes of "religionization." I dedicated a detailed essay to this subject, entitled "Perhaps the Last Taboo," which was published on October 6, 1993 in *Haaretz* and had been also included in a book celebrating the seventy-fifth anniversary of the newspaper. Symbols drawn from the Bible were indeed given secular-national interpretations; however, their religious primeval-ethnic kernel remained and its language, metaphor, and narrative turned into the immigrants' primary title to this land. Therefore, almost from the beginning, the connection between nationhood and religion lay dormant in Zionism like a time bomb whose delayed-action fuse was long enough to last until the 1967 war, in the wake of which the big explosion occurred: the encounter between the ancient Jewish heartland[3] and a militarily powerful society experiencing an even bigger existential anxiety.

Since Gush Emunim and the religious establishment represented the point of view that our right to the entire land is obvious, it was convenient for the secular public to delegate the solution to the whole question about "our right to the land" to them. In the secular public's consciousness, they took the place previously held by the "pioneers" before the state had been established. When Gush Emunim achieved this status, it craved to settle not only throughout the conquered territories but also in people's hearts. The strategy they developed included infiltrating all the old, mostly quasi-socialist and secular elite groups in the army, the educational system, the media, academia, the entire judiciary, and the political leadership in general with members of the young national-religious generation. Their declared, almost explicit, intention was and still is to bring about a silent revolution which would totally change the state's character, transforming it, if not into an absolute theocracy, then at least into a "Jewish" state in which a kind of manufactured Jewishness would dominate the rules of the cultural-political game. Democracy and the attitudes toward minorities and secular Hellenist (licentious) public lifestyle would be pushed to the margins. In this revolution, they entered into a limited or full alliance with the Orthodox, with whom they had an historical rivalry, the traditional Jews of eastern origin, and even with the secular nationalists from the Tabenkin and Jabotinsky schools—in short, all those who had been pushed to the margins of the old regime. There were two reasons why this revolution was not completely successful, but rather was halted in midstream: the Palestinian resistance to the occupation, and the opposition by a portion of the old elite.

There is no doubt that the approach advocating transfer constitutes only one part of the mosaic reflecting the struggle and the culture war over the whole character of Israel. On February 12, 2006, I published an article titled "Kulturkampf" on *Ynet*. In this article too, as in previous ones, I emphasized the disturbing connection between the internal struggles over Israel's political-cultural character and the attitude towards the Palestinians. Thus the request of the former Internal Security Minister, Gideon Ezra, to charge politicians and Israeli peace activists with treason while casting suspicion on them for [allegedly] passing information to the enemy (an approach which until now was implemented at least once—in the trial of Tali Fahima) should not surprise anyone who follows the systematic efforts of many elements in the Israeli and the American Jewish right to take advantage of the current situation in order to mold Israel into a unique kind of regime: a combination of theocracy and fascism. There is no doubt that the Israeli right wishes to exploit this "war" to subdue not only the Palestinians but also anyone within Israeli society who, having a humanistic point of view, opposes them. Even the timing of Ezra's proposal was not coincidental but occurred in light of what appeared to be a partial recovery of the dovish camp after the blows it endured to its morale from Barak, Peres, the suicide terror bombings and Sharon.

A number of years ago, the Israeli intellectual Yoram Hazoni, who was educated in the United States in the lap of American neo-conservatism mingled with Israeli religious-nationalism, published a book in English whose subtitle was *The Struggle for Israel's Soul*. The book, which achieved considerable success among American Jews and their conservative intellectuals, described Hebrew cultural life in Israel in an utterly one-dimensional way. Hazoni's main claim was that most of the writers, poets, artists, and in particular academicians (the author of the present book included) who are not entirely identified with the extreme right or the national-religious stream, have betrayed their mission. In doing so, they have brought upon Israel a cultural and political disaster, which culminated in the attempt to make peace with the Palestinians and could end in the physical destruction of the Jewish state following its moral degeneration.

In the field of literature, for example, Hazoni names Amos Oz, Izhar Smilansky, A.B. Yehoshua, David Grossman, and Meir Shalev. Whoever dared to express themselves on the "Arab problem" with any empathy or to include in their writings an Arab character who is not total scum is, according to Hazoni, "consumed by self-hatred."

Among poets, Aharon Appelfeld, Dalia Rabikovich, Natan Zach, and even Yehuda Amichai are mentioned as complete villains. Also those who did not necessarily empathize with the Arabs or criticize the continued occupation of Palestinian territories and the oppression of their population but had created works of art that are universal in spirit were categorized by Hazoni as enemies of the Jewish people. Hazoni even complained bitterly that most of the recipients of the Israel Prize are anti-Semites. Writers, poets, playwrights, and film directors constitute a special danger as, their anti-Jewish messages, in contrast to those of the academicians, are covert and difficult to oppose. Even a relatively conservative intellectual like Shlomo Avineri didn't escape his criticism, since many years previously he had dealt with Marx.

Despite the fact that even most of the Israeli right could not ignore the superficiality of Hazoni's theories and his detachment from Israeli intellectual reality, the main thesis of his book is worthy of thorough scrutiny. This thesis, it seems to me, even preceded the approach of the "clash of civilizations" between the progressive West and the "dark" non-Western world, in the style of Samuel P. Huntington and George W. Bush. Its Israeli version claims that there exists a culture war with regard to Israeli identity and the political rules of the game, which does not—as is customary—focus specifically on the place of religion in the state, even though this issue constitutes part of the conflict. This internal struggle is conducted between the culture of the allegedly patriotic, sovereign, and Zionist right and that of the anti-patriotic and treacherous left, which is described as shallow and shrouded in false universalism and humanism. Hence the latter allegedly gives preference to the interests of the Palestinians and the Arabs, who are the ultimate existential threat to the Jewish state and thus to Jews worldwide.

The fundamental contention of Hazoni and his ilk is that Jewish intellectuals have a traditional tendency, stemming from a pathological feeling of inferiority and guilt, to adopt for themselves anti-Semitic stereotypes of Jews. This is a kind of axiom which needs only to be stated, does not require proof, and prevents any encounter with reason and debate. Thus there is no attempt to show any sort of difference between anti-Semitic culture and the one attributed by the Israeli right and American conservatives to the Jewish "left," which sometimes is nothing more than moderate liberalism. The use of the labels designating the "left" (reds, Communists!) has the same effect as mass brainwashing. It should be recalled that at that time, this culture war was actually being waged in the form of violent demonstrations accompanied by extreme verbal aggression; it verged on becoming a civil war and culminated with Rabin's assassination.

Hazoni probably began to write his book when the Oslo agreements were being implemented and completed it during the prime ministership of Ehud Barak, who was supposed to continue Rabin's legacy and even promised a "civil revolution," meaning the resolution of the Israeli culture war on both its two intertwined fronts. In between, even Benjamin Netanyahu, for whom Hazoni was an aide, didn't manage to extricate himself from the process, at the end of which could be seen the unmistakable shattering of the colonial idea of a Greater Israel. This explains the tone of frustration and despair that the book exuded.

Even the act of settling in the territory known as Yesha is, in effect, not an end in itself . Both the dogmatic religious ideology and the secular one regard it as the first stage and the means by which, ultimately, a community based on principles of Jewish ethics is being built in Yesha and is supposed to expand throughout the entire land and transform Israel into a Jewish state. Using the narrowest and least inclusive definition of Jewishness, this state would exclude anyone and anything not defined as Jewish and would restrict the canon of what is allowed to be read and taught.

The majority of those espousing this culture consider ceaseless war to be not only a necessary evil but also a natural and sometimes even an exalted situation, as Effie Eitam has recently expressed it. It is ironic that those factions in our midst who are hitching a ride on what Americans consider to be a world war meant to defend "Western" civilization are themselves closer to the regimes of Khomeini and Saddam Hussein than to the liberal democracy which is regarded as suitable by western culture.

However, just as peacemaking and reconciliation between Jews and Arabs in general, and the Palestinians in particular, is perceived by Hazoni and his cohorts as an act of subjugation in the intra-Israeli culture war, we have to consider the policy adopted by the government and the Israeli army against the Palestinians and the Palestinian Authority in a much wider context than usual. It is possible that this policy was not originally intended for this but it is conducted in such a way that it strives toward a simultaneous strategic solution of both the internal and external problems and—in the best of traditions—does not shrink from labeling dissenters as "traitors" and "criminals." Thus incitement replaced public discourse. In general, war—as long as it can be presented as successful—is a comfortable social situation when a regime is attempting to implement social and cultural changes disguised as existential necessities. Every critical voice or thought is pushed either to the margins of or outside the public arena. In a situation like this, ideas such as ethnic cleansing (transfer) and cultural purification, which have increasingly infiltrated into public discourse, thrive like wormwood. The more despair takes hold of the Jewish public, personal security collapses, and the "demographic demon" gathers strength—whether throughout Greater Israel or even within the boundaries of the Green Line—the more these fantasies move from the margins of the collective consciousness closer to its center.

The weakening of personal security is a phenomenon that becomes seven times stronger during a period of deepening economic crisis, unemployment, and inflation, which are themselves largely an outcome of war, even a low-density one. In this way, a kind of vicious circle is created. To the lack of personal security is added the construction of threats to society as a whole: everything from Iran and Iraq to the Hezbollah, in addition to the conflict with the Palestinians, is presented either explicitly or implicitly as a threat to the existence of the state. When a lack of fundamental security in all three areas—the personal, the economic, and the collective-existential one—occurs at the same time, a situation is created which shatters social cohesion within civil societies and transforms people into isolated and passive individuals who lose faith in their ability to exercise influence. On the other hand, under those conditions, a yearning for solidarity, a sense of belonging, and a "strong man" who would act as ruler and savior increases. This situation creates a frightened public (members of the media and intellectuals included) that responds to the regime as if it were clay in the hands of a potter. As stated, this is the most comfortable state of affairs when attempting to achieve an even larger-scale resolution of the cultural conflicts within Israeli society itself, and at least a portion of the people in the position to make decisions are well aware of this fact. Consequently, efforts—which have been quite successful thus far—are made to weaken key institutions of civil culture such as universities, the High Court, or the Broadcasting Authority in particular and the media in general.

If in the past decade it seemed that Israeli society was becoming more open, liberal, and inclined towards multi-culturalism and less militaristic and nationalistic, it looks now as if the cultural pendulum has swung back toward the spirit of Hazoni's vision. Apparently, the turning point was the outbreak of the armed Palestinian rebellion in September 2000, the massacre of Arab citizens one month later, and Barak's proclamation that "we have no partner." These events resulted in rising hatred, a lust for revenge, and Arab-phobia alongside Jew-phobia, all of which deepened the estrangement and hostility between the two civil populations in Israel and caused great confusion to those among them seeking coexistence. Most of the political upheavals which have occurred since then originated principally from the increasing open, mutual hatred coupled with a fear of Arabs that has been transformed into a genuine hysteria by the suicide bombers. During the culture war between the so-called right and left[4] conducted in Israel since the 1970s, all these factors combined, allowing the Israeli right to achieve what seems for now to be a position that enables it to shift the [political and cultural] balance. During the Rabin era and the early part of Barak's term, this same position seemed to have been reached by the secular left, as both Hazoni and his opponents had felt.

This tilt of balance by the secular and religious right will also lead to an attempt to once more gain control over the entire territory of the Land of Israel and, at the same time, over Israeli political culture itself—two loci of control which are supposed to bolster and complement each other. A development of this kind, which could be reflected in all areas of public and even private life, is actually impossible since the present demographic, ethnic, and class realities in the region cannot be changed. It would be possible to shatter the Palestinian Authority and to assassinate or deport its leaders, but it would not be feasible to suppress their people's resistance to the continued occupation and colonization of their land. The ethnic cleansing which was possible in 1948 could not be carried out today under any circumstances without bringing down moral and political devastation on the perpetrators as well. Little by little, even the middle classes, which constitute the backbone of every society, are showing signs of reconsidering and are beginning to properly read the map threatening their political and economic status as well as the moral foundation and the institutional regularization of the whole society—and are therefore reorganizing anew. The success of this reorganization depends on the renewal of the covenant with the Arab citizens of Israel, and this in turn depends upon the reconstruction of Israeliness and the multicultural framework which had begun to be built in the 1970s but has now collapsed as a result of an inter-ethnic war.

## Notes

1. Edward Said was an American literary theorist, a professor of English and comparative literature at Columbia University and a Palestinian political activist.
2. Arab word designating the catastrophe which befell the Palestinians when Israel was established and hundreds of thousands of them lost their lands and homes and thousands also their lives.
3. The ancient Jewish heartland refers here to Judea and Samaria.
4. Both the Israeli right and left are extremely heterogeneous camps containing multiple internal contradictions.

# 23

## POLITICIANS

Both research on and writing about academic subjects, as well as about current political and public issues, are based upon a number of similar fundamental principles and qualities, although each one of those fields uses them in different degrees. The first component is intuition, the nature of which I find difficult to define; I can only testify that I often use this ability to understand things without conscious reasoning, despite the hidden risks. A related component is empathy, i.e., the ability to get inside the head and walk in the shoes of an individual or social group and understand their interests and motives without identifying with them. I believe that one cannot be a good sociologist without the ability to feel empathy for the subjects of a study, an article, or a newspaper survey. A third component is rational thinking, which is intended to balance both intuition and empathy since one must not write and research only under the influence of gut feelings. The fourth is the most important of all: knowledge. Ample and well-founded knowledge and information about the subject are needed. The problem is that knowledge and information are always partial; thus intuition and reasoning are required to complete the crossword puzzle, even if the final result is defective because of errors and unfounded assessments. Also when he knows that he may be mistaken or may express opinions based on incomplete information and sometimes on disinformation, the writer must not let this awareness paralyze him; he is obliged to assume the risk of writing on the basis of information that could be wrong to some degree, as without taking calculated risks, no progress can be made. As the sociologist Ulrich Beck said, we live in a world of increasing uncertainty, and we have to adjust to it.

In retrospect, the predictions and analysis I presented regarding socio-political processes proved to be accurate while I was less successful at reading people. This was probably because I did not have direct acquaintance with them and I relied on others' judgments when they seemed reliable to me or because I fell into the trap of using stereotypes. At the same time, my interpretation of the personality and weaknesses of Ehud Barak was correct, and I tried as hard as I could to reduce the chances of his election as a candidate for the leadership of the Labor Party and the Government to the point that I proposed that his party replace him through a "democratic *putsch*" by repealing the Direct Election Act. On September 12, 1996, in an article entitled "Find the Differences," I compared Barak to Netanyahu, who at the time was at his lowest standing, and I wrote as follows:

> It's a great day for the Labor Party: the Defense Minister gallops like Napoleon on the wings of a white TV set, with a microphone in his hand, to rescue the nation from Bibi, who is so much like him. He's nice, assertive, and compact, expresses himself using four words per sentence, and it will be possible to show a lot of him on television during election programming, wearing a general's uniform (and it's a shame that we don't have the rank of marshall). No one knows, and will ever know what his ideology is—if he has one—and where it is going to lead us. What is important is that, according to the eternal formula, he will lead us to "peace with security." He is a gleaming dowk (combination of dove and hawk), and he exudes aggressiveness. This syndrome of photogenic "securitism" which looks after its own interests is definitely good for whoever believes that a party is a *junta* and that a leadership of major generals is needed in order to make a country march to the polls and is convinced that elections are virtual reality television shows…

Such personal attacks had never been my style, and today I would not be dragged into it again; but then, Barak's candidacy made me lose my temper as I felt that his election would be a disaster for the country. In this case, my considerations went beyond Barak himself since it was part of my struggle against Israeli militarism. A person who is accustomed to simple hierarchical relationships where orders are given, whose personality was almost entirely formed in a military environment, and who lacks experience in sophisticated political negotiations and proper interpersonal relationships cannot be a suitable leader in complex situations like those found in Israel, even if he is directly elected as was customary at the time. Indeed, his unsuitability for the post was confirmed throughout his entire term of office—with the exception of the army's withdrawal from southern Lebanon—and especially by how unsuccessful he was at conducting negotiations with the Palestinians at Camp David, although he was not the only one responsible for their failure. In particular, his unfortunate declaration that "there is no partner" [for peace] led to the collapse of the peace camp and to the election of Ariel Sharon (see "The Way for Sharon was paved by Barak," *Haaretz*, October 1, 2000).

However, while I warned of Barak, I made the big mistake of supporting Shlomo Ben-Ami in the Labor Party's primaries. I saw him as a wise, moderate, and broad-minded man, able to lead Israel at least until the beginning of an internal-social and political path of normalcy. A number of mutual friends confirmed these assumptions. And indeed, in the primaries, Ben-Ami attained a high place in the Labor Party's list. My disappointment was extreme when, in his capacity as Minister of Internal Security, Ben-Ami did not know to rein in the police during the October 2000 riots and in addition, his peculiar testimony before the Orr Commission caused a catastrophic schism between the state and its Arab citizens.

Despite, and perhaps because of, the big collapse caused by Barak, I immediately published an article, intended to be "comforting" for the peace camp, and for myself, entitled "The Premises that Did Not Collapse" (*Haaretz*, June 6, 2001), in which I showed that even though the talks had failed, primarily because of Barak's lack of interpersonal skills, Clinton's situation, and the meeting that was forced upon Arafat without him having been prepared in advance,[1] all of the peace camp's postulates still remained and there was no reason to renounce them or to despair:

> The only members of the peace camp with a good reason to be disappointed are those who assumed it was possible to base the "end of the conflict" on a situation in which the settlements and Israeli control over the occupied territories could be maintained indirectly by turning the Palestinian police into subcontractors whose function would be continuing to guard what is perceived by it as Israel's national, security, and economic interests.

I argued that the interpretation that Israel has no partner for peace, which is based on the assumption that the Palestinians declined the "most generous offers ever made to them," is groundless. The more details became public throughout the years about how Barak conducted the talks and about his "generous" offers to the Palestinians, the more my intuition—based on shreds of information already known then—and the way in which I put the whole picture together from those, were confirmed to be surprisingly accurate and precise.

As for the outbreak of the armed rebellion that spread with the collapse of the talks on which so many hopes were pinned, I again wrote that after thirty-five years of occupation, exploitation, expropriation, and humiliation—with all the concomitant problems—the Palestinian people has a right to use force to oppose the occupation, which itself constitutes a brutal exertion of power. There is no possibility at all of keeping a population of millions under the occupation and rule of another people for entire generations, and whoever thinks otherwise is either ignoring this fact for his convenience or is living in a fantasy. It is possible that the peace camp's most serious mistake was that, for the sake of political and social convenience, it did not have the courage to proclaim this fundamental principle openly, day and night, over and over again. For example, the whole refusal (to serve in the territories) movement, which I supported, was reduced to a tiny group of young people that the army knew very well how to "handle" while gaining the cooperation of "leaders" such as Yossi Sarid and the failed Peace Now[2] movement. If there had been a true peace coalition, it should have united around those principles.

However, from that time until now, as I write these lines, a true peace camp had not yet come into existence, not even in the so called "radical left." Sometimes I reflect on the likelihood and the effectiveness of non-violent civil rebellion by peace activists who are really committed to their worldview. And in fact, most of the power held by hard-core settlers is due more to their concrete actions than to the promulgation of their ideas. Refusal to serve in the territories could initiate a civil resistance of this kind but in our country, "silence is broken" only when military service is over—and those who break it then belong to a small minority, even within the peace camp.

*   *   *

My biggest mistake was to support Amir Peretz, though my initial motives were correct. I didn't have much information on his abilities and personality, yet it seemed to me that the racist attacks on him channeled public discourse into a very unhealthy and unjust direction. Furthermore, the nomination of a person from the "periphery"[3] as the leader of the Labor Party, and possibly afterwards of the government, seemed to me in principle to be both praiseworthy and promising. His interesting interview with Ari Shavit (*Haaretz*, March 3, 2006) reinforced this impression in my mind. Friends assured me, once again, that Peretz definitely had dovish opinions and until he was appointed Minister of Defense, his statements were indeed dovish. Therefore, I wrote in an article entitled "I am an Ashkenazi who is Ashamed" (*Haaretz*, March 6, 2006) about feeling embarrassed by the members of my ethnic group who suddenly gave up their pretense of being Israeli and chose again to openly segregate themselves from other communities. According to the results of surveys carried out among heterogeneous populations and in various places of residence, about half of the traditional Labor Party voters abandoned it when Peretz was elected chairman of the party and nominee for the prime ministership. It is correct and true that Labor (in its Mapai and Ma'arach incarnations) had always been an ethnic Ashkenazi Party despite its pretenses of being non-ethnic and socialist. This "Ashkenazism" was the main characteristic that has brought about the loss of its dominance since 1977. (No, I haven't forgotten Rabin and Barak, yet they too ruled when the right and the religious parties actually had the support of the majority of the public.)

Peretz's surprising election to the leadership of the Labor Party shattered an entire paradigm, not because he is "Moroccan," but because he is an authentic Israeli who did not come from the usual "well" from which the national leadership is drawn. He is warm, intelligent, and learns quickly; he has a sense of humor, is open to new and not necessarily popular ideas, and has a boundless ambition to succeed. He is not without defects and faults, but it has been a long time since we met a candidate so worthy of leading the country on a new, more promising path, both in domestic and in foreign policy. We could have anticipated that the novelty itself would arouse strong antagonism; however, the disclosure of open racism is nevertheless somewhat surprising. This racism was also manifested by the people who jumped on the bandwagon after he was already elected, such as, for example, Avishay Braverman who made the odd statement that he came to "whiten" Peretz. Even the public relations experts who were foisted on him work very hard to root out his enjoyable qualities while claiming that he must be given a "dignified" appearance and be protected by a "white security beehive."

Yet from the moment Peretz chose to serve as Defense Minister in Olmert's cabinet, above (and perhaps under) a dominant and unrestrained Chief of Staff such as Dan Halutz, I knew that he would be drawn into a conceptual and institutional system he could not control and would be dragged along just like anyone else in this situation, especially since the achievements of the Labor Party under his leadership were extremely poor. In an article entitled "Has the Defense Minister Been Taken Prisoner by the Army?" sent to the editorial board on June 10, 2006, I wrote:

> It seems that, since the new Defense Minister took office, the army had escalated its activity against the Palestinians. For a considerable time, even before the mass killing in Gaza last weekend, it was very difficult to see a connection between the actions of the defense forces and the Israeli political pronouncements that expressed the alleged wish to "strengthen" Mahmoud Abbas (Abu-Mazen) and aspired to "pacify the area." Almost every night, the army entered the West Bank to arrest or liquidate one wanted person or another who was always classified as "high-ranking" and responsible for some terror act. Almost every day, our helicopters and planes carried out assassinations in Gaza that, in most cases, injured not only targets considered legitimate by Israel but also "civilians" whose murders should have required, post factum, an apology and the opening of investigations. True, Kassam rockets were fired nearly daily on the Western Negev and it seemed that Sderot was deliberately targeted and no government on earth can let that happen without reacting. However, we have to consider the Kassams in their wider context and it is possible that the implementation of a different policy would have prevented or reduced the number of rockets being launched. First of all, we must not forget that sixteen months ago, Hamas had unilaterally declared a reduction of hostilities (*tahadiah*) and indeed, during this time, no suicide bombings were carried out in its name and almost no rockets were fired into Israel. Nevertheless, last week, Muhammed Abu-Sahila, one of the commanders of the Hamas military wing in northern Gaza, was assassinated north of Jebalia. This elimination was justified on grounds that recently he had launched rockets at Israel and he was, at that time too, on his way to do it again. Regardless of whether this was the case, the Army ceased to be a reliable source of information a long time ago. Its credibility is questionable in this case too because this liquidation fits in well with the policy it adopted in the last few months, which can only be interpreted as being aimed at provoking Palestinians to carry out acts of revenge and bringing the relative calm prevailing during this most recent period to an end. The natural question to be asked is: Where is the new Defense Minister who promised a new policy in defense matters also? Was his intention indeed that we go back to the days of desperate dread on both sides which characterized the second Intifada? Does he now feel so comfortable in the company of his (career) generals and admirals that he, apparently enchanted by their charms and ideas, is able to accept their approaches without thought or objection? This is how he intends to establish himself as a national leader who is from the same mold as Moffaz.
>
> Since before the election I had proposed voting for him and his party, I suggest to Amir Peretz that he return his Defense portfolio to Olmert and as the 2007 budget planning approaches, demand the Treasury portfolio instead. There is hope that in this role, Peretz will not be taken captive by the Treasury's "youngsters" and that he will show deeper understanding. And he is expected not to tell us that Olmert "won't let him." Without his party, Olmert has no government. Let's see him as a true leader and not as a baby under the spell of others.

No less interesting is the reason why this article wasn't published. In checking the facts—which in itself is imperative in every serious newspaper—no documentation about the elimination of Muhammed Abu-Saliha was found in *Haaretz*. A find of this kind could have seriously damaged my credibility in what was supposed to be my field of expertise. I was certain that I didn't invent this assassination and that my notes were not wrong. I went through all the relevant back issues of *Haaretz*, and indeed I found no mention of the assassination. Then I checked on Ynet where that news item was prominently featured. I sent its link to the assistant editor of *Haaretz*; however, she refused to regard that source as a reliable one. As far as she was concerned, what was not published in *Haaretz* did not exist. The incident again created an uncomfortable tension between me and the newspaper.

Later, I became concerned about the growing alienation of the political elite from the Arab public, a process heralded by the new government headed by Olmert and Peretz. As early as April 2006, I guessed that in the political situation which had developed, it was only question of time before the Yisrael Beiteinu[4] party joined the coalition. As these lines are written, it seems apparent that Olmert intends to establish a broad coalition government that will, with the consent and participation of the Labor Party, also include Yisrael Beiteinu. In exchange for the legitimacy granted to this proto-fascist party and for at least one ministerial portfolio, Avigdor Lieberman promised to be "pragmatic," that is, to tone down, for the time being, his anti-Arab rhetoric and even "store it in the basement." However, the problem doesn't end with Lieberman and Yisrael Beiteinu, which ran on an explicitly racist platform, but continues with statements about a government relying on "Zionist parties only," which is a well-known code for "Jewish votes only." Such a government will continue to alienate the Palestinian citizens of Israel, a fact which constitutes a disaster not only for them, but also for the state and its regime. The conduct of Amir Peretz and the Labor Party appears to be more and more problematic. It seems that among the immediate concessions made by Labor to Kadima in exchange for a place in the coalition was the renunciation of their decision not to join a government in which Yisrael Beiteinu participates. In fact, if Kadima itself were a decent party, it too would have refused to deal with Lieberman as a matter of principle. Therefore, when established, this government will indeed be Jewish but at the same time also anti-Israel and not only because of how it deals, both in its use of symbols and its concrete actions, with the Arab citizens. This would perhaps result in the failure of the entire political system and would consequently be the gravest of all of the Labor Party's concessions (see "An Anti-Israel Zionist Government," *Haaretz*, April 16, 2006).

Actually, all Peretz supporters, including Yehoshua Sobol and myself, played a part in this failure. We all thought that sooner or later he would become the Prime Minister and we ignored the fact that Kadima was, relatively speaking, more successful, although it had already begun to lose ground in public opinion polls after Sharon's hospitalization. Certainly no one thought of Peretz in terms of Defense Minister, perhaps not even of Finance Minister, but rather as a top policy planner who would reform the welfare system and promote an agreement with the Palestinians.

However, given the results of the election, there was a certain logic in his appointment to the Defense Ministry and perhaps he could have succeeded as a "socially oriented Defense Minister" if he hadn't been dragged by Halutz and Olmert into the Lebanese adventure. Now it will take another generation to convince the public of the existence of something akin to a "social agenda" and to restore its confidence in politics.

## Notes

1.  Arafat felt that the Camp David summit was premature because, in his view, Israel should have honored the commitments made in the interim agreements before insisting on final status talks. Moreover, in his opinion, there should have been agreements about procedure before the start of negotiations on matters of substance.
2.  Yossi Sarid and the leaders of Peace Now strongly opposed the refusal movement.
3.  Amir Peretz's town of residence, Sderot, is situated in the geographical and social periphery of the country.
4.  Yisrael Beiteinu translates as "Israel is our home." This is a hard-line nationalistic political party, most of whose members are Russian immigrants.

# 24

## BETWEEN DESPAIR AND HOPE

The real problem was that the more I learned about the conflict with the Palestinians and its history, the more skeptical I became about the possibilities of finding a real solution that would satisfy the minimal demands of both people through a territorial partition according to the "two states for two peoples" formula. Even if the Palestinians were to succeed in establishing an independent state within the 1967 borders, with East Jerusalem as its capital and without Jewish settlements in it (which at the moment appears to be a slim possibility)—and this is the maximum that even the most yielding Jewish peace activists are ready to accept—it is doubtful that this minuscule, overpopulated piece of land would provide the needed living space and satisfy the national aspirations of the Palestinians.

Even if Israel were to compensate the refugees in a way acceptable to them and even if it were to assume—justifiably—the responsibility for creating the refugee problem and settle a few hundred thousand refugees within its borders, it would not guarantee the end of the conflict. This would be the case even with the best, most sincere and truthful intentions of the leaders whose actions would at last bring the sides together to sign the long-awaited agreement.

The reason for this does not stem from the Palestinians being conspirators or anti-Semites—although many are and is it any wonder after they have been so maltreated?—but rather from the fact that the structural, social, and geo-political situation of the two intertwined communities does not bode well for a solution. On both sides, there will still exist religious and nationalistic elements striving to keep the entire country undivided and under their exclusive dominance. Hence I was caught in an almost impossible ideological trap as I lacked the ability to propose a realistic solution to the conflict, even though it is possible that this was not expected of me.

It seems that Benny Morris probably reached similar conclusions and kept them to himself until his outburst when he declared that Ben-Gurion should have carried out a total ethnic cleansing in 1948, and that completing this act at the first opportunity should not be ruled out. However, even when disregarding the moral and legal aspects of Morris' approach (which is in itself impossible), it seems that if the Arab countries couldn't take in 750,000 refugees in 1948, they would have found it even more difficult to absorb approximately three times as many and the wound would have taken generations longer to heal.

It is true that in such a case, the focus of the conflict would not have been within the borders of a single territory, but would have been conducted between "the outside and the inside," a fact that perhaps would have made those Jews in Israel or "Eretz Yisrael," who only want to see Arabs through rifle sights, feel better. In this case, would the Palestinians have lost their identity and been absorbed within the Arab world? It's hard to answer such hypothetical questions; however, if we examine the case of Jordan, it doesn't seem that it had much success in trying to achieve that goal in spite of all its attempts.

In addition, it seems to me that Ben-Gurion's argument that the Great Powers in 1948 would not have allowed Jews to rule the entire land is logical. It is more than likely that they would have even compelled Israel to return to the partition borders (as they forced it to withdraw from El-Arish), and to internationalize Jerusalem. Probably, they would also have forced it to accept all the Arab refugees and displaced persons while their houses were still standing and their fields waited to be harvested (a decision very similar to U.N. Resolution 194). It is hard even to imagine what kind of Israel would have been created under such conditions. It is also reasonable to assume that King Abdullah of Jordan would have unleashed the full power of the Arab Legion in an attempt to conquer the whole land. In such a case, the entire balance of power between Arabs and Jews in 1948 would have greatly changed, to the detriment of the latter.

The question of what would have happened "if..." is not legitimate in history as a science, yet since Morris has raised the question, it is permissible to go ahead and play with it in order to refute his argument. As for similar questions regarding the future, the situation is more obvious. Morris and his ilk are calling for the commission of a war crime and a crime against humanity. This time, however, Israel would not be facing a physical-existential threat and the ethnic cleansing would be carried out for the sake of preserving a regime which guarantees the total and "pure" sovereignty of one ethnic entity, to which Morris belongs, over another one which is deprived of its rights. If Zionism does not find another solution to the problems stemming from its existence in the region, I have no doubt that its end will be similar to that of the Apartheid regime in South Africa, or worse, like that of the Pieds-Noir in Algeria and Ian Smith's regime in Rhodesia—a [former] British colony which in 1965 had a minority of white colonists and in 1979, after an international boycott, collapsed and became Zimbabwe.

From its inception, Zionism was to a large extent an anachronistic movement. As a political ideology Zionism was born just as the European colonial era was ending and was based on the premise that Europeans were entitled to emigrate and settle anywhere they wished because of economic advantages, persecution in the old continent, or ideological and religious motives. However, Zionism was not accepted by most of the world's Jews until after the Holocaust. Between 1800 and 1850, of the 65 million Europeans who emigrated to the New World, five million were Jews, i.e. 7.7% of all émigrés (the Jews constituted 1.6% of the Old World's population at that time), while in the first half of the twentieth century, 20% of Europe's Jews emigrated, mostly to North America. Only a few of every thousand came to Palestine and even among those, over half left soon after.

Nevertheless, Zionism was able to establish a colony of immigrant-settlers under the protection of British bayonets. It was also able to save approximately 200,000 non-Zionist German and Polish Jews from extermination at the beginning of the 1930s—Jews who literally had no place else to flee to after the rise of Nazism and the barring of immigration to North America.

It can also be claimed that it provided a haven to Jews from Iraq, Yemen, and North Africa in the wake of the difficulties which its very establishment caused them in their countries of origin. On the whole, the people rescued contributed more to the establishment of Israel than Zionism contributed to rescuing Jews from the global geopolitical situation of the 1930s and 1940s. If, between the mid-1920s and the mid-1930s, Zionism had fired the imagination of millions of European Jews, the extent of the Holocaust could probably have been significantly reduced. The profile of modern Israel would also be different. It is difficult to determine in retrospect who, if anyone, is to be "blamed" for the fact that this didn't happen—Jews, Zionism, or both.

Israel was, without any doubt, "born in sin" on the ruins of the Arab society which had existed in place for centuries—as all immigrants-settlers societies in the distant past were. However, this fact does not negate its right to exist. First, past injustices cannot be erased by the infliction of new ones, and there is no time tunnel in history through which it is possible to travel back—as the Palestinian myth about their right of return assumes —to the situation that supposedly froze in 1947. However, this also holds for the Jewish myth of "return" after two thousand years. Second, a nation with a lively, colorful, creative, and fascinating society, economy, and culture has been built here and, despite its many flaws, has been honorably accepted into the family of nations, an acceptance based on the condition that a suitable and satisfying solution to the Palestinian problem—one that would also be satisfactory to most Palestinians—would be found. Actually, correcting the injustice done to them—even if the solution is not in accordance with the dream they have nurtured— is not only an improvement for them but for all of humanity and, mainly, for ourselves.

However, even if the conflict is unsolvable in the foreseeable future, it can still be managed more wisely and without always resorting to aggression. Wise management will bring about de-escalation of the conflict in its various manifestations, gradual changes in its patterns, and perhaps possible future solutions. The two necessary conditions for this to happen are, first of all, the end of the occupation regime over the Palestinians, which is both morally and practically insufferable, by gradually reducing and shrinking the colonization of the territories; and second, the granting of full and equal rights to the Israel's Arab citizens. Fulfilling this last condition will probably cause Israel to be less Jewish—according to the conventional meaning that the concept of Judaism has in Israel—yet far more democratic and able to survive. Giving everyone a stake in the country's overall welfare will create an interest among Arab citizens both in the state's continuing existence and in coexisting with their Jewish counterparts.

Having delved into the professional literature, I know that intellectuals have the power to change current identities and even to invent and develop new ones, and I consider this to be their function both in Israel and on the Palestinian side. As I've already mentioned, I tried to imagine how this could be done in a small book I published under the title *The End of Hegemony of the Ahusalim*,[1] by which I hoped to stimulate a public debate about the transformation in the country's character.

However, immediately after its publication, the second Intifada—along with the horror inflicted by Palestinian suicide bombers—broke out and instantly halted any real public discussion. In this monograph, I basically suggested transforming Israel into a multi-cultural country under the rule of law, within which the state would maintain neutrality toward ethnic symbols and work to develop an Israeli identity inclusive of all of its citizens regardless of their religion, religiosity, ethnic origin, culture, and language. The proposal was far-reaching for its time, yet I still believe that we should proceed in this, or a similar, direction.

In addition, it would be extremely beneficial if the Europeans were to accept both us and the Palestinian state as members of the [European] Union. A move of this kind might compensate the Palestinians for the territorial and geopolitical state of suffocation to which they would be subjected. At the same time, it could help to fulfill the secret dream of most Israelis to be part of the Western world and at least figuratively escape from the Middle East.

In an attempt to avoid complete despair, I proposed a plan which did not provoke the reactions I had hoped, perhaps because the explanation of the idea was not clear and detailed enough, possibly because its sociological background was not well understood, and mostly because its realization depends upon elements [within the EU] over which neither we nor the Palestinians have influence. It is even possible that the proposal is incompatible with the interests of those same elements. Nevertheless, it seems to me that the idea is worth being developed and marketed. On October 8, 2004, I published an article in *Haaretz* entitled "Israel and Palestine in Europe" in which I wrote:

> With the advent of a new wave of mutual Israeli-Palestinian bloodshed, which has reached another one of its peaks these days, it becomes more and more clear to both sides that each possesses indeed a considerable capacity for attrition; however, neither has the ability to actually shift the balance in this desperate struggle. Not even a "unilateral separation," if it could be carried out, would guarantee an alleviation of hostilities, let alone a real solution to the conflict. At the same time, even if both sides recognize that they cannot overpower their respective opponent and that all of the victims and the destruction are not only unnecessary, but constitute a military and ethical failure and undermine morale, there is no possibility on either side of interrupting this bloody dance. Not only has the situation spun out of the control of the Israeli and Palestinian leadership, but no political change is on the

horizon in the foreseeable future that could stop this chain of events and allow for new political proposals which could serve as a ladder allowing both sides to come down from the tall tree they have climbed. Yet, potentially, there exists such a factor that can immediately replace all the parameters and constraints in which both the Israelis and Palestinians operate and think and can change all the rules of the game: this factor is in fact the European Union and not the United States, as we tend to think.

Up until now, the Europeans, particularly those from central and northern Europe, have invested diplomatic efforts as well as huge sums of money in order to achieve at least the de-escalation of the conflict while building infrastructure and civic, political, and economic institutions within the Palestinian entity. A great deal of this money was lost, both on account of the Palestinians' inept and corrupt management, and the destruction and anarchy caused by the actions of the Israeli army. It seems now that the Europeans, dispirited and disappointed with both sides, are decreasing their level of intervention in the region. At the same time, it does not look as if their fundamental commitment to promoting an agreement in the area has diminished, especially if they could see a really effective way to achieve it without pouring in more billions of Euros in vain.

Such a way, I claimed, does exist. Although it contradicts the European Union's basic principles to a great extent, it would be less costly on the economic level as well as on other levels, maybe to the extent that the Europeans would not even feel it. On the other hand, a development of this kind could cause a substantial change in whatever concerns the reciprocal and global status of the Israelis and Palestinians. This process would involve admitting to the European Union as full members two sovereign states—Israel and Palestine—as the last phase of a final peace agreement between them. In principle, this enormous bonus could be included in programs similar to the Geneva Draft Document[2] or even resembling the American road map, which should be supervised by the quartet. Such a step would have a number of unimaginable advantages.

First, in spite of being divided along national lines, the land would remain under one supra-national, joint umbrella which could ensure non-rigid borders between the two states, enabling freedom of movement, migration, and free access to any place within and outside it. One of the real problems between Jews and Palestinians has always been the minuscule size of the contested piece of land —a territory which has always been perceived as a zero-sum resource. Its inclusion within the European Union would remove most of the territorial problems on the symbolic, material, and military-strategic levels. It would also eliminate the Jewish demographic anxieties and even constitute a suitable answer to the aspirations for a Palestinian return.

Israel has always considered itself part of Europe—as though only a historical accident caused the Holy Land to be placed in the Middle East—and it has aspired both cognitively and physically to escape its position in the East. Since the European Union guarantees multi-culturalism and multi-nationalism to its members, neither the Palestinians nor those Israelis who feel close to the

Eastern culture would necessarily be required, as members—territorially, politically, militarily, and economically—of the European Union, to sever the connection to their Arab identity if they didn't want to. However, many difficulties would undoubtedly arise during the implementation of this process, particularly as it is bound to pre-conditions including arrangements, mutual concessions, and changes in conceptions and identity on both the Israeli and Palestinian side. Yet Europe can include both us and the Palestinians and even benefit from our inclusion almost without noticing us at all. But for this to happen, the Israelis as well as the Palestinians would first have to prove that we do not intend to merely import our troubles, our narrow-mindedness, and our extremism. This would be no easy task, but the benefits would be enormous if we could both pass the test of maturity and wisdom by cooperating and being able to settle differences of interest, as indeed the Europeans have learned to do after centuries of cruel wars, even crueler than ours.

A strong and institutionalized relationship with Europe would also grant the Jews in Israel more existential security, which until now has been based only on military power and, in particular, on the knowledge that we possess nuclear weapons. I've always had the vague feeling that relying on military might is insufficient and unsatisfactory, an opinion that is shared even by right-wing circles. Playing with all these ideas has instilled a spark of hope in me despite the pessimistic conclusions that I have reached. The difference is that my pessimism stems from the given situation here and now, whereas my optimism and hope are pinned on what could develop in the future—what are called "future options," which are presently hidden from us. We, the Jews of Israel, myself included, often tend to adopt the principle and method of the "worst-case scenario" analysis, and see the present and the future in these terms, a kind of perspective that can turn into a self-fulfilling prophecy. How is it possible to jettison this aspect of Israeli political culture especially in light of the fact that the "world," in spite of the abundance of evil in it, does not always produce worst-case scenarios?

## Notes

1.  As mentioned already, *Ahusalim* refers to Ashkenazi, Secular, Long-term Citizen, Socialist and National—a tongue-in-cheek Hebrew acronym for "the old Establishment", similar to WASP.
2.  The Geneva Draft Document was negotiated by MK Yossi Beilin and the Palestinians, led first by Yasser Abd-Rabbo and later, in 1995, by Abu Mazen when an analogous document was prepared. It was supposed to replace the Oslo accords. The draft document was finalized but is incomplete and missing several appendices that are still in the process of negotiation.

# In Lieu of a Conclusion: Question Marks

The story of my life has been told here in terms of three main interlinking circles: my personal history and that of part of my family; my education and professional activity as a sociologist; and a small portion of my work as a "public" sociologist. The question that the reader is likely to ask and perhaps has already asked himself while reading, is what the interrelationships between these circles are and more precisely, how the events of my life and my physical condition influenced my positions and activities in the professional sphere and what impact those in turn had over my activity as a "public sociologist."

It is likely that a certain number of readers have already reflected on this question and found their own answers. In the process of writing and revising this book, I indeed asked myself these kinds of questions, yet I did not find satisfactory answers. Everything that has happened to me throughout my life, at every given point in time up until now, could, with the same degree of probability, have occurred in a totally different way. At the same time, I believe neither in chance nor in fate or predestination.

A friend who read the draft of this book asked who I would have been if my parents had joined a kibbutz, as was suggested to them. It is also possible to ask who I would have become if I had been sent to a "suitable institution," as my teacher Ofra advised, or as a result of any combination of the various additional possibilities I faced at different crossroads during the course of my life. However, these are actually meaningless questions, since they cannot be answered.

Nevertheless, I am almost convinced, as I have written, that being an immigrant in Israeli society has in fact influenced my ideological and professional approaches. Yet this too is a conclusion which doesn't say much since a wide range of possible reactions to being an immigrant exist and most immigrants do not necessarily ask questions but rather aspire to be absorbed into the mainstream, as I myself did in my youth or, alternatively, prefer to detach themselves completely from the society and culture they have found themselves in.

The same can be said about being disabled. There are so many ways of reacting to disabilities that even this condition, which most probably did have a partial impact on the course of my life, is not to be "blamed" for any specific choices I made or for having a substantial influence on who I became.

An additional open question is about the extent to which both circles of my activity, the public and the academic, have affected me. There is no doubt that, not only for me but for anyone who operates in these two arenas, one of the main motivations is the desire to leave a mark. Even during my undergraduate studies, I paid particular attention, though I doubt that I understood its full significance then, to the lecture by one of the founders of modern sociology, Max Weber, who claimed that sociology is not only a profession but also a mission.

As time went by, I adopted "Weberian sociology" as a professional identity. My subjective feeling is that in this narrow sphere, I succeeded in having an influence, yet there's no doubt that this impact will fade away with time. Very few social scientists succeed in entering the "pantheon." It is possible that some of my innovations in this limited field will become "self-evident" but that no one will remember their source anymore. This is the most I can hope for, and it's actually already happening.

Regarding the public sphere, I'm convinced that most experts and commentators on public affairs who preach to the public and, in most cases, directly or indirectly to the political and economic (which is also political) decision-making elite, greatly exaggerate their own influence. In the same way, "professors" and "intellectuals" try to turn the prestige they think they have into some kind of political influence. However, what's written in the newspaper or broadcast on the radio or television is in most cases forgotten the next day, which is a new day with a new newspaper and usually new subjects too.

Even so, two types of influence do occur, if rarely: one has a specific impact while the other has an effect on processes. Regarding the first, it's possible that I had an influence, for instance, on the swap deal for the release of Metulla's guard, Shmuel Rosenwasser, as can be inferred from Golda Meir's furious reaction. Regarding the influence over processes, through a series of articles I published, mostly in a debate with the orientalist Emanuel Sivan, I played a part in consolidating the ideas and arguments behind the Four Mothers movement, which decisively affected the determination to withdraw from Lebanon. However, I wasn't the only one who supported this move and I cannot take all the "credit" for myself.

Another interesting and, in my opinion, important question which I've often asked myself concerns the interrelationship between my professional and public sociology. I always aspired to establish a boundary between the two activities in order to distinguish one from the other since I believed (and to a great extent, still believe) that research and professional writing must be objective and free of ideological opinions. However, the opposite is not the case since public writing must draw on the professional knowledge that has been acquired.

I regarded my book *Politicide* as an unmistakably public piece of writing and in order to underscore this, I did not add any scholarly touches to it, yet I did make extensive use of my research and professional knowledge while writing it. However, justifiably or not, many of my colleagues around the world, and even a few in Israel, regarded it, for better or worse, as a professional product and even began to cite it in their academic works.

I certainly do not hold the opinion, as some of my colleagues do (particularly those who adopted post-modernist approaches), that it is not only impossible to differentiate between the researcher's values and his work, but that this differentiation is not even advisable. In contrast, I think that making this distinction is imperative. Otherwise, what is the difference between a social scientist on the one hand and a mere writer or an ideological orator or religious preacher on the other? Although this differentiation is difficult and perhaps cannot be fully realized, the awareness of the fact that this is indeed a problematic issue is in itself a partial solution.

In his autobiography, Dan Horowitz writes that after his bitter disappoint-ment in communism and the Soviet Union, he and a few friends discovered in (functionalistic) sociology an exciting substitute for communist ideology. I, on the other hand, never considered my professional sociology as a faith of any kind. When I struggled against what I considered as my teacher's paradigm, I did so exactly for this reason, until I felt as though I were falling victim to the same approaches I fought against. I haven't found an unequivocal answer to these questions either.

Being unequivocal is itself a problem, one that has continued to occupy me for years. In the two spheres of activity, but especially in the public one, there is constant pressure to take an unambiguous, mostly simplistic, stand in writing (and to a certain extent also in teaching). The problem is that whenever I am engaged in the creation and dissemination of an idea, I find it difficult to consolidate an unequivocal position, since every issue has more than one facet, a contradiction lies concealed in every development, and every social action has its own prices. There is almost no public controversy in which "justice" lies solely with one side while the other side is completely wrong.

For instance, I knew that evacuating Gush Katif was a mistake since it was not carried out in the framework of a comprehensive agreement with the Palestinians, and it would not have changed a thing in their situation (and it may even have worsened it). On the other hand, the evacuation of settlements was in itself a conceptual breakthrough and a concession on the part of a right-wing leader who had been the driving force behind the appropriation of the Gaza Strip. It was also an admission that the idea of a Greater Israel is a folly.

How is it possible to weigh the costs and benefits of two options and how can an analysis of any option and its alternative be carried out? In most socio-political situations, these kinds of dilemmas exist, especially for those taking a public stand while attempting to pass through the bottleneck of newspaper editors. This is all the more problematic since in a newspaper article, where the writer is allotted 600 words, not only is it impossible to explain a complex idea but in addition, such an article is required to contain an unequivocal resolution to which the writer can remain faithful in good conscience.

I had a similar yet even more severe dilemma regarding the Oslo Accords, which I knew could not lead to an "end to the conflict" and, as mentioned before, I decided to attack them both in the press and professionally. On the other hand, Migdal and I wrote approximately sixty pages in the expanded edition of our book explaining the benefits and costs of the "Oslo process," which my colleague supported.

Finally, there is an additional, tough question to which I have no answer: to what extent do my ethnic, social or class interests dictate my opinions or distort my positions? More than once I have been accused either implicitly or explicitly by Palestinian colleagues and non-Zionist leftists (whose analyses I don't disregard) of stopping my political and social critiques of the regime in Israel at the point where damage could be done to my personal interests as a Jew who belongs to the upper middle class and who is a member, although not a leading one, of the academic establishment. Likewise, they claim that this status does not permit me to take a stand in support of the boycott of Israeli universities or the right of an unconditional return of Palestinians also into the country and that I wriggle in tortuous wordings in order to avoid drawing the allegedly "obvious" conclusions from my analyses and findings.

Yet those who suspect or accuse me of bias have, in most cases, their own personal interests too. This approach leads to the reduction of public discourse to personal motives; therefore, it is my opinion that in public debates we have to consider the arguments themselves and not the people involved. My opinion is that only I, and nobody else, can examine my own motives each time anew; yet I am not certain even about this assertion.

# SELECTED PUBLICATIONS

## Books

1. *Zionism and Territory: The Socioterritorial Dimensions of Zionist Politics.* Berkeley: University of California, Institute of International Studies, 1983. [289 pages]
2. *Zionism and Economy.* Cambridge, MA: Schenkman Publishing Company, 1983. [169 pages]
3. *The Interrupted System: Israeli Civilians in War and Routine Times.* New Brunswick and London: Transaction Books, 1985. [229 pages]
4. Baruch Kimmerling and Joel S. Migdal, *Palestinians: The Making of a People.* New York: Free Press, 1993. [380 pages]
   Paperback enlarged edition: Harvard University Press.
   Italian version: La Nuova Italia Editrice, 1994.
   Enlarged and revised Hebrew version: Keter, 1998. [300 pages]
   Arabic: Haifa: Al-Ithihad, 2001.
5. *The Invention and Decline of Israeliness: State, Culture and Military in Israel.* Los Angeles and Berkeley: University of California Press, 2001.
6. *The End of Ashkenazi Hegemony.* Jerusalem: Keter, 2001 (Hebrew).
7. *Politicide: Sharon's War Against the Palestinians.* London: Verso, 2003.
8. Baruch Kimmerling and Joel Migdal, *A History of the Palestinian People.* Cambridge, MA: Harvard University Press, 2003.
9. *Immigrants, Settlers and Natives: Israel Between Plurality of Cultures and Cultural Wars.* Tel Aviv: Am Oved, 2003 (Hebrew).
10. *Clash of Identities: Explorations in Israeli and Palestinian Societies.* New York: Columbia University Press, 2008.
11. *Marginal in the Center: The Life Story of a Public Sociologist.* Israel: Hakibutz Hameuhad, 2007 (Hebrew).

## Edited book

12. *The Israeli State and Society: Boundaries and Frontiers.* Albany: State University of New York Press, 1989. [330 pages]

## Textbook

13. *Between State and Society: The Sociology of Politics.* Tel Aviv: Open University, 1995 (Two volumes, in Hebrew).

## Journal Guest Editor

1. Political Sociology at Crossroads, *Current Sociology* [special issue on recent developments in political sociology around the world], Vol. 44, No. 3, 1996. [178 pages]

## Papers and monographs in referee journals

1. Dan Horowitz and Baruch Kimmerling, "Some Social Implications of Military Service and the Reserves System in Israel," *European Journal of Sociology*, Vol. 15, No. 2, 1974, pp. 252–276.
2. "Anomie and Integration in Israeli Society and the Salience of the Arab-Israeli Conflict," *Studies in Comparative International Development*, Vol. 15, No. 2, 1974, pp. 64–89.
3. "Sovereignty, Ownership and Presence in the Jewish-Arab Territorial Conflict: The Case of Bir'm and Ikrit," *Comparative Political Studies*, Vol. 10, No. 2, 1977, pp. 155–176.
4. "Determination of the Boundaries and the Frameworks of Conscription: Two Dimensions of Civil-Military Relations in Israel," *Studies in Comparative International Development*, Vol. 14, Spring 1979, pp. 24–41.
5. Victor Azarya and Baruch Kimmerling, "New Immigrants in the Israeli Armed Forces," *Armed Forces & Society*, Vol. 6, No. 3, 1980, pp. 455–484.
6. "A Model for Analysis of Reciprocal Relations Between the Jewish and Arab Communities in Mandatory Palestine," *Plural Societies*, Vol. 14. Nos. 3/4, 1983, pp. 45–68.
7. Baruch Kimmerling and Irit Backer, "Voluntary Action and Location in the System: The Case of Israeli Civilians in the 1973 War," *Journal of Applied Behavioral Science*, Vol. 18, No. 1. pp. 1–16.
8. "Change and Continuity in the Zionist Territorial Politics," *Comparative Politics*, Vol. 14, No. 2, 1982, pp. 191–210.
9. "Making Conflict a Routine: The Cumulative Effects of the Arab-Jewish Conflict Upon Israeli Society," *Journal of Strategic Studies*, Vol. 6, No. 3, 1983, pp. 13–45.
10. Baruch Kimmerling and Irit Backer, "Interruption and Continuity: The Israeli Civilian Institutional Arrangements During Wars," *International Review of Modern Society*, Vol. 15. Nos. 1–2, 1985, pp. 81–98.
11. "Peace for Territories: A Macro-Sociological Analysis of the Concept of Peace in Zionist Ideology," *Journal of Applied Behavioral Science*, Vol. 23, No. 3, 1987, pp. 13–34.
12. Victor Azarya and Baruch Kimmerling "Cognitive Permeability of Civil-Military Boundaries: Expectations from Military Service in Israel," *Studies in Comparative International Development*, Vol. 20, No. 4, Winter 1985–1986, pp. 42–63.
13. "Ideology, Sociology and Nation Building: The Palestinians and Their Meaning in Israeli Sociology," *American Sociological Review*, Vol. 57, No. 4, August 1992, pp. 446–460.
14. "Patterns of Militarism in Israel," *European Journal of Sociology*, Vol. 2, 1993, pp. 1–28.
15. "State Building, State Autonomy, and the Identity of Society: The Case of the Israeli State," *The Journal of Historical Sociology*, Vol. 6, No, 4, 1993, pp. 397–429.

16. Dahlia Moore and Baruch Kimmerling, "Individual Strategies of Adopting Collective Identities: The Israeli Case," *International Sociology*, Vol. 4, 1995, pp. 387–408.
17. "Academic History Caught in the Cross-Fire: The Case of Israeli-Jewish Historiography," *History and Memory*, Vol. 7, No. 4, 1995, pp. 41–65. [enlarged Hebrew version: "History, Here and Now," in Y. Weitz (ed.), *Zionist Historiography: Between Vision and Revision*. Jerusalem: Yad Ben Zvi, 1997].
18. "Changing Meanings and Boundaries of the 'Political'," *Current Sociology*, Vol. 44, No. 3, 1996, pp. 152–176.
19. Baruch Kimmerling and Dahlia Moore, "Collective Identity as Agency, and Structuration of Society: Tested by the Israeli Case," *International Review of Sociology*, Vol. 7, No. 1, 1997, pp. 25–50.
20. "Between Hegemony and Dormant *Kulturkampf* in Israel," *Israel Affairs*, Vol. 4, Nos. 3–4, 1998, pp. 49–72.
21. "Process of Formation of Palestinian Collective Identities: The Ottoman and Colonial Periods," *Middle Eastern Studies*, April 2000, Vol. 36, No. 2, pp. 48–81.
22. "Religion, Nationalism and Democracy in Israel," *Constellations*, Vol. 6, No. 3, 1999, pp. 339–363. Hebrew version: *Zmanim*, Tel Aviv: Tel Aviv's University School of History, 50, December 1994.
23. "Legislation and Jurisprudence in an Immigrant-Settler Society," *Bar Ilan Law Studies*, Vol. 16, No. 1, 2001, pp. 17–36.

## Chapters in books

1. Baruch Kimmerling and Moshe Lissak, *Inner Dualism: An Outcome of the Center-Periphery Relationships During Modernization Processes in Uganda*, Sage Research Papers in Social Sciences, Studies in Comparative Modernization Series. Beverly Hills: Sage Publications, 1979. [45 pages]
2. "The Israeli Civil Guard," in Louis A. Zurcher and Gwyn Harries-Jenkins (eds.), *Supplementary Military Forces: Reserves, Militias, Auxiliaries*. Beverly Hills: Sage Publications, 1978, pp. 107–125.
3. "The Economic Interrelationships Between the Arab and Jewish Communities in Mandatory Palestine." Cambridge, MA: Center for International Studies, MIT, 1979. [79 pages]
4. "Social Interruption and Besieged Societies: The Case of Israel," Amherst: The Council of International Studies, The State University of New York at Buffalo, 1979. [38 pages]
5. "A Conceptual Framework for Analysis of Behavior in a Territorial Conflict: The Generalization of the Israeli Case," Jerusalem: Leonard Davis Institute for International Relations, the Hebrew University, 1979. [30 pages]
6. "Between the Primordial and Civil Definitions of the Collective Identity: The State of Israel or Eretz Israel," In: E. Cohen, M. Lissak and U. Almagor (eds.), *Comparative Social Dynamics: Essays in Honor of Shmuel Eisenstadt*. Boulder, CO: Westview Press, 1984, pp. 262–283.
7. "Between 'Alexandria-on-Hudson' and Zion," in *The Israeli State and Society: Boundaries and Frontiers*. Albany: State University of New York Press, 1989. [Hebrew version in *Yahadut Zmanenu*, Vol. 4, 1987].

8. "Boundaries and Frontiers of the Israeli Control System- Analytical Conclusions," in *The Israeli State and Society: Boundaries and Frontiers*. Albany: State University of New York Press, 1989.
9. "Discontinuities in Elite Recruitment in Israeli Society," in I. Lustick (ed.), *Books on Israel*. Albany: State University of New York Press, 1988, pp. 72–78.
10. "The Power-Oriented Settlement: Bargaining between Israelis and Palestinians," in M. Ma'oz and A. Sela (eds.), *The PLO and Israel: From The Road to the Oslo Agreement and Back?* New York: St. Martin's Press, 1997, pp. 223–251.
11. "Political Subcultures and Civilian Militarism in a Settler-Immigrant Society," in D. Bar-Tal, D. Jacobson and A. Kliemann (eds.), *Concerned with Security: Learning from Israel's Experience*. Greenwich, CT: JAI Press, 1998, pp. 395–416.
12. "Elections as a Battleground over Collective Identity," in A. Arian and Michal Shamir (eds.), *Elections in Israel: 1996*. Albany: New York State University Press, 1999, pp. 27–44.
    [Hebrew version published by Israel Institute for Democracy]
13. "Elites and Civil Societies in Middle East," in E.S. Brezis and P. Temin (eds.), *Elites, Minorities and Economic Growth*. Rotterdam: Elsevier, 1999, Chapter 4.
14. "The Social Construction of Israel's National Security," in Stuart A. Cohen (ed.), *Democratic Societies and their Armed Forces: Israel in Comparative Context*. London: Frank Cass, 2000, pp. 215–252.

## Encyclopedic entries

1. "Arthur Rupin," "Alfred Bonne," "Yonina Gerber-Talmon," in *Internationales Soziologenlexikon*. Band 1. W. Bernsdorf und H. Knospe (eds.). Stuttgart: Ferdinand Enke Verlage, 1980. [German]
2. "Israel," in *The Oxford Companion to Politics of the World*, Joel Krieger (ed.). New York: Oxford University Press, 1993 [revised edition 2001].

## Semi-professional publications (selected)

1. "The Battle Over the Hegemony," *Politika*, 31 March 1991 ([Hebrew).
2. "On Knowledge of the Place..." ("Al-Daat Ha'Makom"), *Alpayim*, Vol. 6, 1992, pp. 57–68 (Hebrew).
3. "La graande missere des ideologues: La paix possible, on peut enfin etudier la realite du passe, sans fard," *Courrier International*, Vol. 210, 10–16 November 1994 (French).
4. "On Elections in Israel," *Middle East Report*, Vol. 26, No. 4, 1996, pp. 14–18.
5. "Between Celebration of Independence and Commemoration of al-Nakbah: The Controversy over the Roots of the Israeli State," *MESA Bulletin*, July 1998.
6. "Al-Nakbah," 50 to 48, special issue of *Theory and Critique*, April 1999 (Hebrew).
7. "The Political Culture of Israel," in M. Lissakand and B. Knei-Paz (eds.), *Israel Towards the 2000's*. Jerusalem: Magnes, 1996 (Hebrew).
8. "Shaking the Foundation," *Index on Censorship*, Vol. 3, 1995, pp. 47–52.
9. "Unholy Covenant," *Index on Censorship*, Vol. 4, 1996, pp. 146–148.
10. "Weder demokratisch noch judisch," *Informationsprojectkt Naher und Miltterer Osten*, Vol. 13, 1998, pp. 12–15 (German).
11. "The Roots of Zionist Culture" (review essay), *Middle East Studies Association Bulletin*, Vol. 33, Winter 1999, pp. 154–159.

# Index